Procedural 3D Modeling Using Geometry Nodes in Blender

Discover the professional usage of geometry nodes and develop a creative approach to a node-based workflow

Siemen Lens

‹packt›

BIRMINGHAM—MUMBAI

Procedural 3D Modeling Using Geometry Nodes in Blender

Copyright © 2023 Packt Publishing

All rights reserved. No part of this book may be reproduced, stored in a retrieval system, or transmitted in any form or by any means, without the prior written permission of the publisher, except in the case of brief quotations embedded in critical articles or reviews.

Every effort has been made in the preparation of this book to ensure the accuracy of the information presented. However, the information contained in this book is sold without warranty, either express or implied. Neither the author, nor Packt Publishing or its dealers and distributors, will be held liable for any damages caused or alleged to have been caused directly or indirectly by this book.

Packt Publishing has endeavored to provide trademark information about all of the companies and products mentioned in this book by the appropriate use of capitals. However, Packt Publishing cannot guarantee the accuracy of this information.

Group Product Manager: Rohit Rajkumar
Publishing Product Manager: Vaideeshwari Muralikrishnan
Senior Content Development Editor: Debolina Acharyya
Technical Editor: Simran Ali
Copy Editor: Safis Editing
Project Coordinator: Sonam Pandey
Proofreader: Safis Editing
Indexer: Hemangini Bari
Production Designer: Arunkumar Govinda Bhat
Marketing Coordinator: Nivedita Pandey

First published: March 2023

Production reference: 1200223

Published by Packt Publishing Ltd.
Livery Place
35 Livery Street
Birmingham
B3 2PB, UK.

ISBN 978-1-80461-255-2

www.packtpub.com

I dedicate this book to my parents, Geertje and Diego, who have always been my guiding light and the foundation of my success. Their unwavering love, support, and belief in me have been the driving force behind my passion for graphic design.

– Siemen Lens

Foreword

I have had the pleasure of working with Siemen Lens on various visualization projects, from furniture visualization to visualizing biotech installations, where moving elements were also particularly important. So, for both still images and moving images, Siemen has already gained a lot of experience, despite his young age. The skills he displays testify to a high professional level.

What is particularly striking is that Siemen repeatedly manages to have enough information with a small brief to realize a professional rendering. Siemen thinks visually and can effortlessly translate this into a strong way of working out graphics within a parametric environment.

Siemen is always looking for ways that a visualization can be improved, preferably by harnessing the processing power of a platform, and making maximum use of parametric functions and Geometry Nodes. As a result, he achieves the desired visualization faster.

With this book, he shows the thinking frameworks you need to get to a result quickly. Always seen from a practical angle, Siemen takes you into the world of Blender.

Wouter Adriaensen,

Owner of Mercurius 3, a full-service design agency

Contributors

About the author

Siemen Lens is a CG artist who excels at photorealism. He currently studies multimedia in Antwerp. His specialty is creating abstract yet photorealistic renders using Geometry Nodes, physics, texturing, and various other techniques in Blender. He also uses other software such as After Effects, Illustrator, and VEGAS Pro. Siemen has worked as a product render designer in a furniture company. He has also worked at PartydoosMedia, a Dutch digital graphic design agency. His goal is to create visually convincing CG art that is pleasing to the eye. With this book, he aims to get you well versed with Geometry Nodes.

I would like to express my deepest gratitude to all those who have supported me throughout the writing process of this book. I would also like to extend my appreciation to Mihir Roy for recommending me to Packt Publishing.

About the reviewers

Maurice Gysin is a student from Switzerland and finishes school this year. He has been using Blender for over a year and made a 3D animation as his graduation project. He is passionate about 3D modeling and creating art with Blender. He loves to explore the capabilities of Blender and create unique and innovative projects. He is eager to push the boundaries of 3D design and continues to learn and grow with the software. He is currently studying and learning new skills to improve his 3D modeling and animation abilities.

Van den Eynden Jeroen is a graphic media student in Antwerp, Belgium.

While he is an aspiring Blender artist, with the help of this book and the great programs covered in it, he started to improve his understanding of the software.

Table of Contents

Preface   xiii

Part 1 – Familiarizing Yourself with the Node System

1

An Introduction to Geometry Nodes   3

Technical requirements	4	The different node connections and how to use them	7
Understanding the Geometry Node system	4	Exploring different shapes	7
In what situations are Geometry Nodes applicable?	5	Exploring different node connection colors	8
		Multi-connection inputs	11
Understanding the Geometry Node editor	5	Exercise – accessing the Geometry Node system	11
Exploring the standard Geometry Nodes blocks	6	Summary	14

2

Understanding the Functionality of Basic Nodes   15

What are basic nodes?	15	Understanding how to manipulate Points	19
Exploring Mesh nodes	15		
The Subdivision Surface node	16	The Distribute Points on Faces node	20
The Join Geometry node	17	The Mesh to Points node	21
The Set Shade Smooth node	18	The Instance on Points node	22
The Extrude Mesh node	18		

Instance nodes	23	The Curve to Mesh node	25
Translating Instances	23	The Mesh to Volume node	26
The Geometry to Instance node	24	Volume to Mesh	27
The Realize Instances node	24	**Summary**	**28**

3

Must-Have Add-ons for Building Node Trees — 29

Exploring must-have add-ons	29	The Node Arrange add-on	34
The Node Wrangler add-on	29	How to use the add-on	34
How to use the add-on	30	**Exercise – how to install add-ons in Blender**	**36**
Shortcuts	33	Enabling add-ons	36

Part 2 – Creating a Mesh in the Geometry Node System

4

Making Use of Node Primitives — 41

Introduction to Node Primitives	**41**	**Curve nodes**	**48**
Why use Node Primitives?	42	Where can you find Curve Primitive Node?	48
Where can you find Node Primitives?	42	The Curve Line Primitive Node	49
Mesh nodes	**43**	The Curve Circle Primitive Node	50
Where can you find Mesh Primitive Nodes?	43	The Bezier Segment Primitive Node	51
The Cube Primitive Node	43	The Star Primitive Node	52
The Grid Primitive Node	44	The Spiral Primitive Node	53
The UV Sphere Primitive Node	44	**Exercise – your first Geometry Nodes project**	**54**
The Ico Sphere Primitive Node	45	**Summary**	**58**
The Mesh Line Primitive Node	46		
The Cone and Cylinder Primitive Nodes	47		

5

Distributing Instances onto a Mesh — 59

Distributing the points on a Grid primitive — 59
Exploring the nodes we will be using — 60
Building up the node tree — 60

Instancing objects on points — 63
Randomizing instances — 66
Experimenting with Group Inputs — 68
How to utilize Group Inputs? — 69

Exercise – creating a grassy field — 70
Sketching the idea — 70
The nodes we will need — 70
Modeling the terrain — 71
Modeling a blade of grass — 71
Setting up your Geometry Node editor — 72
Distributing and instancing the points — 72
Randomizing the grass — 75
Linking a material to your mesh — 76
Cleaning up your node tree — 78
Using Group Inputs to add sliders to the modifier — 79

Summary — 80

6

Working with the Spreadsheet in Blender — 81

Introduction to the Spreadsheet — 81
What does the Spreadsheet do? — 82
Exploring the different datasets in Spreadsheet — 82
Filtering items using the Spreadsheet — 84

Demonstrating how the Spreadsheet can be useful — 85
Introducing the nodes you'll need — 85
Building the structure of the node tree — 86

Exercise – creating a rotated tesseract cube — 90
Sketching the basic idea — 90
Introducing the nodes you'll need — 90
Building the node tree — 91
Adding a material to your tesseract cube — 96

Summary — 97

7

Creating and Modifying Text in the Geometry Node Editor — 99

Introducing strings — 99
The various nodes we will use in this chapter — 100
Where can you find String nodes? — 100
Introducing you to the different String nodes — 102

Converting strings into a usable mesh — 107
The String to Curves node — 107
The Fill Curve node — 108
The Extrude Mesh node — 108

Exercise – making a procedural countdown — 109
Sketching the basic idea — 109
Exploring the nodes required to make a procedural countdown — 110
Building the node tree — 110

Summary — 114

Part 3 – Modifying Meshes and Curves in the Geometry Node System

8

Editing Curves with Nodes — 117

Adding noise to your Curves — 117
Offset by Random values — 118
Offset by Noise Textures — 121

Giving thickness to your Curves — 124
Basic thickness control — 126
Advanced thickness control — 127

Exercise – making a simple lightning bolt — 129
Sketching the basic idea — 129
Making the node tree — 130

Summary — 136

9

Manipulating a Mesh Using Geometry Nodes — 137

Extruding your mesh — 138
Demonstrating the Extrude Mesh node — 138

Using Booleans in your mesh — 141
Demonstrating the Difference mode — 142

Adding noise to your mesh — 144
Demonstrating how to add noise to your mesh — 144

Exercise – making a procedural tree — 146
Making the node tree — 146

Summary — 153

Part 4 – Hands-On Projects Involving Advanced Workflow Techniques

10

Creating a Procedural Plant Generator — 157

Creating the node tree	157	**Utilizing group inputs**	169
Creating the stem	158	What inputs will we include?	169
Creating the leaves	162	Renaming the group inputs	170
		Summary	173

11

Creating a Procedural Spiderweb Generator — 175

Creating a scene in our Viewport	176	Adding detail and randomization	182
Creating our node tree	178	**Group inputs**	184
What's a convex hull?	178	**Organizing your node tree using Reroutes**	186
Creating a convex hull around our objects	179		
Making a wireframe from the convex hull	179	**Summary**	187

12

Constructing a Procedural LED Panel — 189

What are named attributes?	189	Storing the RGB values in named attributes	196
How do LED panels work?	190	Creating materials	199
Creating the node tree	191	Linking the named attributes to the materials	201
Creating a single subpixel	191		
Creating an array of pixels	192	**Adding group inputs to the node tree**	202
Creating an array for every subpixel	193		
		Summary	205

Part 5 – Best Practices to Improve Your Workflow

13

Tips and Tricks for the Geometry Node Editor — 209

Converting a mesh to a wireframe	210	Linking weight paint with Geometry Nodes	219
Remeshing in the Geometry Node editor	212	Making use of geometry proximity	224
Using volumes to model in the editor	214	Manual calculation	225
		Using the Geometry Proximity node	228
Aligning instanced objects along a normal	216	Exercise – making two meshes merge together	230
		Summary	233

14

Troubleshooting the Most Common Problems in Geometry Nodes — 235

Exploring the most common problems in Geometry Nodes	235	When the chosen material doesn't appear on the model	247
My shading behaves weirdly	235	Applying a modifier makes parts of the mesh disappear	248
My node tree is very slow	245	Summary	248
Common mistakes when working with Geometry Nodes	247		

Appendix

Important Shortcuts — 249

Index — 251

Other Books You May Enjoy — 260

Preface

Welcome to *Procedural 3D Modeling Using Geometry Nodes in Blender*!

This book is designed to provide a comprehensive guide to understanding and utilizing Geometry Nodes in your 3D modeling workflows.

Geometry Nodes are a powerful tool in the world of Blender modeling, allowing for greater flexibility and control over your models. With the ability to create complex shapes, manipulate vertices and faces, and generate intricate patterns, Geometry Nodes can take your 3D modeling skills to the next level.

In this book, we will explore the various types of Geometry Nodes, their functions, and how they can be used to enhance your models. We will also cover advanced techniques such as scripting and animation, providing you with the skills and knowledge necessary to take your 3D modeling career to the next level.

Who this book is for

Whether you are a professional 3D artist or just starting out, this book will provide you with the tools and techniques needed to master the art of Geometry Nodes. With the knowledge and skills gained from this book, you will be able to create stunning, highly detailed models with ease and efficiency.

What this book covers

Chapter 1, *An Introduction to Geometry Nodes*, teaches you about the different node inputs and outputs, how the node system works, and the flow of the node system in Blender.

Chapter 2, *Understanding the Functionality of Basic Nodes*, covers the basic nodes we will be working with in this book, which include Math nodes, Curve nodes, and Mesh nodes, and their functions, inputs, outputs, and parameters as the building blocks for the rest of the book.

Chapter 3, *Must-Have Add-ons for Building Node Trees*, explains the various free add-ons available inside Blender and how to download them, along with their functionality and technicality in depth to enhance your node tree-building journey.

Chapter 4, *Making Use of Node Primitives*, explores the functions of the primitive nodes in Blender, including the Curve primitives and the Mesh primitives.

Chapter 5, *Distributing Instances onto a Mesh*, teaches you how to apply the skills and techniques learned in previous chapters to distribute points on a plane, and helps you learn about handy nodes, such as the **Random value** node, to add randomization to your projects.

Chapter 6, *Working with the Spreadsheet in Blender*, teaches you how to use the **Duplicate elements** node to duplicate elements procedurally. You will also learn how to work with the **Spreadsheet** feature.

Chapter 7, *Creating and Modifying Text in the Geometry Node Editor*, teaches you how to create and modify text in the Geometry Nodes editor.

Chapter 8, *Editing Curves with Nodes*, explains how to modify curves using noise and thickness nodes and apply the skills in a lightning bolt exercise.

Chapter 9, *Manipulating a Mesh Using Geometry Nodes*, teaches you how to use Geometry Nodes to manipulate mesh by extruding, subdividing, smoothing, and applying Boolean effects.

Chapter 10, *Creating a Procedural Plant Generator*, explains how to create a plant generator using custom curves, distribution, and instancing leaves and how to make a pot using Geometry Nodes.

Chapter 11, *Creating a Procedural Spiderweb Generator*, explains how to create a procedural web generator by making use of the **Convex Hull**.

Chapter 12, *Constructing a Procedural LED Panel*, covers how to create a procedural LED panel by creating an array of red, green, and blue pixels and using **Named Attributes** to link the Material editor to the Geometry Nodes editor.

Chapter 13, *Tips and Tricks for the Geometry Nodes Editor*, explores various tips and tricks for the Geometry Nodes editor, including techniques for vertex proximity, weight painting, and remeshing to enhance your modeling workflow.

Chapter 14, *Troubleshooting the Most Common Problems in Geometry Nodes Editor*, covers troubleshooting techniques for Geometry Nodes, including methods for fixing shading, optimizing slow node trees, and addressing common issues.

To get the most out of this book

To get the most out of this book, you will need to have Blender version 3.3 LTS installed. You should possess basic knowledge of basic material nodes, modeling, and viewport control within Blender. This will enable you to follow the instructions and create the desired results from the book. Without these prerequisites, the book may be difficult to understand and follow.

Software/hardware covered in the book	Operating system requirements
Blender 3.3	Windows, macOS, or Linux

Download the supporting files

To download and view the complete node trees of the relevant chapters, click on this link: `https://packt.link/UvynW`.

To make it easier for you, we have included all of the node trees we cover in this book as scenes in this blend file (link above).

You can switch these scenes by looking at the top right of your screen, where you see the name of the exercise. If you click this, you'll get the option to select your preferred chapter.

Download the color images

We also provide a PDF file that has color images of the screenshots and diagrams used in this book. You can download it here: `https://packt.link/IDhC9`

> **Important**
> Some of the images might not be clear in the printed book, so it is recommended that you download the graphic bundle.

Conventions used

There are a number of text conventions used throughout this book.

Bold: Indicates a new term, an important word, or words that you see onscreen. For instance, words in menus or dialog boxes appear in **bold**. Here is an example: "To do this, let's go to the **Layout** workspace and press the *Tab* key to enter **Edit Mode**."

> **Tips or important notes**
> Appear like this.

Get in touch

Feedback from our readers is always welcome.

General feedback: If you have questions about any aspect of this book, email us at `customercare@packtpub.com` and mention the book title in the subject of your message.

Errata: Although we have taken every care to ensure the accuracy of our content, mistakes do happen. If you have found a mistake in this book, we would be grateful if you would report this to us. Please visit `www.packtpub.com/support/errata` and fill in the form.

Piracy: If you come across any illegal copies of our works in any form on the internet, we would be grateful if you would provide us with the location address or website name. Please contact us at `copyright@packt.com` with a link to the material.

If you are interested in becoming an author: If there is a topic that you have expertise in and you are interested in either writing or contributing to a book, please visit `authors.packtpub.com`.

Share your thoughts

Once you've read this book, we'd love to hear your thoughts! Scan the following QR code to go straight to the Amazon review page for this book and share your feedback.

`https://packt.link/r/1804612553`

Your review is important to us and the tech community and will help us make sure we're delivering excellent quality content.

Download a free PDF copy of this book

Thanks for purchasing this book!

Do you like to read on the go but are unable to carry your print books everywhere? Is your e-book purchase not compatible with the device of your choice?

Don't worry! With every Packt book, you now get a DRM-free PDF version of that book at no cost.

Read anywhere, any place, on any device. Search, copy, and paste code from your favorite technical books directly into your application.

The perks don't stop there; you can get exclusive access to discounts, newsletters, and great free content in your inbox daily.

Follow these simple steps to get the benefits:

1. Scan the QR code or visit the following link:

   `https://packt.link/free-ebook/9781804612552`

2. Submit your proof of purchase.

That's it! We'll email your free PDF and other benefits to you directly.

Part 1 – Familiarizing Yourself with the Node System

Welcome to the first part of this book, where we will be introducing you to the world of node-based geometry manipulation in Blender. In this section, you will familiarize yourself with Geometry Nodes and understand the functionalities of basic nodes and must-have add-ons for building node trees.

This section comprises the following chapters:

- *Chapter 1, An Introduction to Geometry Nodes*
- *Chapter 2, Understanding the Functionalities of Basic Nodes*
- *Chapter 3, Must-Have Add-Ons for Building Node Trees*

1
An Introduction to Geometry Nodes

In this book, you'll learn how to work with **Geometry Nodes**. You will find basic and intermediate-level information about Geometry Nodes here. This book will help you learn various topics, such as distributing points, modifying meshes, creating meshes, and covering the basic nodes.

If you are learning any kind of Blender workflow, Geometry Nodes will surely be a handy tool to know about. They open up new possibilities for procedural modeling and animation.

You'll also get the chance to try your skills with fun exercises throughout this book; these include exercises such as making a procedural plant, a procedural landscape, and a Procedural LED panel.

In this chapter, we'll talk about the practicality of Geometry Nodes, why they might be useful for you, and some scenarios in which this new tool will be helpful. We will also go over the different node inputs and outputs. Finally, at the end of this chapter, you will learn how to access the Geometry Node system.

In this chapter, we will cover the following topics:

- Understanding the Geometry Node system
- In what situations are Geometry Nodes applicable?
- Understanding the Geometry Node editor
- The different node inputs and outputs
- And finally, how to access the Geometry Node editor

Technical requirements

In this book, we will use Blender version 3.3, which can be downloaded from this link: `https://download.blender.org/release/Blender3.3/`

If you do not have certain nodes, then you might have an outdated version of Blender. While newer versions of Blender might work with this book, we cannot guarantee that everything will match the explanations we give. For the best experience, we recommend using **Blender 3.3**.

To download and view the complete node trees of the relevant chapters, click on this link: `https://packt.link/UvynW`.

To make it easier for you, we have included all of the node trees we cover in this book as scenes in this blend file (link above). You can switch these scenes by looking at the top right of your screen, where you see the name of the exercise. If you click this, you'll get the option to select your preferred chapter.

Understanding the Geometry Node system

The Geometry Node editor is a new feature in **Blender 3.0**. Over the months, it has evolved into a very useful tool that every CG artist should know. Geometry Nodes is all about procedurally modeling your mesh. This can help with big scenes where you need lots of objects to have variation. For example, if you are making a forest, every tree needs to have a bit of variation; otherwise, the scene will look like a render. To easily add variation to trees, we use Geometry Nodes.

Previously, creators would use hair particles to scatter objects along a mesh. With Geometry Nodes, this is no longer needed. Geometry Nodes will help in scattering all objects just the way you want. There are lots of ways to scatter your objects. We will also go over the various ways to randomize these instances. The idea of Geometry Nodes is to procedurally generate a complex mesh out of a basic and simple input.

Unlike the Material Nodes editor, which does not use a Modifier, the Geometry Node editor is a Modifier that can be applied from the **Modifiers** tab. This Modifier can be combined with other Modifiers like any other would. The Geometry Nodes Modifier consists of a few parts:

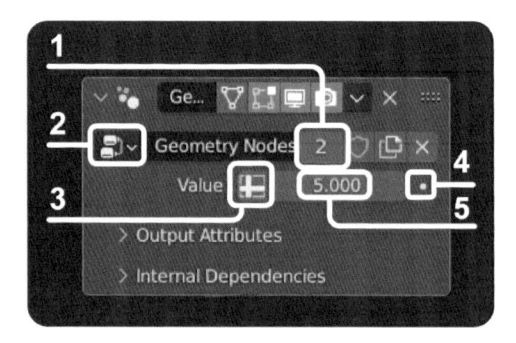

Figure 1.1: The Geometry Nodes Modifier

Part 1 refers to how many times the node tree has been used. If the node tree is only being used by one object, this number will not be there. The button in part 2 allows you to select a node tree out of the different node trees in your project.

Part 3 allows you to link various attributes to this variable. For example, you can link weight paint values with this for a simple stone distribution solution.

The button in part 4 allows you to animate the value of part 5. This can also be done by pressing *i* on any value field.

Lastly, part 5 defines the current value that is being inputted into the node tree. You can change this value by clicking on it or by holding down your mouse cursor while sliding.

Behind this Modifier lies the Geometry Node system. It consists of various nodes to procedurally model your objects.

In what situations are Geometry Nodes applicable?

Many people think that Geometry Nodes are the new way to model in Blender, and for certain scenarios, this is true. But there are times when you're better off using the normal modeling workflow.

Geometry Nodes are usually used to procedurally generate multiple objects at once and to scatter objects around on a mesh, for example, scattering grass onto a field, generating roads procedurally, or generating multiple buildings at once.

Geometry Nodes are generally not used to model complex organic structures with lots of features, for example, faces, human figures, clothes, etc.

While it is certainly possible to model these objects via Geometry Nodes, it's very impractical to do so because the amount of detail in these objects is near impossible to program mathematically using Geometry Nodes. It's much more practical to model the structures via the normal modeling workflow in Blender.

Now that we've got a better understanding of when Geometry Nodes are applicable, we'll talk about everything you need to know about the Geometry Node editor.

Understanding the Geometry Node editor

The Geometry Node system makes use of the node tree design in Blender, like the material node editor. Much like the material node editor, the node system flows from left to right. Geometry Nodes can modify and create different types of geometry, such as the following:

- Meshes
- Curves
- Point clouds
- Volumes
- Instances

Let's take an in-depth look at these terms.

A mesh is a structural build of a 3D model consisting of faces. 3D meshes make use of the three axis points, x, y, and z. A mesh is made up of vertices, which make up edges, which, in turn, make up faces.

A curve is a way to define paths in Blender; this can be used on multiple occasions. For example, if you want a camera to follow a specific path, this can be done with curves. These can also be modified, used, and created in the Geometry Node editor. This will be explained in *Chapter 8*, *Editing Curves with Nodes*.

A point cloud is a selection of scattered points around a mesh. These point clouds are only visible in the viewport and not in the render.

A volume is a semi-transparent effect that can also be experimented with in the Geometry Node editor. Volumes are usually used to create abstract effects in the Geometry Node editor but can also be used to create a foggy atmosphere in your scene.

An instance is best explained as a copy of the original mesh. This can be used to copy multiple objects around a mesh, much like we used to do with hair particles. This is mostly used to scatter rocks or grass onto a base mesh.

All of these datatypes will use the same connection type, a Geometry connection. This node connection is green. Let's have a look at the input and output node connection of the Geometry Node system.

Exploring the standard Geometry Nodes blocks

The first node that this book will introduce you to is the **Group Input** node.

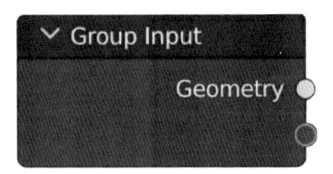

Figure 1.2: Group Input node

The standard **Geometry** output of this node returns the base mesh of your object before any modifications have been made. This mesh basically returns the mesh you've inputted into the object's **Edit** mode.

This node is used to add variables to the Geometry Nodes Modifier so that you can have easy access to the most used variables. To create these variables, just slide a value into the unused node socket, and it will automatically occupy the node socket.

At the end of the node tree, you will use a **Group Output** node.

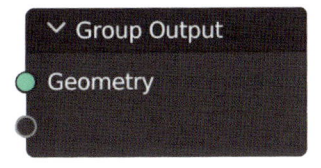

Figure 1.3: Group Output node

This will define the end of the Modifier. Just like the **Group Input** node, the **Group Output** node has an unused node socket to output extra data to the Modifier. This can be used to define UV maps, for example.

The different node connections and how to use them

Now that we've looked into the group input and group output nodes, let's go over the various node connection inputs and outputs.

Let's start by explaining the various input and output shapes in the Geometry Node editor.

Exploring different shapes

Let's take a closer look at the input and output shapes in the Geometry Node editor.

The round node connection

This is what a round input/output node connection looks like:

Figure 1.4: The round input/output node connection

This is a round input/output node connection. This defines a single node value. For example, in geometry nodes, a single node connection can send through multiple values from other locations. With a round connection, this is not the case. This will likely result in the value being rounded to one value or returning an error value.

The squared input/output node connection

This is what a squared input/output node connection looks like:

Figure 1.5: The squared input/output node connection

It accepts multivalue fields. This means that every vertex on our mesh will be calculated separately according to the node tree. This feature in Geometry Nodes is very fun to play around with because each point gets its own flow of calculation, which opens up a world of interesting possibilities. An example of this feature is adding noise displacement to your mesh; each vertex will get its own displacement because each vertex is being calculated separately thanks to the square input/output node connection.

Exploring different node connection colors

Here's an in-depth look at the different colors in the Geometry Node editor.

Boolean node connection

This node connection offers Boolean values.

Figure 1.6: The Boolean input/output node connection

This node connection will define either an *on* or an *off* value; in other words, this is a value with either a 1 or a 0. As explained previously, this can either be a single value (circle shape) or multiple values (square shape).

Vector node connection

This is a vector node connection.

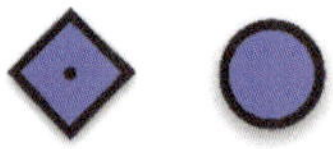

Figure 1.7: The vector input/output node connection

This carries three values combined into one. These values can be separated with a **Separate XYZ** node. It can also be combined with a **Combine XYZ** node. The vector node is used to define positions, rotations, scales, and offsets. It can also be used to define UV maps in the material node editor.

Geometry node connection

This is a geometry node connection.

Figure 1.8: The geometry input/output node connection

This defines geometry and instances. When you slide an object from the outliner into the Geometry Node editor, you will see this connection to add this instance to your Geometry Nodes project. This is also the connection you will see when you generate a point cloud with the **Distribute Points on Faces** node. This node will also show up on both sides when you use any geometry-modifying node, such as **Transform Instance** node, **Scale Instance** node, and any primitive mesh node. All of these nodes will be explained in *Chapter 2, Understanding the Functionalities of Basic Nodes*.

Integer node connection

This is the integer node connection.

Figure 1.9: The integer input/output node connection

This defines or accepts any value that is an integer; some examples of integer values are 0, 1, 2, 3, and 4. These values are basically values without a decimal point. These are usually used to define indexes of certain things, for example, duplicate objects. This node connection can be found on nodes such as the **ID** node, the **Duplicate Elements** node, and the **Index** node.

Value node connection

This is the value node connection, also known as the factor node connection.

Figure 1.10: The value input/output node connection

This defines a plain value. The difference between this and an integer node connection is that the value node connection can contain decimal points. Some examples of nodes containing this node connection are the **Noise Texture** node and any math node. This value can also make use of multivalue fields, just like the square symbol we previously discussed.

Color node connection

This is a color value.

Figure 1.11: The color input/output node connection

This node connection contains three values, an R channel (red), a G channel (green), and a B channel (blue), also known as the RGB channels. These can be separated into their respective RGB values using a **Separate RGB** node. They can also be combined using a Combine RGB node. Just like the examples explained in the *Exploring different shapes* section, this node connection can also make use of multivalue fields.

String node connection

This node connection defines a string of text.

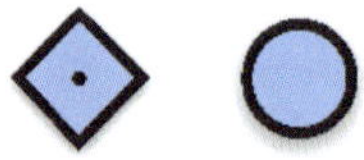

Figure 1.12: The string input/output node connection

This value will mainly be seen on nodes that are made to create or modify text, such as the **String** node, the **String to Curves** node, and the **String Length** node. This will be explained in depth later on in the book.

Material node connection

This node connection defines a material.

Figure 1.13: The material input/output node connection

It can be used to set the material of selected geometry in the node editor. This node basically refers to a material you've already made and one that is included in the project file. Some nodes that make use of this node connection are the **Material** node, the **Set Material** node, and the **Replace Material** node.

Multi-connection inputs

Let's look into some special node connections.

Multi-Connection inputs allow you to connect multiple output connections into one input socket. This is generally used to join multiple datatypes of the same type into one output.

Figure 1.14: Geometry multi-connection input

The node connection seen here is usually used to combine elements; for example, the input shown in the preceding figure is used to join geometry together.

Figure 1.15: String multi-connection input

The preceding socket is used to join strings together. It works in the same way as the geometry multi-connection input.

Exercise – accessing the Geometry Node system

Now, you'll learn how to access the handy Geometry Nodes tool in Blender.

Make sure you at least have **Blender 3.2**, but in this book and chapter, we will be using **Blender 3.3**. Let's begin:

1. Firstly, let's start by opening Blender.
2. Then, you can head on to the **Geometry Nodes** tab in the top section of your screen. Now your journey begins.

12 An Introduction to Geometry Nodes

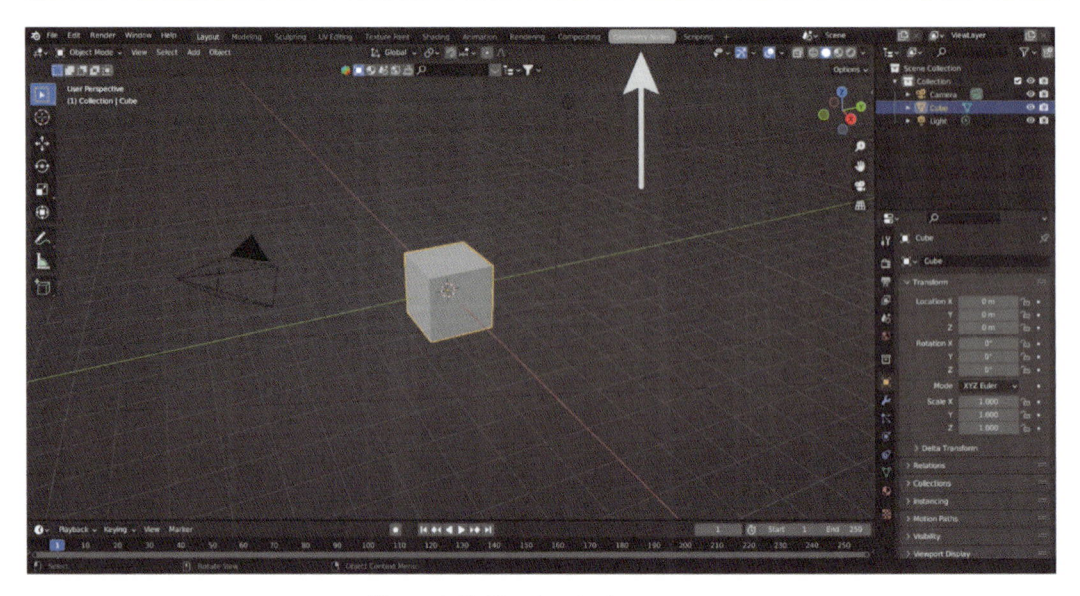

Figure 1.16: Blender startup screen

When you click on the **Geometry Nodes** tab at the top of your screen, you'll see the following:

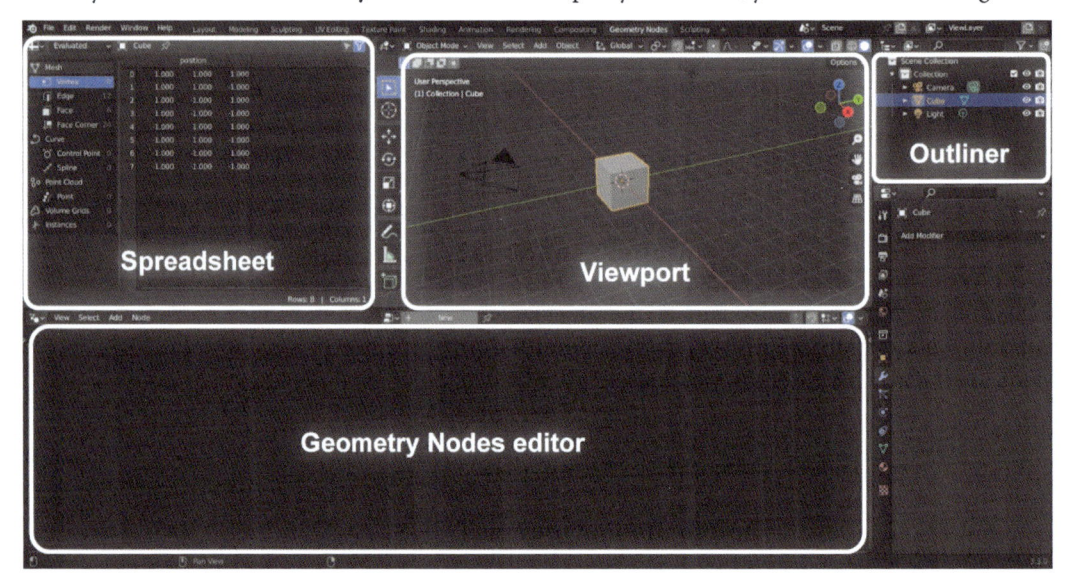

Figure 1.17: Geometry Node editor tab with info overlayed

This might look overwhelming at first sight, but don't worry, this book will guide you through all the parts of this node editor.

There are four parts you'll need to know about on this screen:

- **Spreadsheet**

    This is a separate window that allows you to see various bits of information about elements of your geometry, such as, for example, the properties of instances.

- **Viewport**

    This is your main view in Blender. It allows you to see the project in 3D space.

- **Outliner**

    This is a list of all the objects in your current scene. This makes it easy to create instances by sliding your object from the outliner right into the Geometry Node editor.

- **Geometry Node editor**

    The Geometry Nodes editor is your main editing workspace for working with Geometry Node trees.

To start working on Geometry Nodes, it's important to learn how to add a node tree to your projects. There are two ways to do this:

- One way to do this is to add a Geometry Nodes Modifier from the **Modifiers** tab in the **Properties** tab:

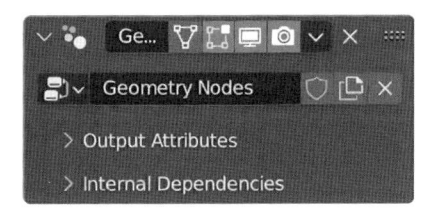

Figure 1.18: Geometry Nodes Modifier

    After you've added the Modifier to the Modifier stack, you'll need to press the **New** button. You've now successfully created a new node group.

- The other way to do this (and the quicker way since we're already in the Geometry Nodes workspace) is to just click the **New** button in the Geometry Node editor. This automatically adds a new Geometry Nodes Modifier along with a beginning and end node. The following figure shows the **New** button you'll find at the top of the Geometry Nodes workspace to add a new node tree, along with all the functions of the button.

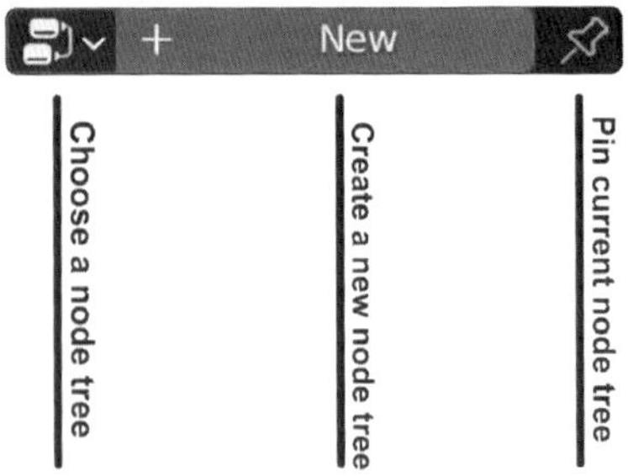

Figure 1.19: Node group selection box

This is the end of the chapter. In this chapter, you've learned about the various node connections you will come across in the node editor, along with how to access the node editor.

Congratulations! You now know the basics of the Geometry Node editor.

Summary

In this chapter, we've covered the various node connections. This includes the Vector, Boolean, Color, Integer, Value, String, Material, and Geometry Inputs, along with the different shapes of node connections. We have explained how to access the Geometry Node editor in various ways, how the node system works, how it flows, and everything there is to know about this new system in Blender. Having read this chapter, you will now understand how this Geometry Node system works and what kinds of node connections are available in the Geometry Node editor.

In the next chapter, we'll go over the basic nodes you'll be needing the most in your basic projects. This is important because we will be using these nodes in the coming chapters.

2
Understanding the Functionality of Basic Nodes

In the last chapter, you learned how to use the Geometry Node system; in this chapter, we will be explaining the building blocks, or *nodes* of the Geometry Node system.

To get started, we'll introduce you to the basic nodes that you will be using throughout this book. The basic nodes are the nodes that you will use in most of your projects to perform basic commands, such as combining meshes, converting meshes, instancing points on your mesh, and more. We will also explain what every input, output, and value means with visual examples.

In this chapter, we will cover the following topics:

- Exploring Mesh nodes
- Understanding how to manipulate Points
- Instance nodes
- Converter nodes

What are basic nodes?

The basic nodes are the nodes that you will use the most in your Geometry Nodes projects, not only in this book but also when you will start creating Geometry Nodes projects on your own. These nodes perform the basic operations that you will need regularly, such as the **Subdivision Surface** node, the Join Geometry node, the Extrude Mesh node, and many more nodes that you will need most of the time.

Exploring Mesh nodes

Let's start by explaining the nodes you'll need the most, the Mesh nodes. These are used to modify the mesh you are working with. In this chapter, we will go over the most basic nodes you are likely to use with any Geometry Nodes project.

The Subdivision Surface node

We are all familiar with the **Subdivision Surface** modifier.

Figure 2.1: Subdivision Surface node

To easily explain this node, we will be comparing it to the modifier. The input node called **Mesh** refers to the mesh you give the node to process. The **Level** integer value refers to the iterations of subdivision, just as the modifier offers.

The next values you'll see on the node aren't values we see on the modifier. These are *creasing values*. These define how much the mesh should be affected by the **Subdivision Surface** modifier. As you can see by the square node connection shape, the node has a multivalued field. That means that this node can process multiple values of creasing at different points.

Now, let's look at different creasing examples.

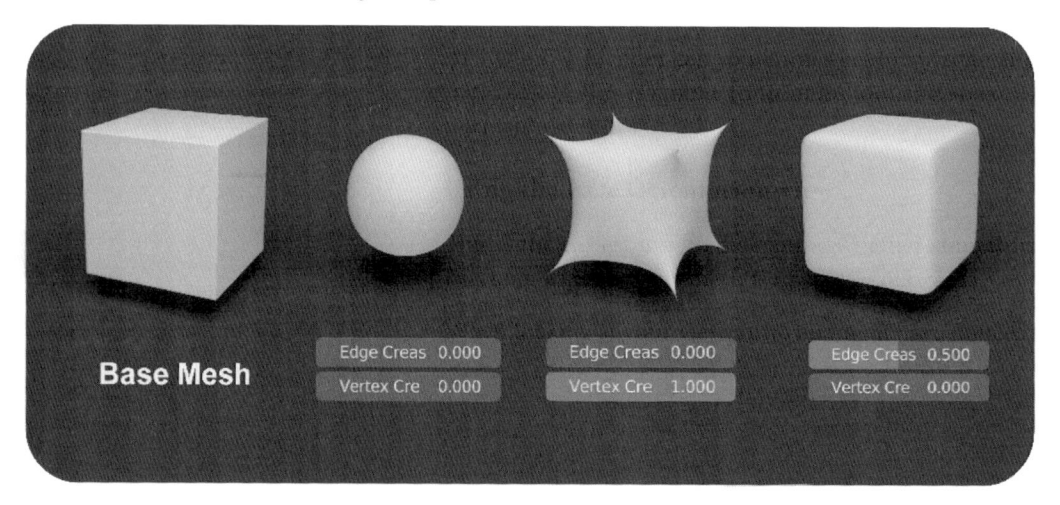

Figure 2.2: Different creasing examples

As you can see in the preceding screenshot, there are two types of creasing values.

Edge Creasing defines how much each edge is impacted by the **Subdivision Surface** modifier. 0 means 100% impact, and 1 means 0% impact.

Vertex Creasing works in the same way, except that instead of the edges being impacted, you're now impacting each vertex, respectively.

The Join Geometry node

Next, we'll explain the usage of the **Join Geometry** node.

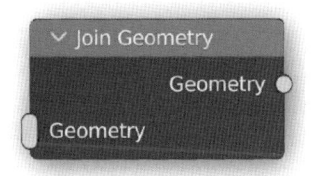

Figure 2.3: Join Geometry node

As explained in *Chapter 1*, *An Introduction to Geometry Nodes*, this node makes use of a multi-connection mesh input. This means, you can connect multiple node connections into this socket. The **Geometry** output node connection contains all the objects you've joined into one object.

The **Join Geometry** node is best explained as the **Join** function in **Object Context Menu** found when you want to merge (or join) multiple objects into one object.

Figure 2.4: Object Context Menu

> **Note**
> **Object Context Menu** can be found when right-clicking on the viewport.

You can see **Object Context Menu** in *Figure 2.4*.

The Set Shade Smooth node

The **Set Shade Smooth** node has a lot of resemblance to the **Shade Smooth** function in **Object Context Menu**.

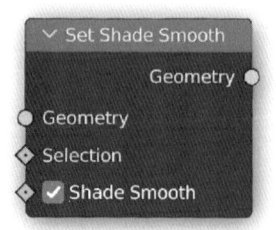

Figure 2.5: The Set Shade Smooth node

The difference between this node and the function inside of Blender is that this has a **Selection** Boolean input. This means that by using the **Geometry** input, we can selectively choose what parts of our inputted mesh can be shaded smooth and which can be shaded flat.

Using this node, we can also choose what parts of the mesh can be shaded flat using the last Boolean value. If the **Shade Smooth** Boolean node value has been turned off, the mesh will be shaded flat. The output value named **Geometry** outputs the mesh that has been shaded according to your selection inputs.

The Extrude Mesh node

The screenshot below shows the **Extrude Mesh** node.

Figure 2.6: The Extrude Mesh node

This can be compared to the **Extrude** function in **Edit Mode** (**Edit Mode** can be accessed by pressing **Tab** in the viewport). This node accepts the base mesh as an input, along with a selection of the mesh you want to extrude. If no value is given, it will select all the mesh to be extruded. The **Offset** value defines the offset that the extruded faces will use. This value is a vector value and can be controlled using values of the same purple socket.

Offset Scale defines how much the faces will be extruded.

The **Individual** Boolean value defines whether the extruded parts of the mesh should stay together or not. If the value is unchecked, the extruded parts will form additional faces in between the gaps of the extruded faces.

The **Mesh** output gives the extruded mesh, along with all the modifications. The two other Boolean values define the sides and tops of the extruded mesh.

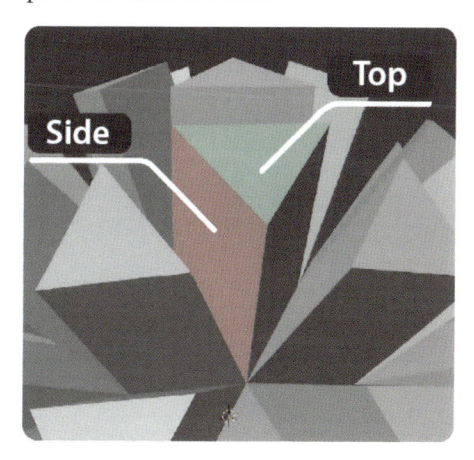

Figure 2.7: Tops and sides of the extruded mesh

Now that we've explained the basic Mesh nodes, let's go over the basic points nodes that you will be using.

Understanding how to manipulate Points

Points are used to distribute instances onto a mesh, but they can also be converted to volumes. Learning how to distribute points onto a mesh is a crucial step in learning about Geometry Nodes, as you will be using them the most. So, without further ado, let's get right into this section.

The Distribute Points on Faces node

This node is used to randomly distribute points onto a mesh.

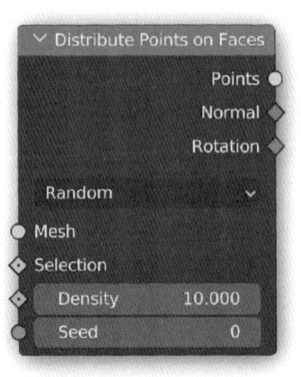

Figure 2.8: The Distribute Points on Faces node

It gets a base mesh as an input, such as a plane or Ico Sphere, but any mesh works.

It will randomly scatter points all over your inputted mesh with the distribution method of your choice. The only requirement to be able to place points is that the mesh must contain faces. If your mesh does not contain faces, you must use a **Mesh to Points** node (*Figure 2.10*).

There are multiple point distribution methods:

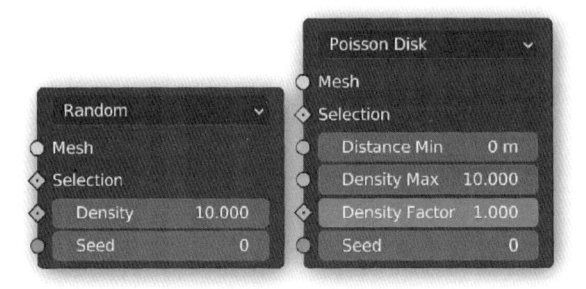

Figure 2.9: Different distribution methods

- **Random**: This will scatter the objects randomly around a mesh with no regard for the distance between each point:

    - The **Density** value defines how dense the point distribution is
    - The **Seed** value defines how it will be randomly distributed

- **Poisson Disk**: This will scatter the objects with a Poisson sampling method, which means that you'll have finer control over the placement of the points:

  - **Distance Min** controls the minimum radius each point should have from another point.
  - **Density Max** controls the max density of the placement of the points.
  - **Density Factor** controls the density by a factor of 0 to 1, which can also be controlled via a multivalued field. This means we can control this with a noise map using a texture node. You'll learn how to do this in *Chapter 9, Manipulating Mesh Using Geometry Nodes*.
  - The **Seed** value, just like the **Random** distribution, controls the random placement of the points.

The node has a **Points** output, which is a geometry output that does not contain the base mesh. If you want the base mesh, you'll have to add it back with a **Join Geometry** node. The node also has the **Normal** and **Rotation** vector outputs, which define the way that each point is facing along the mesh.

The Mesh to Points node

This node will convert mesh to points without randomization.

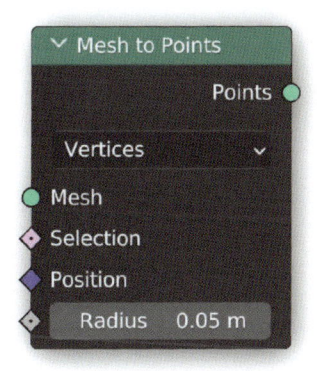

Figure 2.10: Mesh to Points

It will place a point at every vertex. This can also be useful for distributing along a grid or mesh.

Once again, we have the **Selection** Boolean value to select which of the mesh will be converted to points, 0 means no points, and 1 means there will be points.

The **Position** vector value defines the position of each point. This is useful for placing the points in a custom position, for example, on a line or along the normal of the original mesh.

The last input is the **Radius** value. This defines the radius of each point. This radius does not serve much of a purpose other than a Viewport visual.

The Instance on Points node

This is one of the nodes you will be using the most in your Geometry Nodes projects.

Figure 2.11: Instance on Points

This node will project your instances onto defined points.

This node takes a **Points** input. These are generated using the nodes of the previous subheadings.

The **Selection** Boolean value defines whether the point should be instanced or not.

The **Instance** value defines the instance that should be used. You can use any mesh as an instance if you use a **Geometry to Instance** node, this is because, by default, we can't use normal geometry as an instancing object.

The next input, the **Pick Instance** Boolean value, is a value that will only be useful with instanced collections. When not using collections, this value will not affect anything. Collections are basically groups of objects. This is useful in the Geometry Node editor for tasks such as scattering various rocks, for example.

The **Pick Instance** Boolean value comes into play if you want to place different objects of the collections as separate objects, which can be chosen using the integer value below the **Instance Index** value. We will do a project on this in the advanced part of the book (*Part 4*).

The **Rotation** and **Scale** values define the rotation and scale of each instance separately. These nodes make use of multivalued fields that can be connected to the **Random Value** node, for example.

Instance nodes

In the previous heading, we talked about how to place and instance points. In this section, we will explain how to edit these instances and modify them accordingly.

Translating Instances

These nodes are used to position your instanced objects.

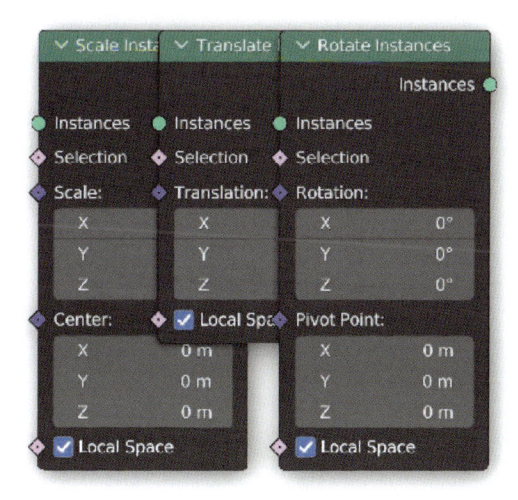

Figure 2.12: Translating Instances nodes

These nodes include the **Translate Instances** node, the **Scale Instances** node, and the **Rotate Instances** node. These three nodes are generally the same in terms of input and output node connections.

The **Instances** value accepts the instanced objects. These can be used to individually translate objects along the multivalued vector value.

The **Selection** Boolean input defines whether the instance should be influenced by the node. 0 means not influenced, 1 means influenced.

The last input is the **Local Space** input. If this is checked, the local space will be used as a positioning system; otherwise, the world space will be used as the standard positioning system.

On the **Scale Instances** node, there is an option called **Center**. This defines the center where the scaling happens. It's a multivalued node, so this can also be influenced by, for example, a noise texture or a random value.

The **Rotate Instances** node has an extra option called **Pivot**. Just like the **Center** option in the **Rotate instances** node, this defines the center of where the rotation will happen.

The Geometry to Instance node

This is a very widely used node.

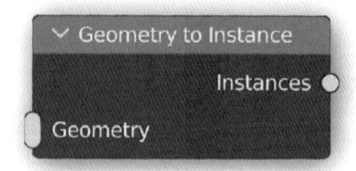

Figure 2.13: The Geometry to Instance node

This node will convert **Geometry** to **Instances**. What this means is that the geometry will be divided into separate objects that can be moved separately. For example, if you want to move multiple objects, you'll convert them to instances first, because the normal **Translate** node does not contain a multivalued socket. This might be a problem if you want to move objects separately from each other.

On the other hand, the **Translate Instances** nodes do contain multivalued sockets.

The only input socket on this is a multi-connection socket that accepts multiple geometry inputs and joins them as an instanced object.

The Realize Instances node

This node is used to convert Instances back to **Geometry**.

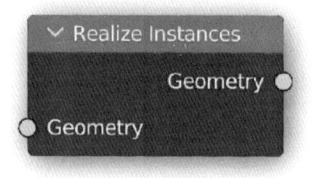

Figure 2.14: The Realize Instances node

The main problem that you might face if you apply the Geometry Nodes modifier is that instances might disappear from your mesh.

This happens because instances are a mere illusion of mesh. They are not real geometry, but they appear as real geometry. To make them real geometry, we need to realize the instances.

This node will solve that by converting, or realizing **Instances** back to a **Geometry** mesh.

Let's now go over the **Converter** nodes; you'll need these nodes a lot if you want to create sculptures with lots of Curves, and with this step comes a lot of problem-solving and creative thinking. We will be discussing **Converter** nodes last since these nodes will bind all the previous sections together.

Converter nodes

The following nodes are used to convert certain types of geometry to other types of geometry, such as mesh, Curves, instances, volumes, and points. Most of these nodes are just input-output nodes. So, I will only go over the special ones that need more explanation.

The Curve to Mesh node

This node will convert Curves to meshes. We also have the option to add a profile to the curve.

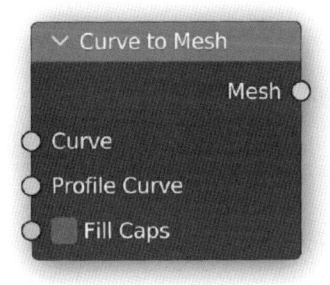

Figure 2.15: The Curve to Mesh node

The **Profile Curve** value accepts a curve node connection such as, for example, a curve circle. It can also be modified in thickness using a **Set Curve Radius** node.

The **Profile Curve** value defines what shape your curve will have. If you just want it to be a tube, you can use a circle. If you want it to be a custom shape, you can use any curve you want to define the shape of your curve profile.

The **Fill Caps** Boolean value defines whether the caps will be filled in or not. The *caps* are the ends of the curve profiles.

The opposite node, the **Mesh to Curve** node, converts a mesh to a curve by disregarding the faces.

The Mesh to Volume node

This is the **Mesh to Volume** node, one of the handier nodes to use in your Geometry Nodes journey.

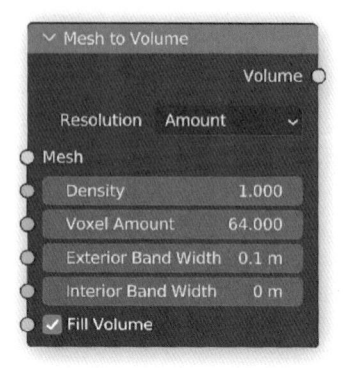

Figure 2.16: The Mesh to Volume node

It allows you to convert your mesh to a volume. The upside of using this technique is that we can convert this back to a mesh using a **Volume to Mesh** node to get a clean topology on our models.

The **Mesh to Volume** node has six inputs. For starters, it has the standard **Mesh** input that most Mesh nodes have.

Below the **Mesh** input, you will see the **Density** input. This value will define the density of the volume. A higher value means more densely packed volumes.

Voxel Amount defines the resolution of your volume. In other words, it defines the number of *voxels* your volume is allowed to contain. A *voxel* is a volume element; it literally stands for *volumetric pixel*. Below, you can see a visual demonstration of how the voxel amount progresses and affects a model.

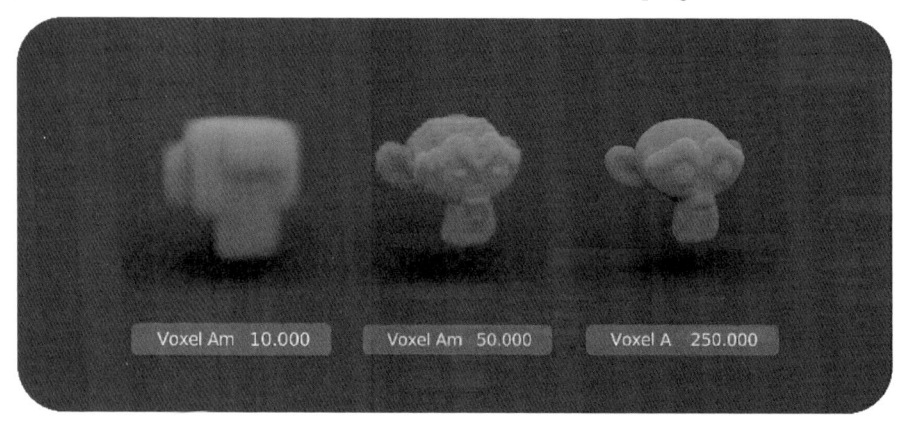

Figure 2.17: Voxel Amount demonstration

There are three inputs left in this node. Firstly, **Exterior Band Width** defines the size of the outer voxels of the volume. The larger this value, the thicker your volume is going to appear.

Interior Band Width defines the size of the inner voxels of the volume, which is less noticeable on a high exterior scale. In certain situations, it might benefit performance to turn this value down.

Lastly, we have the **Fill Volume** Boolean. This defines whether the volume should be hollow or not. If you are struggling with performance issues, please leave this unchecked. If you are noticing hollow fields in your volume, you might fix this by enabling this option.

Volume to Mesh

Last but not least of the nodes in our list is the **Volume to Mesh** node.

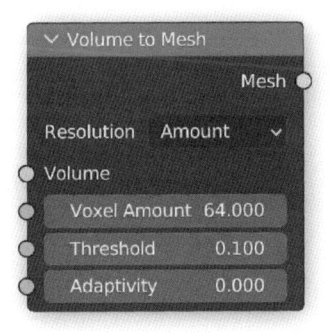

Figure 2.18: The Volume to Mesh node

This node, as the node name suggests, will convert volumes to mesh data. There are three options for defining the resolution of this converter node:

- **Grid**: This allows you to divide your volume into a grid of vertices. This option comes with the **Threshold** and **Adaptivity** values.
- **Amount**: This allows you to control the amount of voxels you will take into consideration when converting this mesh. This option comes with the **Voxel Amount**, **Threshold,** and **Adaptivity** values.
- **Size**: This allows you to control the size of each voxel. This might be more appropriate for your needs but will be less simple to control on a large-scale mesh.

We will be covering **Amount** since it gives the most control over what you're trying to achieve. You might find another option handier for your projects, so be sure to experiment with the different options.

This node contains the standard **Geometry** input, which accepts volumes, the **Voxel Amount** value, and the **Threshold** and **Adaptivity** values.

We have already covered the **Voxel Amount** value in *Figure 2.17*. It's the same concept but in reverse. So, instead of converting a mesh to a volume, we're now converting volumes to meshes.

The **Threshold** value defines at what density the volume should be turned into a mesh.

For example, if we want every single voxel to be turned into a mesh, we can use a really low threshold such as `0.001`. But you might need to fine-tune your threshold to get the result you desire.

Adaptivity will decimate your final mesh into a less performance-hungry mesh. You can experiment with this value if you're having performance issues.

The **Mesh to Volume** and **Volume to Mesh** nodes we covered can also be combined to make an excellent **Remesh** node with a lot of control. The **Remesh** function inside Blender is basically a way to clean up your topology simply and efficiently. It rewires your topology by using an algorithm. We will cover this in the advanced parts of this book.

With the **Volume to Mesh** node, we have come to the end of the chapter.

Summary

In this chapter, we covered what nodes you'll be using most frequently, along with the reason why these nodes are useful. We went over the inputs and outputs of the nodes and explained each parameter in depth.

Knowing about these parameters will help you better understand future nodes and develop a sense of how the Geometry Node system works.

Now that you have a clear understanding of all the basic nodes you will be using, let's move on to the next chapter!

In the next chapter, we will go over the add-ons that might be useful when working in the Geometry Node editor.

3
Must-Have Add-ons for Building Node Trees

In the previous chapter, you learned what the basic nodes do. In this chapter, let's have a look at the different add-ons you can use with the Geometry Node editor. These add-ons have some cool features, and they can help speed up your workflow greatly. We will also show you how to use these add-ons and where you can find them. This chapter is useful to know about the various add-ons that are present in the Geometry Node editor.

In this chapter, we will cover the following topics:

- **Node Wrangler**
- **Node Arrange**
- Exercise – how to install add-ons in Blender

We will begin this chapter by learning about the **Node Wrangler** add-on. This is a tool that you will use a lot in your Geometry Nodes workflow.

Exploring must-have add-ons

If you have watched any Blender tutorials on YouTube or other tutorial platforms, you'll have noticed that the **Node Wrangler** and **Node Arrange** add-ons are widely used add-ons because they offer a wide variety of handy tools that could be useful in any node editor inside Blender. In fact, every tutorial expects you to have these add-ons installed, so we really recommend installing them before continuing with this chapter and the rest of this book.

The Node Wrangler add-on

The **Node Wrangler** add-on was developed by *Bartek Skorupa*, *Greg Zaal*, *Sebastian Koenig*, *Christian Brinkmann*, and *Florian Meyer*. It provides tons of great tools and features to speed up your workflow in any node editor inside Blender. In this section, we will go over how to use the add-on, along with shortcuts this add-on makes use of.

This is a built-in add-on inside Blender and does not need additional installation to get it working.

The **Node Wrangler** add-on is mainly designed to be used with shortcuts. So, we will be explaining the usage of some of the most useful shortcuts that can be applied using this add-on.

It is notable to mention that this add-on isn't only usable in the Geometry Node editor but is made for use in every node editor in Blender. This includes the Compositor and the Material editor.

How to use the add-on

Let's start by explaining how to easily connect nodes. Usually, you'll have to connect node sockets by dragging one dot to another dot. With this trick, you'll be able to drag one node to another to automatically connect them.

Many users struggle with efficiently connecting nodes, but this add-on makes that really easy.

By using the *Alt + right-click* shortcut while dragging from one node to another, the **Node Wrangler** add-on will automatically create an appropriate link between both nodes. It will check what the most plausible way to connect the two nodes is.

By using the *Alt + X* shortcut, **Node Wrangler** will delete any unused or unconnected nodes from your node tree. This is very useful when you have finished a big node tree and you want to clean it up.

By using the *Shift + S* shortcut, you can easily and efficiently switch the node type you are working with. Pressing this shortcut will bring up the **Switch Type to…** menu. From here, you can choose what node to replace the current node with.

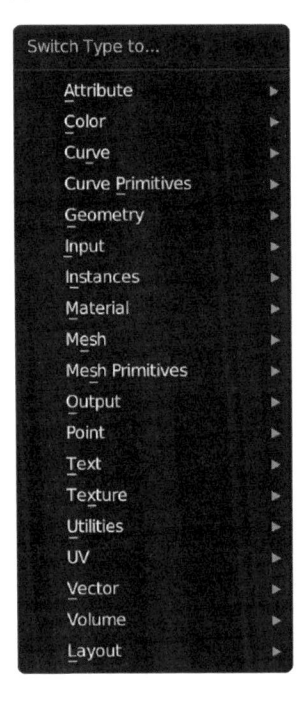

Figure 3.1: Switch Type to… menu

It will also adapt its inputs and outputs accordingly to make the swap as convenient as possible for the user.

The *Shift + C* shortcut allows you to copy the settings from one node to another. Keep in mind that these nodes have to be of the same type. This might be useful if you have a node that you want to append inside of a node tree, but you don't want to disconnect it.

By selecting the receiver node first, and then the main node, the main node will transfer its attributes to the receiver node. In this menu, you also have the option to copy and transfer various types of labels from the selected nodes.

If you want to clear a label from a node, you can always use the *Alt + L* shortcut.

Along with clearing labels, of course, we also have the option to modify our node labels.

To modify a label using the **Node Wrangler** add-on, you can press the *Shift + Alt + L* shortcut. This will allow you to quickly rename any node or node group.

Using the / (slash) shortcut, you can conveniently add reroutes to your node tree.

"What's a reroute?" I hear you ask.

Figure 3.2: Reroute connection

A reroute is a type of node connection that is not dependent on a node. It is used to organize your node tree, as well as to easily connect large amounts of nodes to other nodes. The color of the reroute depends on the color of the node connection that it is inputted into. As said before, a reroute acts much like a normal node connection. This reroute can also be moved around by pressing *G* on your keyboard.

We will get into organizing your node tree in a further chapter.

When you press the / key, you'll see this menu appear.

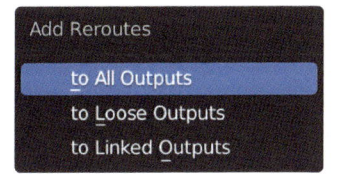

Figure 3.3: Add Reroutes menu

to All Outputs means that the **Node Wrangler** add-on will add reroutes to all the outputs of the nodes.

to Loose Outputs means it's only going to add reroutes to the node outputs that aren't occupied by a node connection.

to Linked Outputs means it's only going to add reroutes to the node outputs that are occupied by a node connection. Additionally, you can also add reroutes by pressing *Shift + right-click* and dragging over a node connection line.

By pressing *O*, you can connect the selected node to the end node, the Group output node.

This is useful to see the effects of the selected node. Let's say you want to see what a certain node is outputting. Pressing *O* on this node will connect it to the Group output, allowing you to see the effects of the selected node.

You can reverse this connection by pressing *Ctrl + Z*, like in any program.

The quick access panel

Let's also cover the quick access panel of **Node Wrangler**. This might be more useful to users that aren't big fans of using many shortcuts in Blender. The panel can be accessed from the right side of the Geometry Node editor or by pressing *Shift + W*.

Figure 3.4: Node Wrangler menu

At the top of this menu, we see the **Merge Selected Nodes** option, which allows you to merge any type of data, such as geometry or math data, in a convenient manner. We have four main options to merge geometry data:

- **Join Geometry**
- **Intersect**
- **Union**
- **Difference**

We also have the option called **Use Math nodes**, which allows us to conveniently add **Math** nodes in Blender.

Below the first option, we see the familiar **Switch Node Type** option, which is equivalent to the **Switch Type To** or *Shift + S*. Instead of using the shortcut, you can use it from this menu too.

The **Detach Outputs** button does exactly as the name suggests; it detaches the outputs of the current node that you have selected. Here, we also have the option to swap links, as we explained before.

The next button, **Frame Selected**, will group the selected nodes in a frame; this is convenient for when you want to clean up your node tree or make your node tree easier to understand for other people. You can also use this to add comments to your node trees.

Below that, we have the **Align Nodes** button. This is useful for aligning all nodes on a straight line. While learning about the next add-on, we'll cover how to easily clean up node trees with the click of a button.

Shortcuts

Let's go over the shortcuts we've learned in this chapter so far.

Shortcut	Action
Alt + (click)	Auto-connect nodes
Alt + X	Delete unused nodes
Shift + S	Switch node types
Shift + C	Copy node attributes
Alt + L	Clear a node label
Shift + Alt + L	Modify a node label
/	Add reroutes

Shift + 🖱	Drag and add a reroute
O	Connect a node to Group Output
Shift + W	Open the quick access panel

> **Note**
> Keep in mind that this shortcut list is based on the Blender default shortcut settings.

Now that we've successfully covered the **Node Wrangler** add-on, we can move on to the next section, where we'll tell you all about the **Node Arrange** add-on.

The Node Arrange add-on

The **Node Arrange** add-on is a simple add-on that allows you to easily clean up your node trees with the click of a button. This add-on was developed by *JuhaW* and can be found in the sidebar of the Geometry Node editor, where there will be an entry named **Arrange** after activating the add-on. You can bring up the sidebar using the shortcut *N*.

This is a very small add-on, but it achieves quite a lot. That's why we will be covering it in this chapter.

How to use the add-on

Let's start by taking a look at the layout of the add-on menu. This menu can be found on the right-hand side of the Geometry Node editor screen.

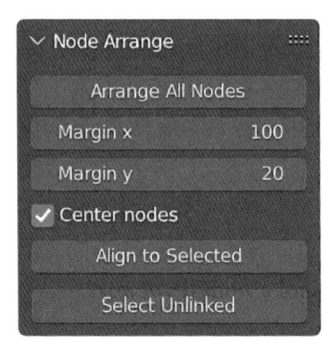

Figure 3.5: Node Arrange menu

This is a really easy add-on to use. There is one main button, the **Arrange All Nodes** button, which will automatically organize your nodes via an algorithm that will make your node tree look way more organized.

The margin value will add a specific margin between each node. This is useful for spacing out each node to create more room between them.

In the following figures, we see the differences in a node tree before and after the implementation of **Node Arrange**:

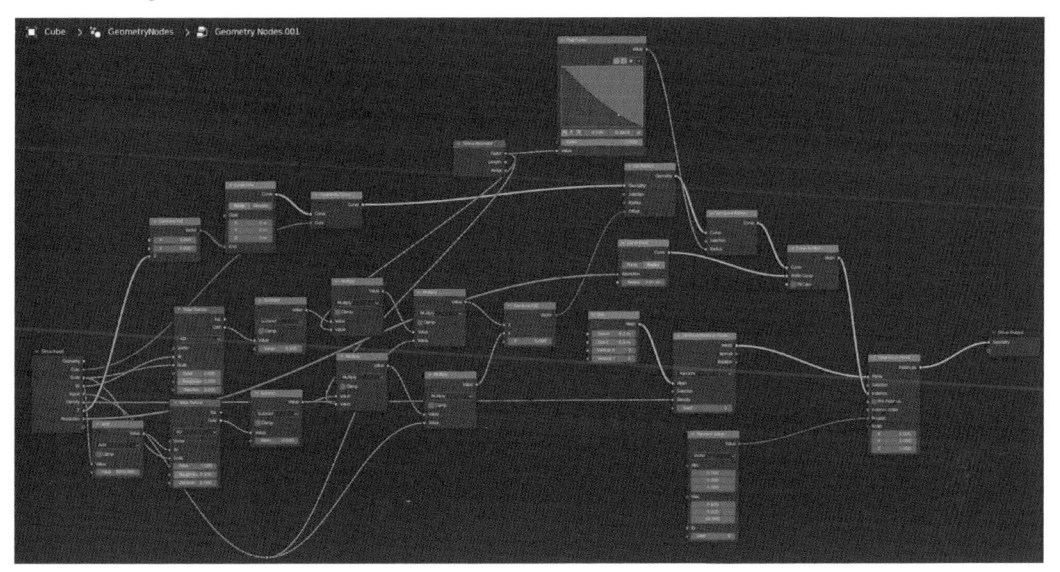

Figure 3.6: Node tree before using Node Arrange

In the preceding figure, you can see that the node tree is not organized at all; some nodes are very tangled up. In the following figure, using **Node Arrange** (*Figure 3.7*), we can see that all the nodes are nicely arranged into a logical structure.

If some node cables are still hard to see, we can use reroutes to route them to make the node tree even nicer.

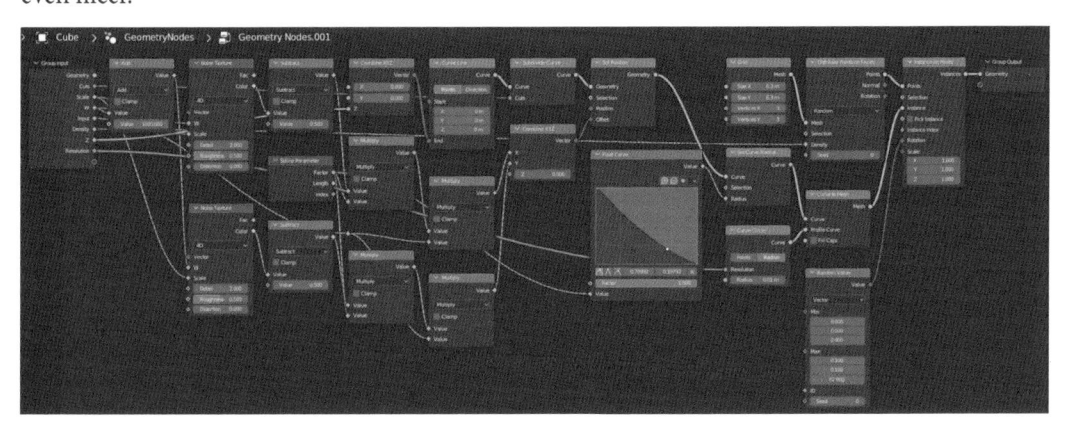

Figure 3.7: Node tree after using Node Arrange

Now that you have learned about the **Node Arrange** add-on, you're ready to learn how to add add-ons to Blender and access them.

Exercise – how to install add-ons in Blender

In this section, we will show you how to install add-ons in Blender. All of these add-ons are official Blender add-ons and can be installed through Blender itself.

We will need to enable these add-ons for them to work; they're not enabled by default.

Enabling add-ons

Let's quickly cover how to enable these add-ons:

1. Let's start by heading over to the **Blender Preferences** dialog inside Blender.

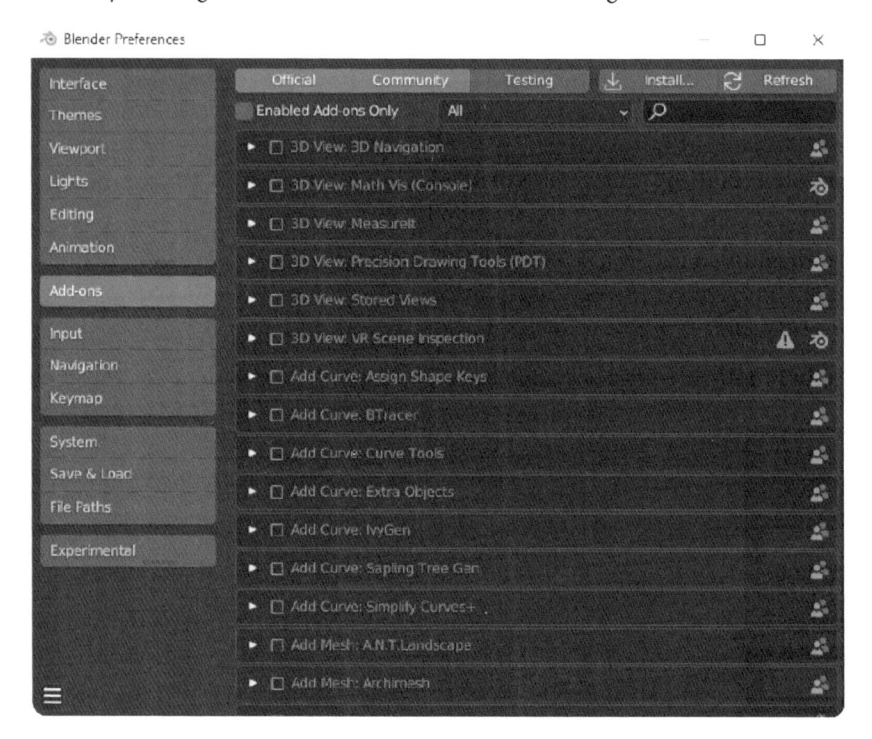

Figure 3.8: Blender Preferences Dialog

2. When you are in the **Blender Preferences** dialog, please click on the **Add-ons** tab.

3. When you are in the **Add-ons** tab, search for **Node Wrangler**.

Figure 3.9: Node Wrangler add-on entry

4. You can enable this add-on by clicking the square on the left-hand side of the title.

This will add the **Node Wrangler** add-on to your Blender preferences and will stay there even if you open another project. To disable the add-on, just uncheck the check mark and the add-on will be removed from your system.

Here, we've seen how you can install the **Node Wrangler** yourself. This progress is the same for any other official Blender add-on. Now, let's take a look at how we can access the functions of these add-ons,

Accessing these add-ons

Once the desired add-on(s) is enabled, you can find it on the right-hand side of any node editor, including the Geometry Node editor.

To expand the right-hand menu of the Geometry Node editor, you'll have to press the arrow you see on the right of the Geometry Node editor. You can also press *N* to open this.

Figure 3.10: Geometry Nodes right-hand menu expander

Pressing this will reveal the tab where the add-ons reside. Clicking each button will lead you to the menu of each add-on.

Figure 3.11: Right-hand tab of the Geometry Node editor

This brings us to the end of this chapter.

Summary

In this chapter, you learned how to use the **Node Wrangler** add-on with both shortcuts and the quick access panel. This chapter also showed you how to use the **Node Arrange** add-on. It showed how to access as well as install these add-ons.

These add-ons will help you greatly by offering tools that are useful in the Geometry Node editor, as well as in other node editors such as the Material editor and the Compositor.

In the next chapter, we'll go over the primitive shape nodes. You will learn how to add these nodes to the node editor, what all the nodes do, and their options.

Part 2 – Creating a Mesh in the Geometry Node System

In the second part of this book, we will delve deeper into the capabilities of node-based geometry creation in Blender. The chapters will cover making use of node primitives, distributing instances onto your mesh, working with the spreadsheet, and creating and modifying text in the editor.

This section comprises the following chapters:

- *Chapter 4, Making Use of Node Primitives*
- *Chapter 5, Distributing Instances onto a Mesh*
- *Chapter 6, Working with the Spreadsheet in Blender*
- *Chapter 7, Creating and Modifying Text in the Geometry Node Editor*

4
Making Use of Node Primitives

In the previous chapter, we introduced you to the various add-ons we can use along with the Geometry Node editor. In this chapter, we will introduce you to the Node Primitives of the Blender Geometry Node editor, why you should use them, where you can find them, the different kinds of nodes, and lastly, we'll end the chapter with an exercise on Node Primitives.

In this chapter, we will be covering the following topics:

- Introduction to Node Primitives
- Why use Node Primitives?
- Where can you find Node Primitives?
- The different Mesh Primitive Nodes
- The different Curve Primitive Nodes
- Exercise – your first Geometry Nodes project

Introduction to Node Primitives

Node Primitives allow you to place primitive shapes into your scenes by using various nodes.

But firstly, what are primitives? Primitive shapes are shapes that are relatively simple in terms of geometry or can be calculated using a mathematical equation. In Blender, these objects include a cube, a cylinder, and two different types of spheres.

Curves also have various primitives. These include a line, a circle, a star, a spiral, and a Bezier curve.

Each Node Primitive will likely convert a bunch of parameters into a single mesh/curve object that will be output as a geometry output node socket. Some nodes also allow you to output the sides and tops of the generated primitive using Booleans.

Why use Node Primitives?

Node Primitives are really easy to use. They are really useful because we can change the properties of these shapes while working in the Node editor. It's a matter of changing a value or slider to change the shape of the primitive.

Primitives do not nearly use as much RAM as instances do. If you can use a primitive instead of an instance, you are better off doing so.

Where can you find Node Primitives?

Node Primitives can be found in the **Add** menu in the Geometry Node editor. The **Add** menu can be accessed by clicking on **Add** at the top of your **Geometry Nodes** window or by pressing *Shift + A*:

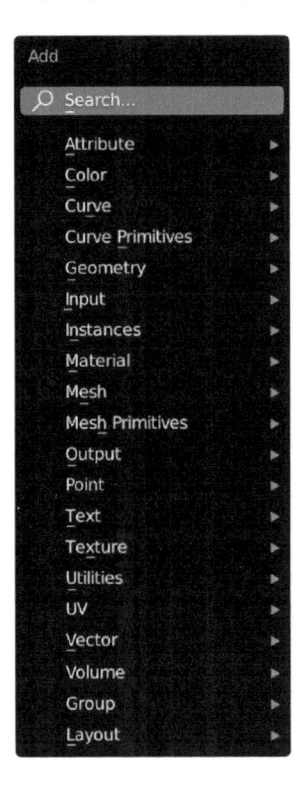

Figure 4.1: The Add menu

This menu will have all the nodes of the Geometry Node editor, including the ones we'll cover, the curve primitives, and the Mesh primitives. Hovering with your mouse over these entries will expand the chosen menu.

We will begin with the Mesh Nodes.

Mesh nodes

Mesh nodes will generate a primitive shape of your choice in the form of a mesh output. These include **Cone**, **Cube**, **Cylinder**, **Grid**, **Ico Sphere**, **Mesh Circle**, **Mesh Line**, and **UV Sphere**. These nodes will basically generate mesh inside your Geometry Node editor.

Where can you find Mesh Primitive Nodes?

Mesh nodes can be found in the **Add** menu. As stated before, the **Add** menu can be found by pressing *Shift + A*. You will find the **Mesh Primitives** entry in the dropdown that appears *(Figure 4.1)*. When hovering your mouse over the **Mesh Primitives** menu option, you will see the menu shown in *Figure 4.2*:

Figure 4.2: Mesh Primitives menu

This menu will show all the primitive mesh nodes that we will be explaining in this section. Let's get into it!

The Cube Primitive Node

The **Cube** Node Primitive is one of the most basic Node Primitives that you will be using. This allows you to place cubes in your Geometry Nodes projects:

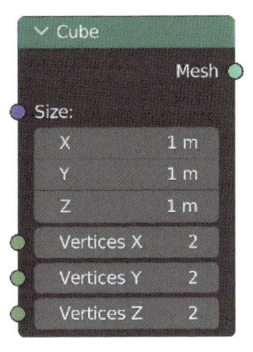

Figure 4.3: Cube Node Primitive

As you can see in *Figure 4.3*, we have a vector input that defines the X, Y, and Z dimensions of the cube. Using this node, we can also control the number of vertices that this cube will contain on each axis. This is comparable to adding loop cuts to a cube in **Edit Mode**. The node outputs the generated cube mesh using a geometry output.

The Grid Primitive Node

The **Grid** Node Primitive allows you to create a mesh that is essentially a plane. This will be useful when you want to start your Geometry Nodes project with a plane shape (also referred to as a grid):

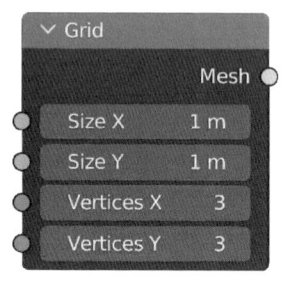

Figure 4.4: Grid Node Primitive

Much like the **Cube** Node Primitive (*Figure 4.3*), we can control the X and Y dimensions of this plane by using the value input sockets or by changing the values directly. We also have the option to change the X and Y Vertex count again. This will add subdivisions on each of these axes, much like with the **Cube** Node Primitive.

The UV Sphere Primitive Node

The **UV Sphere** Node Primitive will allow you to create a sphere while having control over the **Segments, Rings, and Radius** of the output sphere. This is useful when you want to control the vertical and horizontal resolution of your sphere:

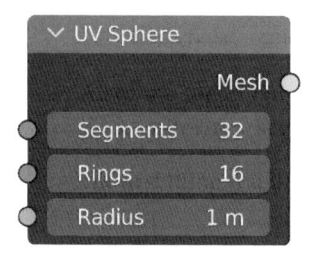

Figure 4.5: UV Sphere Node Primitive

Segments are the vertical rings that the sphere will have; in other words, the vertical resolution of your sphere.

Rings are the horizontal rings that the sphere will have; in other words, the horizontal resolution of your sphere.

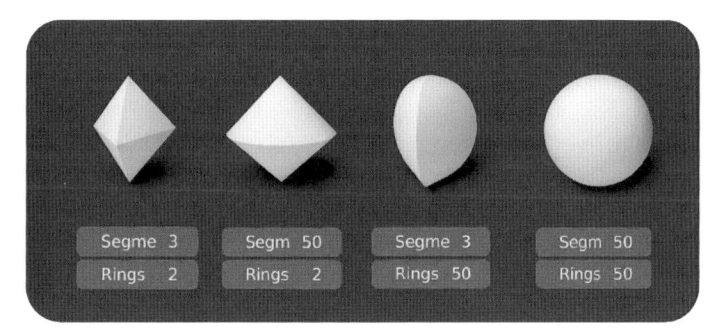

Figure 4.6: Segments and Rings demonstration

The Ico Sphere Primitive Node

Like **UV Sphere**, **Ico Sphere** is also a sphere. The difference is that **Ico Sphere** is made up of triangular faces and they're not connected with segments and rings, but instead, they form an even topology.

Figure 4.7: Ico Sphere Node Primitive

While **UV Sphere** and **Ico Sphere** might both be spheres, there is a crucial difference in the topology of the two options. In the following figure, you can see the difference in the topology:

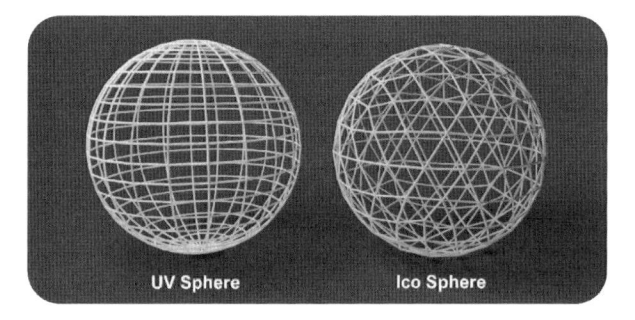

Figure 4.8: Difference between UV Sphere and Ico Sphere

The UV Sphere consists of segments that connect to a single vertex at the top and bottom, along with rings that stretch around the sphere.

The Ico Sphere has a better-defined, more even topology. A great topology is crucial if we want to modify any kind of mesh, such as when you want to displace your mesh, which we will explain in *Chapter 9*, *Manipulating Mesh Using the Geometry Node Editor*.

As shown in *Figure 4.7*, the **Ico Sphere** Node Primitive consists of a **Radius** value and a **Subdivisions** value; the **Subdivisions** value simply defines the resolution of the Ico Sphere, while **Radius** controls the scale of the sphere by increasing its radius.

The Mesh Line Primitive Node

The **Mesh Line** Node Primitive defines a simple line mesh:

Figure 4.9: Mesh Line Node Primitive

There are two different options for this node, **Offset** and **End Points**, as seen in *Figure 4.10*:

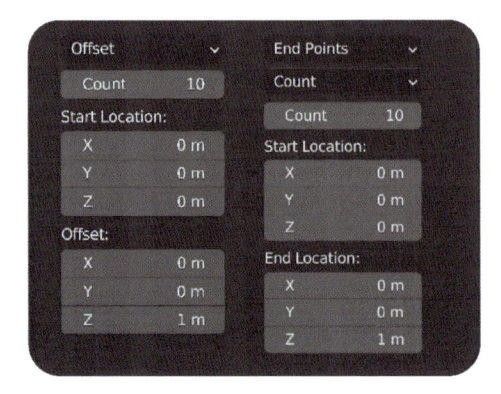

Figure 4.10: Different Mesh Line modes

In the **Offset** mode of this node, we can control the **Start Location** and **Offset** values. Both of these can be controlled via a vector node socket.

The **count** defines how much each offset should be repeated with a new **mesh line** iteration. The **count** also defines how many vertices are contained in the mesh line.

The **End Points** mode of this node will add points to your line by first defining the start point and the end point, and then allowing you to add points in between these two vector locations. Using the **Count** option, you will get precise control of how many vertices there will be in your mesh line. Using the **Resolution** option, you will be able to control how many vertices there will be in the mesh based on the allowed distance per vertex. For example, a resolution of 0.7 meters will place a vertex every 0.7 meters apart from each other.

The Cone and Cylinder Primitive Nodes

The **Cone** and **Cylinder** Primitive Nodes are two of the more advanced primitive nodes in the Geometry Node system:

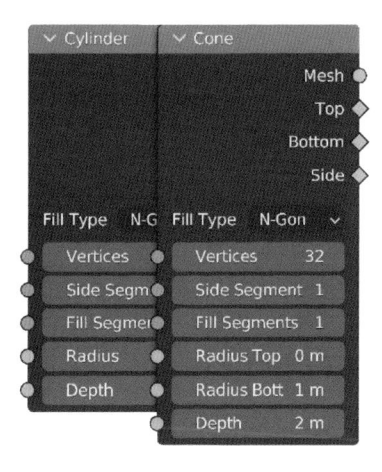

Figure 4.11: Cylinder and Cone Primitive Nodes

The **Vertices** integer value defines how many vertices each ring will contain (the rings are the horizontal lines of the object).

The **Side Segment** integer value allows you to control the number of these horizontal lines or rings.

The **Fill Segments** integer value allows you to control the inner rings of the top and bottom face. These rings will stay and loop around on only the top and bottom faces.

The two radius values (one radius value in the case of the **Cylinder** node) define the radius at the top and bottom of the object. For example, to make a cone correctly, you have to set **Radius Top** to 0.

The last value, the **Depth** value, defines the height of your cylinder or cone.

Both nodes share the same output sockets; one output socket is used to output your object geometry, and the other three Boolean values define the top, bottom, and sides of your mesh. These node outputs can be used on Boolean node inputs for cases such as mesh selection and other Boolean node connection use cases.

When we click on the **Fill Type** menu, we are presented with three fill type options, as you can see in the following figure:

Figure 4.12: Fill Type menu

None means that it will not fill in the top and bottom faces; the faces will be open.

N-Gon means that the center faces at the top will be joined into one N-Gon face.

Triangles means that the center faces at the top will be joined into a star shape or multiple triangles to prevent N-Gons since we do not want messy topology!

Curve nodes

Curve nodes are the basic Curve shapes that you can use in the Geometry Node editor. These include **Arc**, **Bezier Segment**, **Curve Circle**, **Curve Line**, **Curve Spiral**, and more.

Where can you find Curve Primitive Node?

Just like the **Mesh Primitive Nodes**, the **Curve Primitive Nodes** can be found in the **Add** menu (*Figure 4.1*), under the **Curve Primitives** entry. Once you hover your mouse over this entry, the menu shown in *Figure 4.13* should pop up:

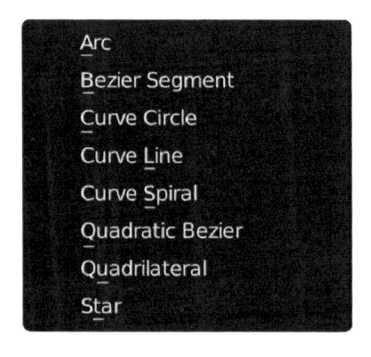

Figure 4.13: Curve Primitives menu

Curve nodes | 49

Each entry in the menu is a Curve Primitive Node. We will explain the commonly used ones in this heading, so without further ado, let's get right into the Curve Primitive Nodes.

The Curve Line Primitive Node

Using the **Curve Line** node, we can define a straight path. This will be useful when you want to align objects along a straight line or when you want to create a pole. This can be done by giving the Curve thickness:

Figure 4.14: Curve Line Node Primitive

There are two different modes in which we can use this node. These two modes are called **Points** and **Direction**. In the following diagram, you can see the values each mode presents:

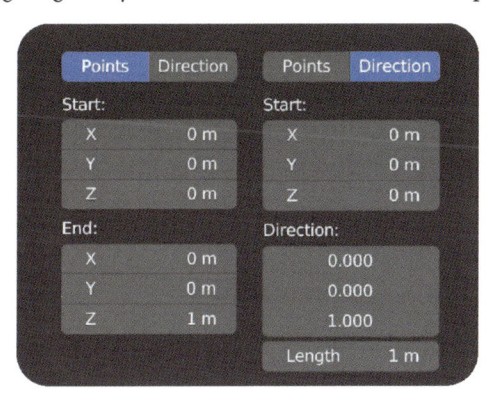

Figure 4.15: Different modes

Using the **Points** mode, we can simply define the **Start** vector location and the **End** vector location of the line. If you want to make the line longer, you must modify the **End** location and move it further away from the **Start** location vector.

Using the other mode, the **Direction** mode, we can define the **Start** location and give a direction that it should follow, depending on the use case; for example, if you want to define a direction, this might be a better choice. Along with the **Direction** vector, we also get the option to define the length of the line. The output of this node will give the finished Curve following the parameters you have entered.

The Curve Circle Primitive Node

The **Curve Circle** node will add a circle to your Geometry Node editor by making use of Curves. This can be useful to make shapes aligned in circles or to make a donut by giving the **Curve Circle** shape thickness by using a **Curve to Mesh** node. Keep in mind that the **Curve to Mesh** node will also require a **Profile Curve** input. This will be explained in the coming chapters.

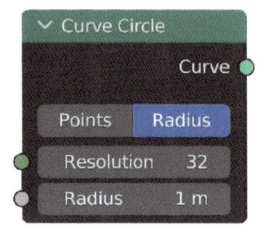

Figure 4.16: Curve Circle Node Primitive

Just like the **Curve Line** node, we are presented with two different modes for defining the shape of this circle: **Points** and **Radius**.

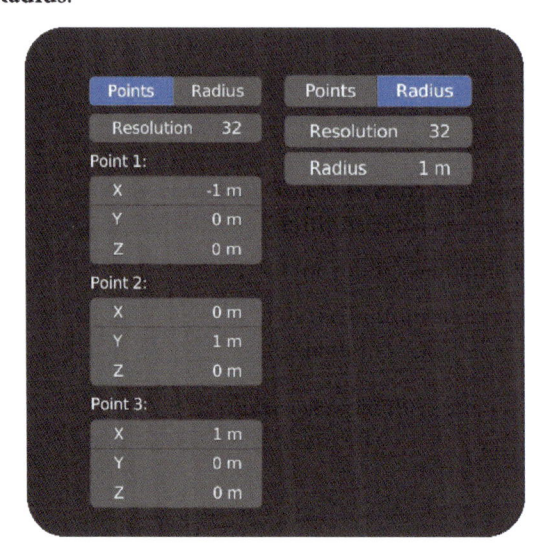

Figure 4.17: Different modes

The **Points** mode is used to create a circle based on the placement of three X, Y, and Z points. These points can also be controlled by a vector node input.

The **Resolution** integer value defines how many vertices this curve circle should contain.

When we switch over to the **Radius** mode, we are presented with a much simpler interface, and this is the option you will be using the most. In this mode, we can only change the radius and resolution of the circle. Just like in the **Points** mode, the resolution defines how many vertices the curve circle should contain.

The Bezier Segment Primitive Node

The next primitive is **Bezier Segment**. This will define a Bezier curve using four vector values – **Start**, **Start Handle**, **End Handle**, and **End**:

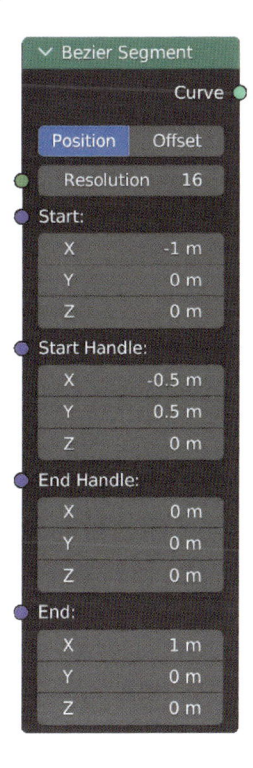

Figure 4.18: Bezier Segment Node Primitive

Once again, this node has been equipped with two different modes to define a primitive curve. If you have ever worked with Blender curves before, you will know what handles are.

For those who have not worked with handles in Blender, they essentially define the tangent that your Curve will follow by defining two extra locations:

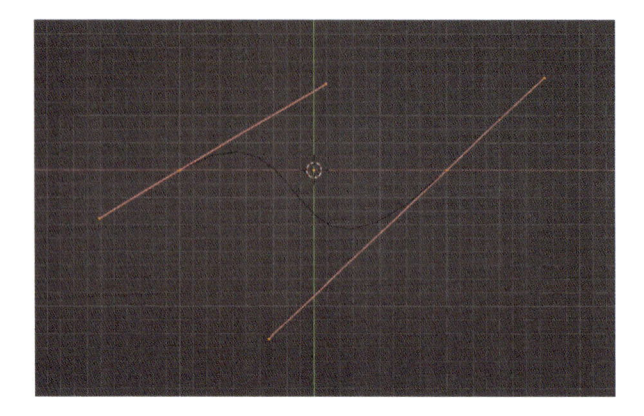

Figure 4.19: Tangents in Blender

The red lines you see in this diagram are handles. Let's start explaining the node now.

The **Start** vector value defines the beginning position of your Bezier segment. The **Start Handle** vector defines where your handle (the red line) should begin. Logically, the **End Handle** vector defines where the handle should end.

Finally, the **End** value defines the end position of your Curve.

The differences between the modes are that the **Position** mode makes sure that the **Start** and **End** handles are in a fixed position.

On the other hand, if we use the **Offset** option, the **Start** and **End** handles will be defined by offsetting them from the start and end of the Curve.

The Star Primitive Node

This node will define the shape of a star with various levels of control:

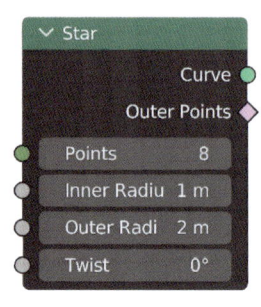

Figure 4.20: Star Node Primitive

Here are the various input values for it:

- **Points** will control the number of points your star contains. This will also define how many vertices your Curve will contain. If you double the points value, you get the vertex count of the star curve.
- **Inner Radius** defines how thin your star is. You can imagine this as an inner circle inside of your star.
- **Outer Radius** defines how long the spikes of your star should be.
- The **Twist** value will twist the inner part of your star, creating a twisting effect:

Figure 4.21: Star twisting

The Spiral Primitive Node

The **Spiral** Node Primitive will define a spiral shape with a Curve:

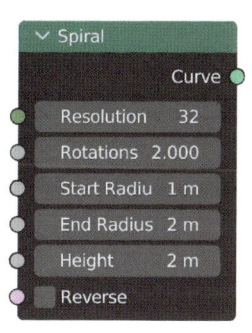

Figure 4.22: Spiral Node Primitive

This node can be useful when you want to align objects in a spiral shape. So, without further ado, let us get right into teaching you all about this node:

- The **Resolution** integer value defines the number of vertices the spiral curve should contain. The amount reflects the number of vertices each layer should have.
- The **Rotations** value will rotate the spiral X number of times before it reaches the **Height** value.

- **Start Radius** defines the radius that the spiral will follow at the beginning of the spiral.
- **End Radius** logically defines the radius that the spiral will follow when it nears the end.
- **Height** defines the height of the spiral; as stated before, the rotations will define the max rotations fitted in the given height.
- The **Reverse** Boolean value defines whether the Curve should be mirrored or not.

To wrap things up, we will teach you how to combine two primitives using a **Join Geometry** node. This will be your first Geometry Nodes project.

Exercise – your first Geometry Nodes project

Let's start by creating your first simple Geometry Nodes project; we will be combining two primitive nodes.

Let us first start by thinking about what nodes we will need. If we want to combine a plane and a cube, we will need three nodes:

- **Cube**
- **Grid**
- **Join Geometry**

We will need **Join Geometry** to combine the two objects.

Let us add a Geometry Nodes workspace to the default cube (or any other object; we won't be using the mesh itself), and let's open the Geometry Node editor:

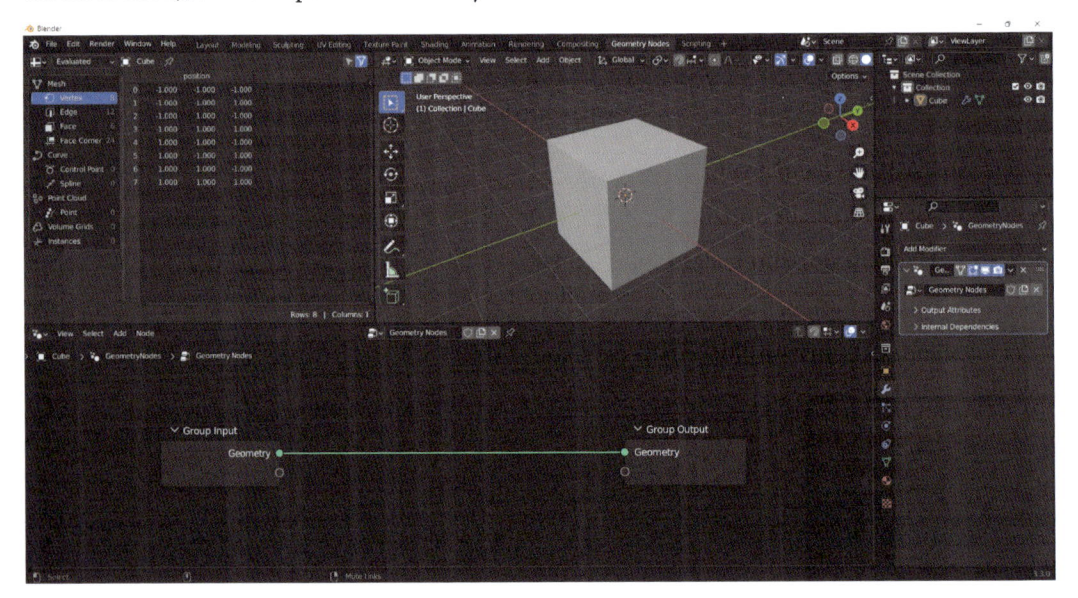

Figure 4.23: Geometry Node editor

Exercise – your first Geometry Nodes project   55

We will not need the **Group Input** node since we will just use Primitive nodes, so you can go ahead and delete the **Group Input** node.

Let us start by adding the **Cube** node to our Geometry Node editor. Start by clicking **Add** at the top of your screen and hovering your mouse over the **Mesh Primitives** tab.

After that, click on **Cube**.

This will add the **Cube** node to your Geometry Node editor.

Let us repeat this step for **Grid**. After that, your Geometry Node editor should look something like this:

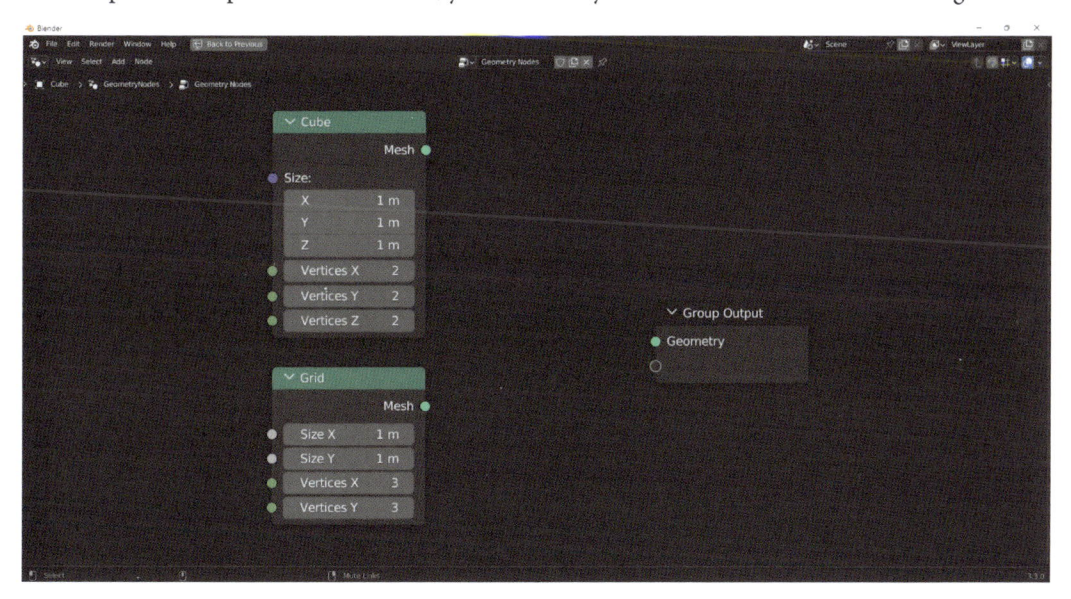

Figure 4.24: Primitives

You will not see anything appear in the viewport; this is normal and is because **Group Output** is still empty.

Try connecting the **Mesh** output of **Grid** to **Group Output**. Once doing so, you will see that the grid (plane) will appear in the viewport.

56　　Making Use of Node Primitives

We cannot directly combine the cube to the grid; to combine them, we will need a **Join Geometry** node. This will allow us to join two geometry outputs together. Let us disconnect the **Grid** node and add the **Join Geometry** node:

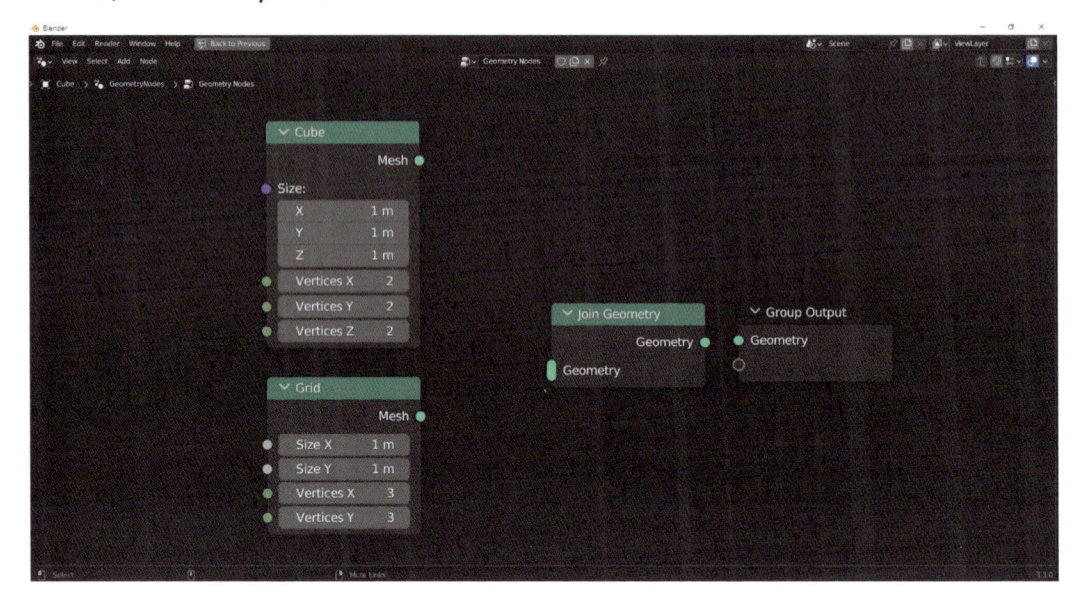

Figure 4.25: Add a Join Geometry node

Now it is time to connect these nodes. Let us start by connecting the **Cube** output to the **Join Geometry** input socket. This can be done by left-clicking the **Mesh** output of the **Cube** and sliding it to the **Geometry** input of the **Join Geometry** node.

Since the **Join Geometry** node contains a multi-connection node socket, we can connect multiple node connections to the same socket. Let us now connect the **Grid** node to the socket as well. Your node tree should now look something like this:

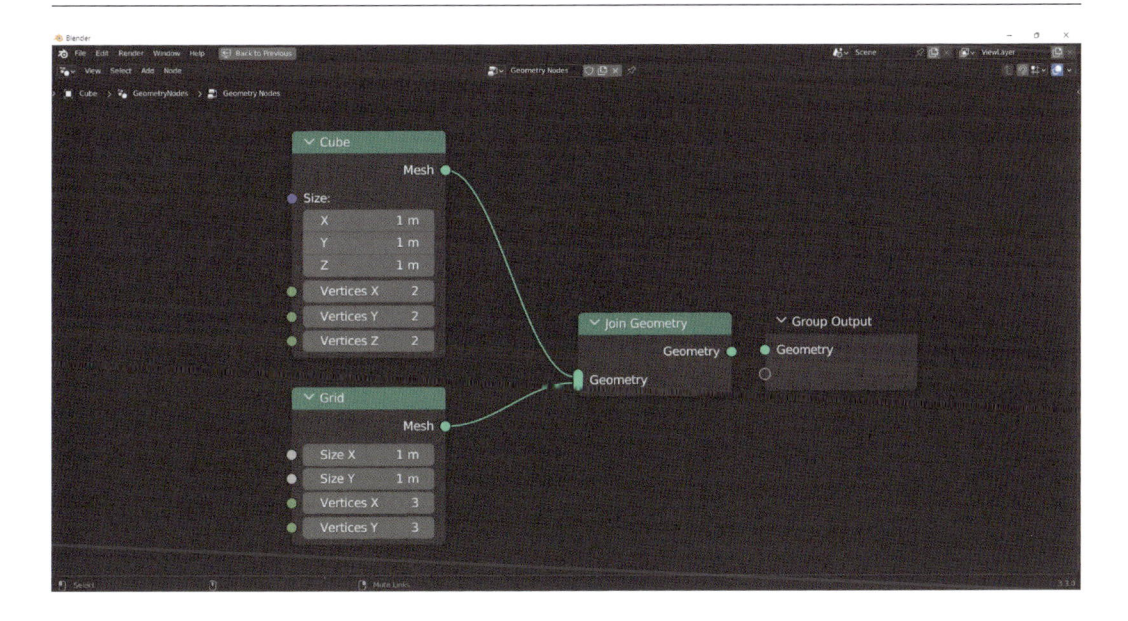

Figure 4.26: Connect the primitives to the Join Geometry node

All that is left to do now is to connect the output of the **Join Geometry** node to the **Group Output** node:

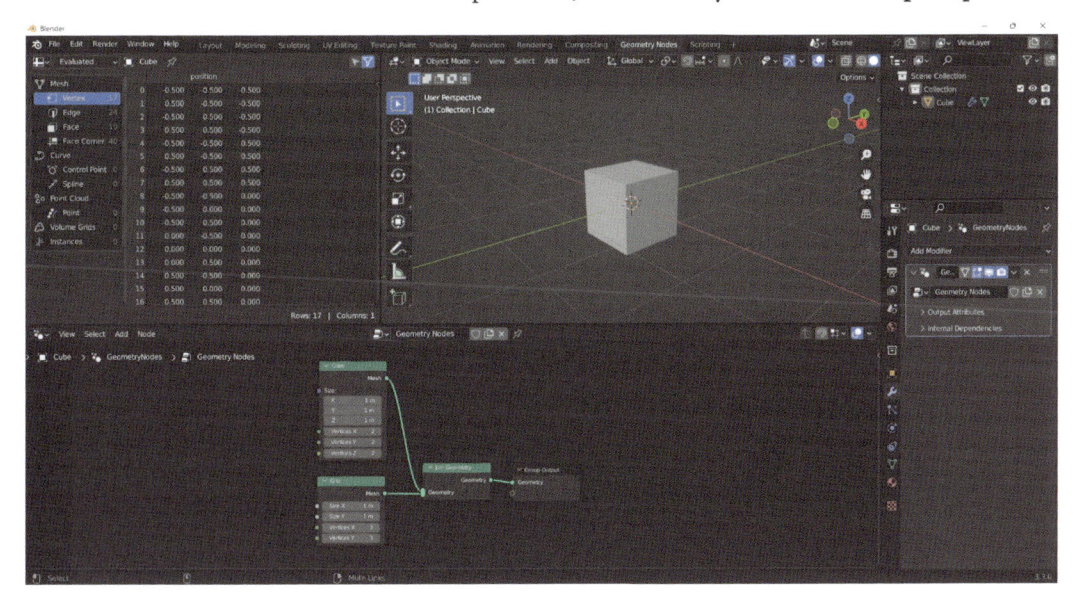

Figure 4.27: Connect Join Geometry node to Group Output

Looking at the viewport, we can see that only the cube appears to be visible; in reality, the grid (plane) is covered up by the cube since they are the exact same size. Let us fix that by increasing **Size X** and **Size Y** of the grid:

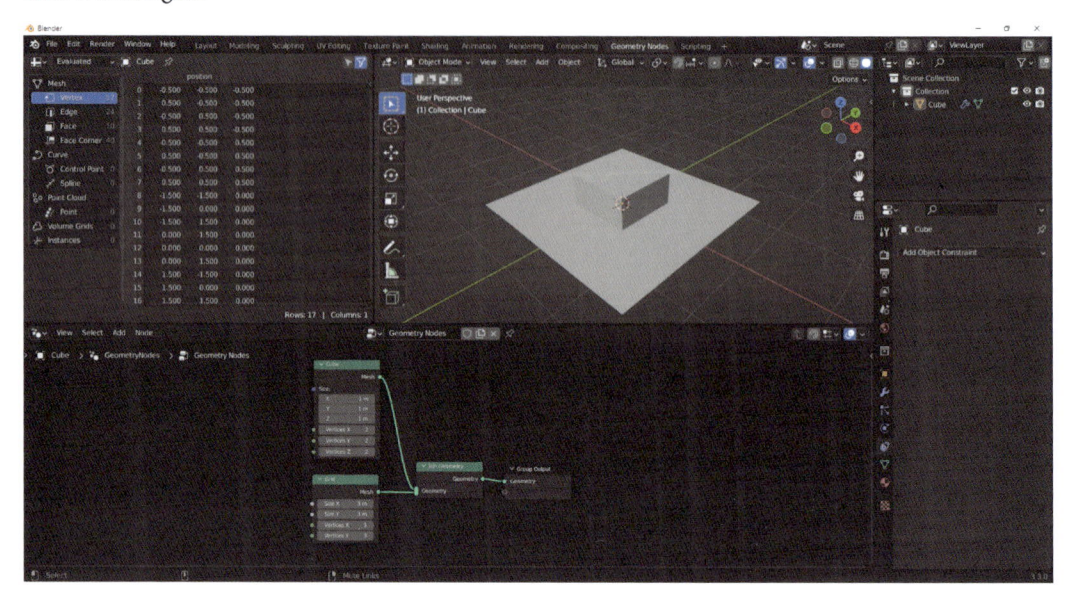

Figure 4.28: Increase the size of the grid

And that is it! Your first Geometry Nodes project!

This brings us to the end of this chapter. We've successfully combined two primitive nodes together.

Summary

In this chapter, you've learned how to use the various Mesh Primitive Node and the various Curve Primitive Nodes. We've also shown you how to combine two primitive objects together using the **Join Geometry** node.

Now that you know about Node Primitives, you can move on to the next chapter. In the next chapter, you will learn how to distribute points onto a plane to start instancing objects or primitives onto a mesh.

5
Distributing Instances onto a Mesh

In this chapter, we will show you how to distribute instances onto your mesh. To do that, we first need to distribute points on a Grid primitive, and only then can we distribute instances on those points. Being able to distribute instances on your mesh is crucial when you want to scatter multiple objects around your scene; for example, in a forest scene where the rocks, grass, and leaves are scattered throughout the scene. We will also show you how to randomize these instances and the use cases that randomization presents. Randomization is one of the most important factors for photorealism - it can be the make-or-break factor for many of your scenes. You will also learn the first steps in making a useful Geometry Nodes project.

In this chapter, we will be covering the following subjects:

- Distributing the points on a Grid primitive
- Instancing objects on points
- Randomizing instances
- Experimenting with Group Inputs
- Exercise – creating a grassy field

Distributing the points on a Grid primitive

The first topic we will be covering in this chapter is distributing points onto a Grid Primitive. These steps can also be applied to any other mesh. This step is crucial to instance objects in the Geometry Node editor.

Exploring the nodes we will be using

To get started with this demonstration, we will have to think about what we want to achieve. In this case, we want to distribute points onto a grid. To do this, we will need a total of three nodes, the **Grid** node primitive, the **Distribute Points on Faces** node, and the **Join Geometry** node.

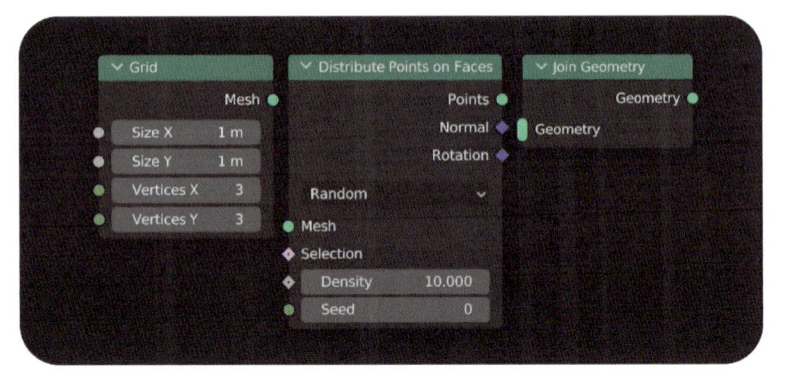

Figure 5.1: The different nodes you'll need

Let's start by explaining what these three nodes will do in this demonstration:

- The **Grid** node: This will be the base input, the mesh that we will get started within the Geometry Node editor, in this case, a Grid primitive.

- The **Distribute Points on Faces** node: This node will, as the title of this node suggests, distribute points on the faces of an inputted mesh. The output of this node will only contain the points.

- The **Join Geometry** node: As mentioned in the previous node, the **Distribute Points on Faces** node will output just the points. To add back the base mesh, we will need to use the **Join Geometry** node to join the original mesh with the **Points** geometry.

Now, we'll jump into building the node tree.

Building up the node tree

We will start by visualizing a Grid primitive. To do this, we will not need the **Group Input** node, because we are using a primitive node as our base mesh input. So, you can go ahead and remove the **Group Input** node:

1. Let's start the process of building a node tree by creating a 5-meter by 5-meter **Grid**. We can do this by adding a **Grid** node primitive and setting **Size X** and **Size Y** to five meters each. We won't make use of the **Vertices X** and **Vertices Y** values. So, we can put these values to 2. The reason that we won't put it on 0 or 1 is that you need at least 1 face to distribute points onto. So, we will need a minimum of four vertices to make up one face.

2. The next step is to connect the **Grid** node to the **Group Output** node to visualize this node primitive.

If you did everything correctly, your window should now look like *Figure 5.2*.

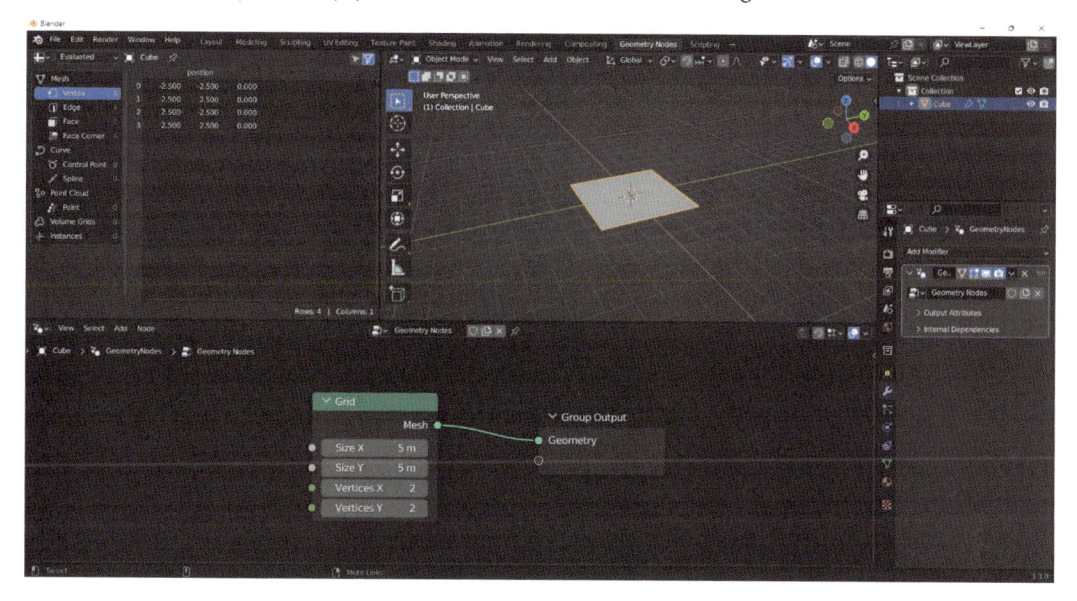

Figure 5.2: Visualizing the grid

Now, it's time to distribute the points onto the **Grid**, as the heading describes.

3. To do this, press *Shift + A* to open the **Add** menu. Let's head over to **Point**, and then we'll click **Distribute Points on Faces**.
4. When you drop this node onto the node cable, the node will be automatically connected.

If you've followed these steps correctly, your node tree should look like *Figure 5.3*.

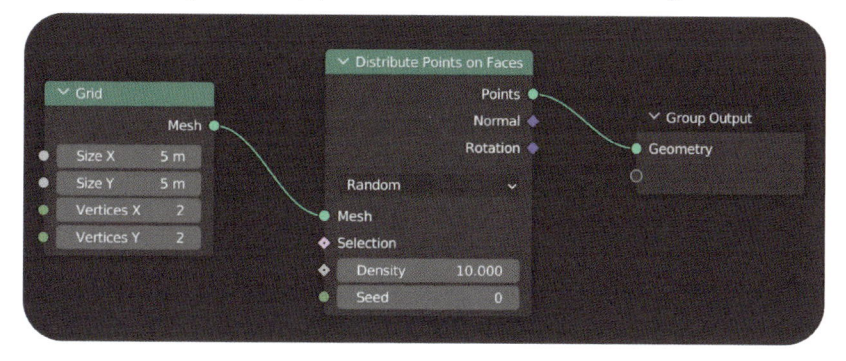

Figure 5.3: The current node setup

As you can see on the viewport, the grid disappears. This is normal because the **Distribute Points on Faces** node will only output points. If we want to make the grid appear again, we will have to use a **Join Geometry** node to join the grid and the points together.

This is how you can do that:

1. Go ahead and press *Shift + A*.
2. Then click on **Geometry**.
3. Finally, press **Join Geometry** to add a **Join Geometry** node.

> **Note**
> If you find it difficult to remember these categories, you can also use the search function to search for all of your desired nodes.

4. Let's drop the **Join Geometry** node into our editor between the **Distribute Points on Faces** node and the **Group Output** node. We will see that nothing changes. This is because we're not joining anything together yet.
5. Let's drop in the output of the **Grid** node into the multi-connection input of the **Join Geometry** node.

If you've followed these steps correctly, you will now see the **Grid** primitive with various points scattered along the surface, as shown in *Figure 5.4*.

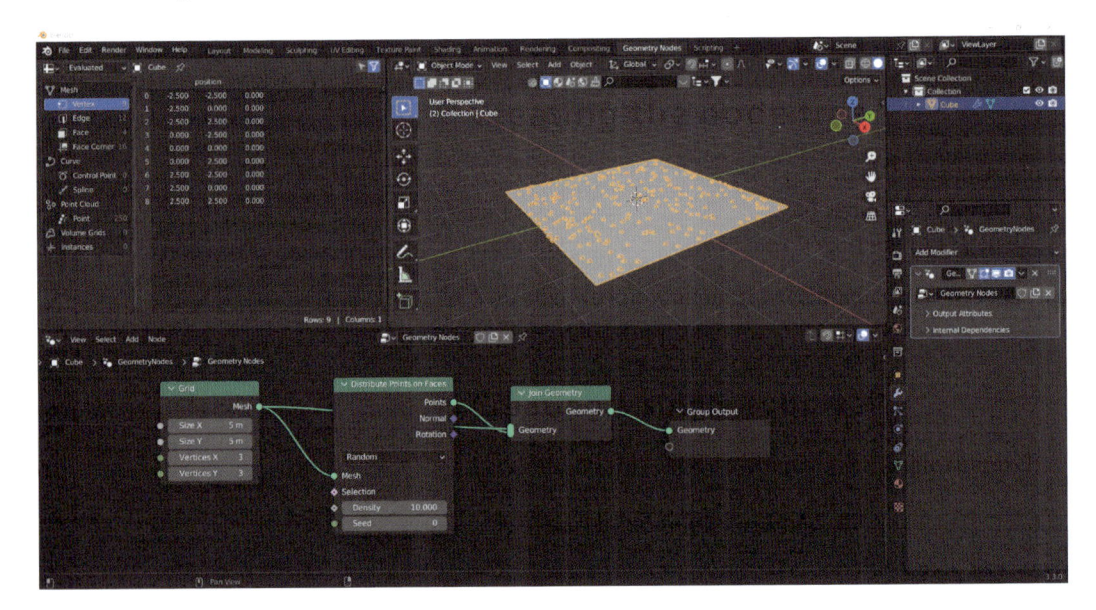

Figure 5.4: The current node setup

Congratulations! You now know how to scatter points onto a grid or plane.

Instancing objects on points

Now that you've learned how to distribute points onto a mesh, let's learn how to instance objects onto these points. For this, we will need the **Instance on Points** node.

To start instancing objects, we will have to input the base mesh along with our instance object.

We will be continuing with the same project from the last heading.

To get started, add an **Instance on Points** node. We need to drop this node in between the **Distribute Points on Faces** node and the **Join Geometry** node.

Drop it on the node cable as highlighted in *Figure 5.5*.

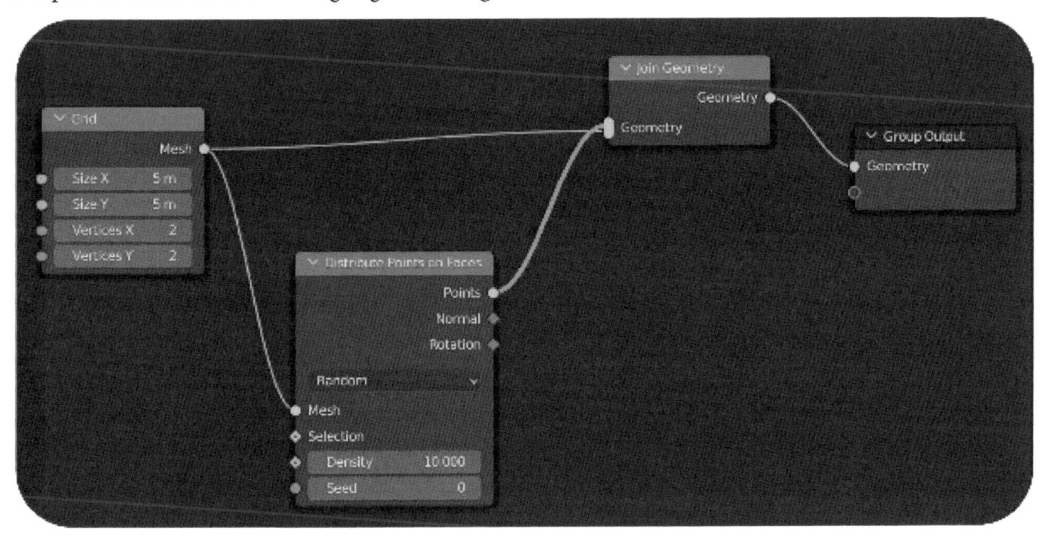

Figure 5.5: Node cable where the node should be dropped

We want to have a bare input of just the points since the **Instance On points** node only accepts a **Points** input in the first socket. That is why we have to place the node right after we distribute the points onto the grid.

When you drop this node onto the node cable, Blender will auto-connect the node to the **Points** input, which is correct.

Now, we will need to choose an object to instance. Let's add a simple **Cube** node primitive as our **Instance** object. Let's plug in the mesh output of the cube into the **Instance** input on the **Instance on Points** node.

Distributing Instances onto a Mesh

If you've followed the steps above correctly, your node tree should look like *Figure 5.6*.

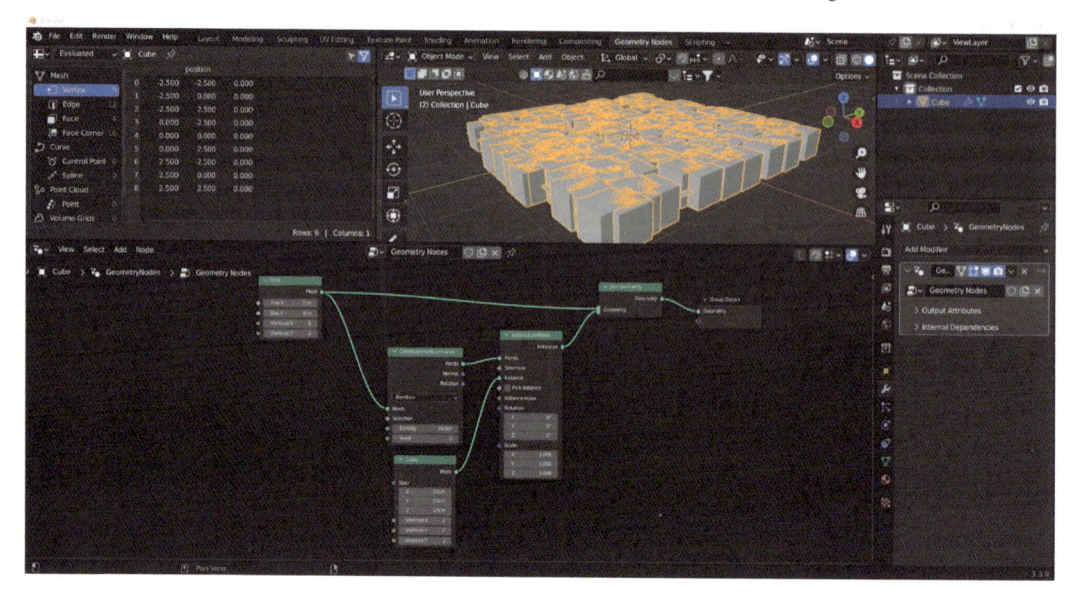

Figure 5.6: Instancing objects onto a grid

There are two problems we see at first sight:

- The cubes are intersecting into the grid
- The cubes are intersecting with other cubes

Luckily, the customizability of Geometry Nodes makes this really easy to fix.

Let's start with the first problem, the cubes are intersecting into the grid. To fix this, you simply have to change the location where the instances (or cubes) are placed. To do this, let's add a **Translate Instances** node after the **Instance on Points** node. We need to place it after the **Instance on Points** node because otherwise, we will be raising the points, which we don't want. We will be raising the **Z** translation to 0.2 meters. This will raise the cube 0.2 meters up the *z* axis.

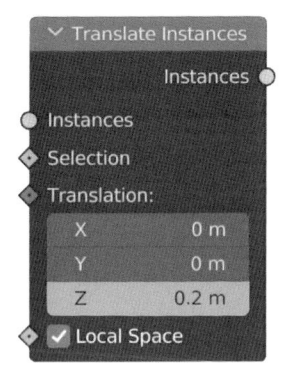

Figure 5.7: Translate Instances node

We will see that the cubes are now raised from the surface. We can now check that issue off the list.

The next problem, the cubes intersecting into each other, is easier to fix than you might think; all we have to do is to change the distribution method that the **Distribute Points on Faces** node uses. This will change the way that the cubes are distributed.

Let's use the **Poisson Disk** distribution method, as this allows us to define a minimum distance that the points should follow. Let's give the node a **Distance Min** of 0.4 meters. The node should end up looking like *Figure 5.8*.

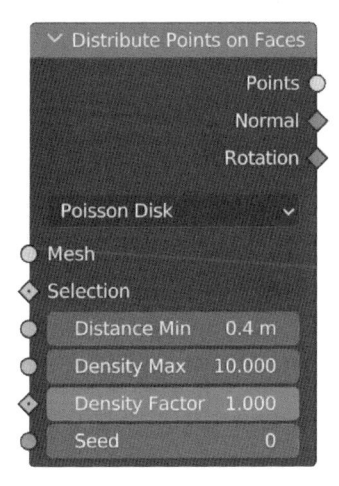

Figure 5.8: Poisson Disk distribution method

When we look back at our viewport, we can see that the cubes have socially distanced from each other.

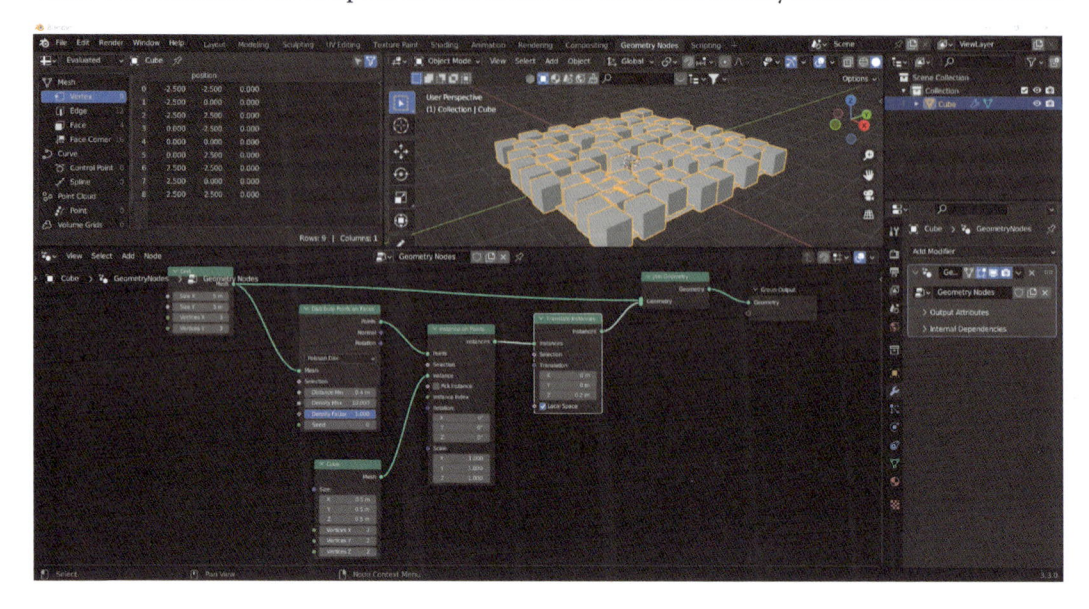

Figure 5.9: Distance Min on Instanced objects

We can now see that both issues are fixed. Let's now move on to the next step.

Randomizing instances

Now that you know how to distribute points onto your mesh and place instances on those points, it's time to learn how to randomize these instances. Randomization is important because the human eye is very good at noticing patterns in geometry. To fix this, we have to randomize factors in our projects. For this, we will be using the **Random Value** node.

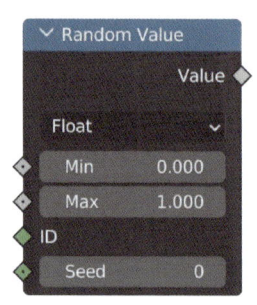

Figure 5.10: Random Value node

This node will output various random values for other flows of the node tree, thanks to the multivalued field node connection.

Randomizing instances   67

The **Random Value** node can output various data types. When clicking on the selection box at the top of the node, you can see a list of all the different data types this node can generate.

Figure 5.11: Different data types

For this part of the tutorial, we will be randomizing the rotation of the cubes.

Let's choose the **Vector** data type from the list since we want to have a different random value for each of the *x*, *y*, and *z* axes.

To link this **Random Value** node to the project from *Figure 5.9*, we will need to add a **Rotate Instances** node. This node needs to be added *after* the **Translate Instances** node, otherwise, the cubes will be translated in a different direction following its rotation value.

Let's plug the **Random Value** node into the **Rotation** input of the **Rotate Instances** node. If you have followed these steps correctly, your node tree should look like *Figure 5.12*.

As you can see, each cube is now randomly rotated.

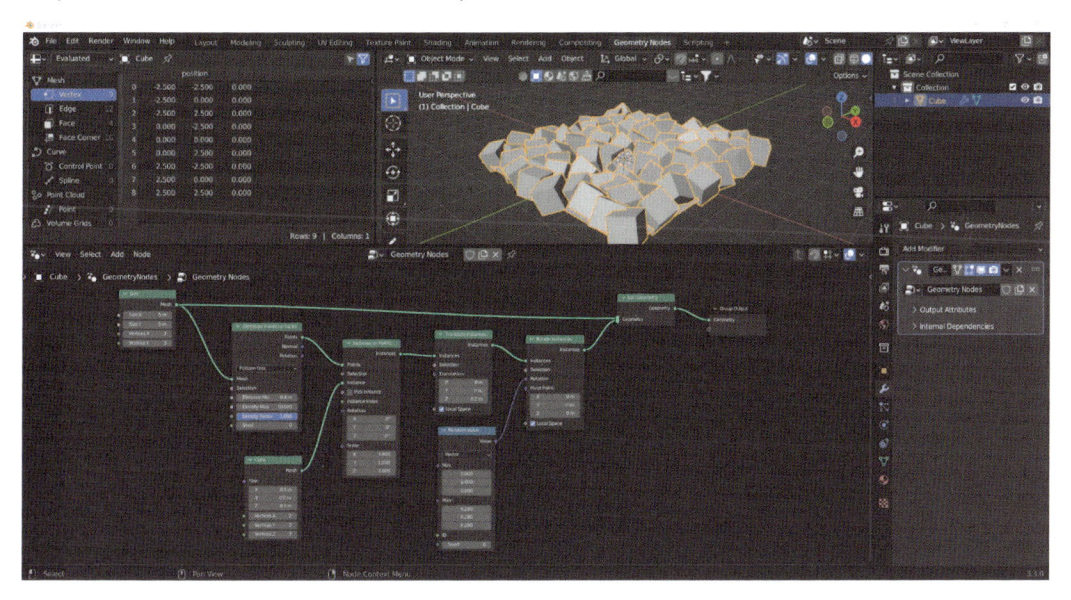

Figure 5.12: Your current node tree

As you might notice in *Figure 5.12*, the **Rotate Instances** node does not make use of the degrees system, instead, it makes use of the radians system.

To explain radians quickly, 1 radian equates to about 57°. Radians are useful in this use case because radians are dimensionless, they can just be treated as numbers. They define a very natural description of an angle.

For a full circle, we will need 6.28 radians, because 2 times pi equals 6.28. This equates to 360°.

Let's enter `6.280` as our **Max** value on each axis in the **Random Value** node. This will allow the cubes to rotate in any direction.

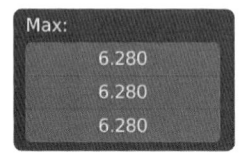

Figure 5.13: Max values of randomization to get a full rotation

Now we have learned how to distribute points onto a mesh, how to instance objects onto these points, and how to give these objects a randomization using the **Random Value** node.

Next, we'll experiment a bit with Group Inputs since they can enhance the user experience with the help of your node tree.

Experimenting with Group Inputs

Group Inputs can be seen as easy-access variables in our modifier stack.

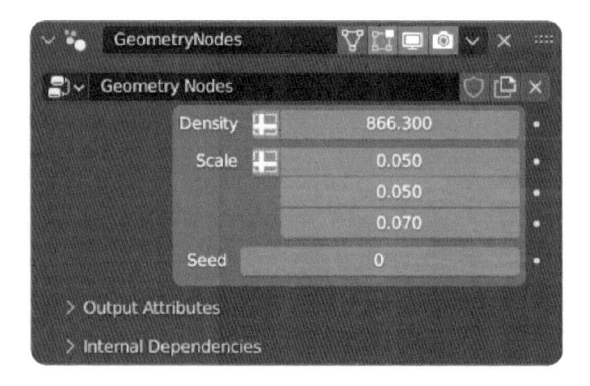

Figure 5.14: Group Inputs

Group Inputs make it easier for the end user to change commonly used variables right from the modifier stack.

How to utilize Group Inputs?

We can add various Group Input values by adding in a **Group Input** node (this gets automatically added when you create a node tree) and sliding an input node connection into the dark gray node connection on the **Group Input** node as seen in *Figure 5.15*. Sliding an input node into this dark gray node connection will automatically add a Group Input to your modifier. You will mostly be using Group Inputs when you have values that you want to have easy access to, for example, the density of grass.

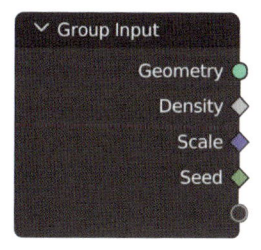

Figure 5.15: Group Inputs

Group Inputs also have advanced settings for when you want to have finer control over the different data types, the names of your values, and the min-max limits of your values. To access the advanced settings of the Group Inputs, head to the right-hand side of the Geometry Node editor, where the Add-ons reside. Instead of clicking on an Add-on, let's click on the **Group** tab. We will see the various inputs that we have put into our **Group Input** node.

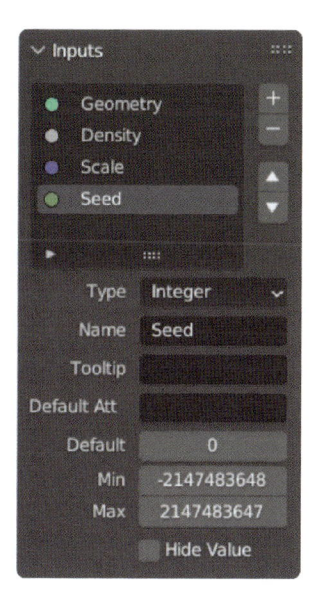

Figure 5.16: Group Inputs advanced settings

We can edit various things about these values, such as the type of the value, the name of the value, the default value, and a minimum and maximum value. This addition to the Geometry Node system will make it easier for you or an end user to easily modify key variables of your node tree right from the **Modifier** tab.

Exercise – creating a grassy field

In this exercise, you will be creating a grassy field using the nodes you learned in this chapter. We will start by distributing points onto a terrain mesh, then we will make and instance blades of grass, and then we will give these blades of grass some randomization.

Sketching the idea

In this section, we will think about what steps we need to complete to achieve the goal of creating a grassy field. We will need to model a basic terrain mesh and distribute some points on it; we will also need to model a single blade of grass to use as an instance object. After that, we will randomize the rotation of each blade of grass. To finalize this project, we will also show you how to link materials to your procedural mesh.

The nodes we will need

In this section, we will talk about the nodes we will need to create a grassy field.

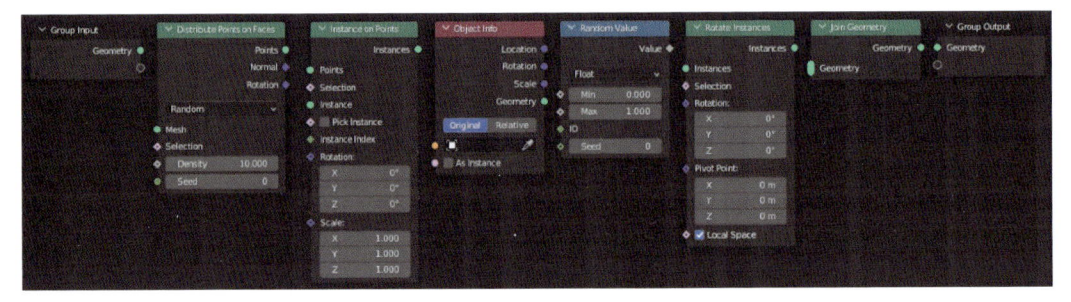

Figure 5.17: The nodes you'll need in this exercise

It's a good practice to have a clear idea about the nodes required for an exercise. Here are the nodes we will need for creating a grassy field:

- A **Group Input** node to input the terrain mesh
- A **Distribute Points on Faces** node to distribute points on the terrain mesh
- An **Instance on Points** node to place grass on the terrain mesh

- An **Object Info** node to load in an instance object
- A **Random Value** node to add randomization to each blade of grass
- A **Join Geometry** node to join the points and base terrain back together after distributing the points
- And lastly, a **Rotate Instances** node to rotate each blade of grass

Next, we will be showing you how to model the various assets we will need for this project.

Modeling the terrain

While we can model the terrain procedurally in the Geometry Node editor, this will be covered in the more advanced chapters of the book. For now, we will explain this exercise by modeling the various assets in **Edit Mode**.

Let's start by creating a new project in Blender, and clearing the default scene because we don't need the included **Camera**, **Cube**, or **Light**.

Add a **plane** and press *Tab* to enter **Edit Mode**.

Let's subdivide this plane and let's start pulling up parts of the plane with proportional editing. Once you're happy with your terrain, you can continue to the next step, where we'll model a single blade of grass.

Modeling a blade of grass

In **Object Mode**, add a **Cylinder** with a vertex count of 3.

Figure 5.18: Cylinder with vertex count of 3

The reason why we only want three vertices is that we will instance these objects a lot, so to save your computer's performance, you should have as few vertices as possible.

Let's scale down the top face by pressing S. We can also add horizontal loop cuts to the vertical lines of the cylinder to give it a bit of randomization.

Once you're happy with the blade of grass, let's continue to the next step.

Setting up your Geometry Node editor

Let's head over to the **Geometry Nodes** workspace inside of your current project. This button can be found at the top of your screen, as shown in *Figure 5.19*.

Figure 5.19: The Geometry Nodes workspace button

In the workspace, click the terrain mesh and then click the **New** button to add a new node tree to the terrain mesh.

Distributing and instancing the points

Let's start building our node tree by adding a **Distribute Points on Faces** node and dropping it between the **Group Input** and the **Group Output** nodes. You can change the **Density** and **Seed** values until you are happy with the result.

The **Group Input** node will make sure that the terrain mesh from edit mode will be used in the Geometry Node editor.

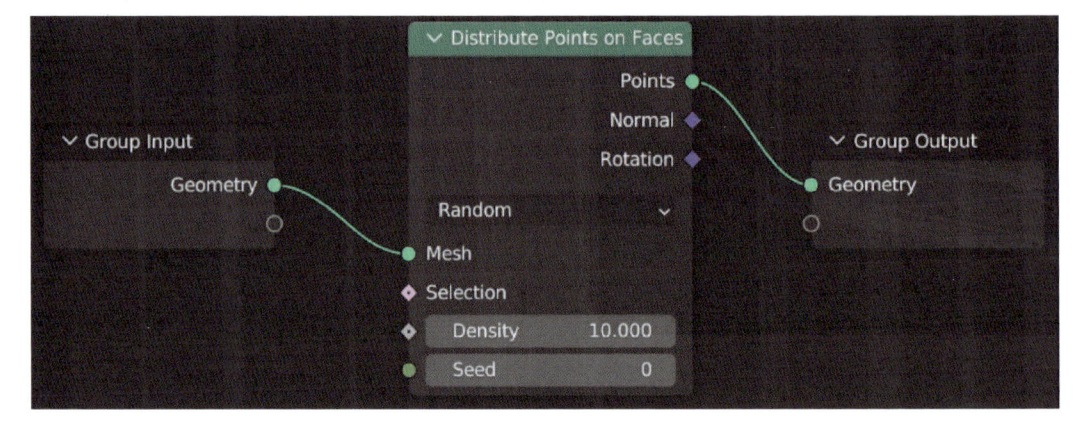

Figure 5.20: Your current node tree

In your project, you will see that the terrain mesh itself is not visible anymore, so let's make it visible again by using a **Join Geometry** node as we've done previously in this chapter. We will join the **Group Input** node connection together with the distributed points.

Exercise – creating a grassy field   73

If you've followed these steps correctly, your node tree should look like this:

Figure 5.21: Your current node tree

Now, we'll instance a blade of grass on each of these points as we've done before in this chapter. The difference now is that we will now use an existing object as an instance object, in this case, the blade of grass.

We can do this by adding an **Object Info** node. You can find this node by using the **Search** function in the **Add** menu.

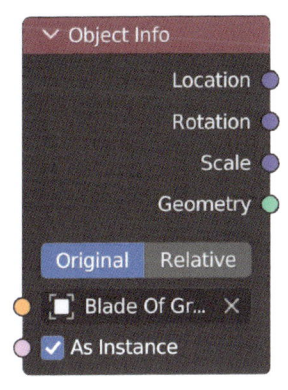

Figure 5.22: The Object Info node

This node will place any existing object as a node in the Geometry Node editor. We have various options here, the first input is an object selection box to choose your desired object, and the second checkbox defines whether the object should be imported as an Instance or not.

At the output side of this node, we see four output node connections. **Location**, **Rotation**, and **Scale** will define each of these attributes as a vector output. The last output, **Geometry**, will define the geometry of the chosen object.

Select your blade of grass in the object selection box and tick the **As Instance** Boolean value so it will be imported as an instance.

Drop in an **Instance on Points** node after the **Distribute Points on Faces** node.

Now, connect the **Geometry** output of the **Object Info** node to the **Instance** input of the **Instance on Points** node.

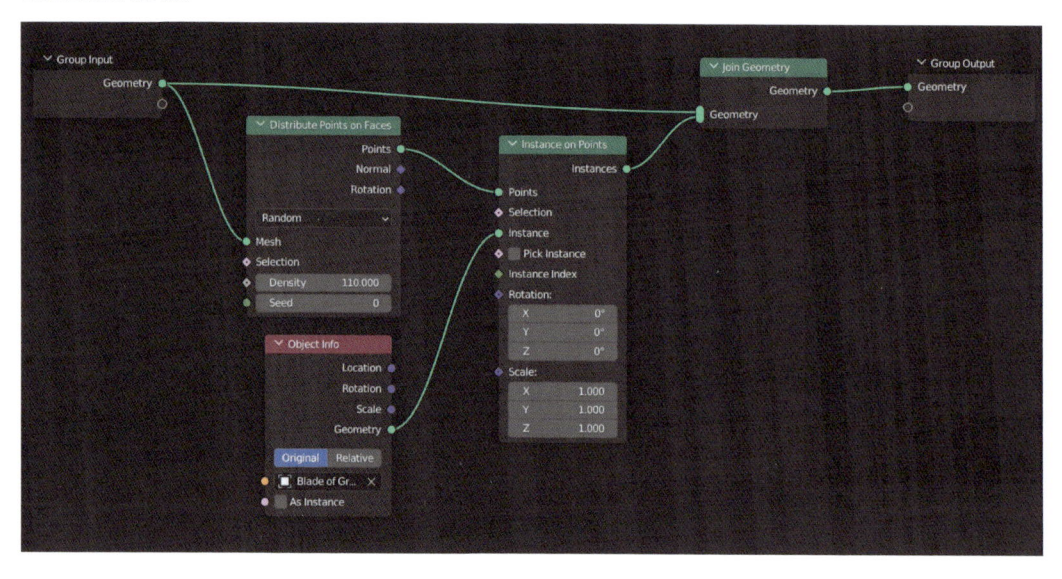

Figure 5.23: Your current node tree

We can see that the grass appears now, but it is way too large.

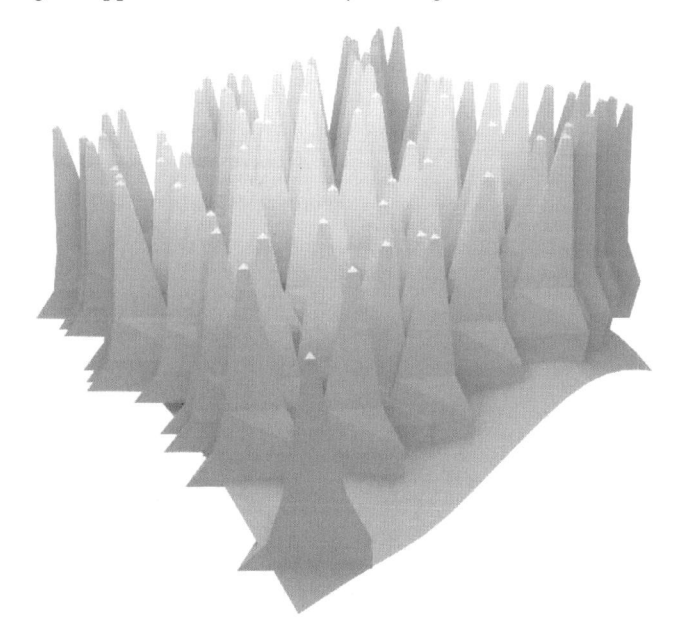

Figure 5.24: Grass appears too large

We can set the scale of the grass by turning down the **Scale** value of the **Instance on Points** node.

> **Note**
> You might face an issue where the blades of grass are situated in the middle of the terrain rather than on the terrain; you can fix this by changing the origin point of the blade of grass. After that, the blades of grass will be nicely situated on the terrain.

Just like the previous demonstration we performed; the next step will be giving randomization to the grass.

Randomizing the grass

Let's now randomize the rotation of the blades of grass. For that, we will be using a **Random Value** node as we used before in this chapter.

Let's set this node to **Vector** and put **X max** and **Y max** on `0.3` and put **Z max** on `6.28`. This will allow the grass to rotate more on the *z* axis than it will on the *x* and *y* axis.

Let's plug this **Vector** output value into the **Rotation** input of the **Instance on Points** node.

This is also a good moment to experiment with different shapes of grass or to modify some values to get a result that you are satisfied with.

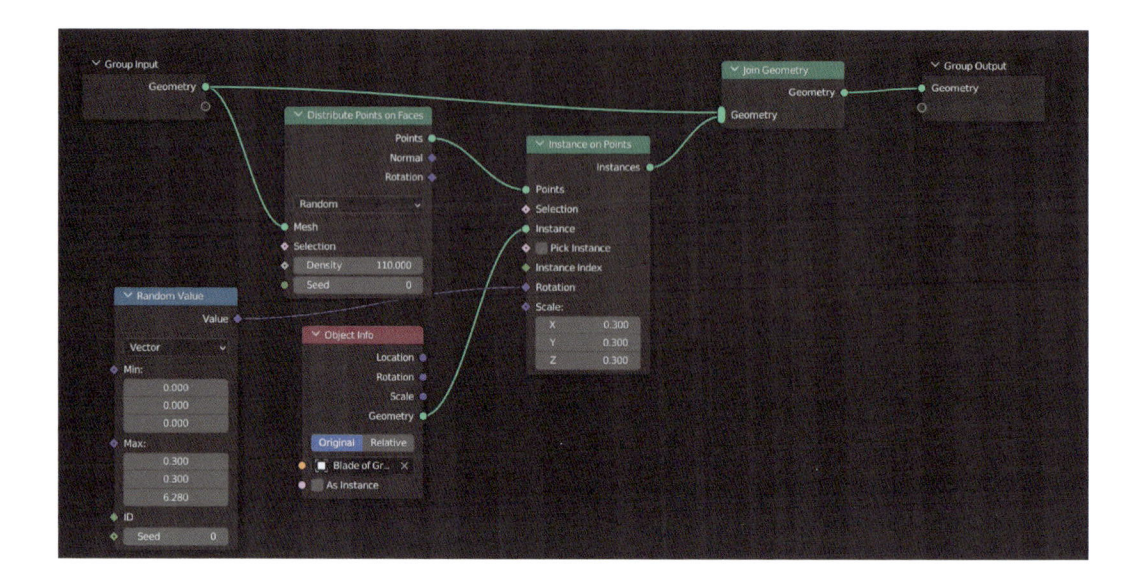

Figure 5.25: Your current node tree

If you followed the steps correctly, your node tree should look like *Figure 5.25*.

Linking a material to your mesh

Let's add a material to your grass now. Start by heading over to the **Shading** workspace at the top of your screen.

Add a new material to the terrain object. Give this material a dark green color to appear like grass.

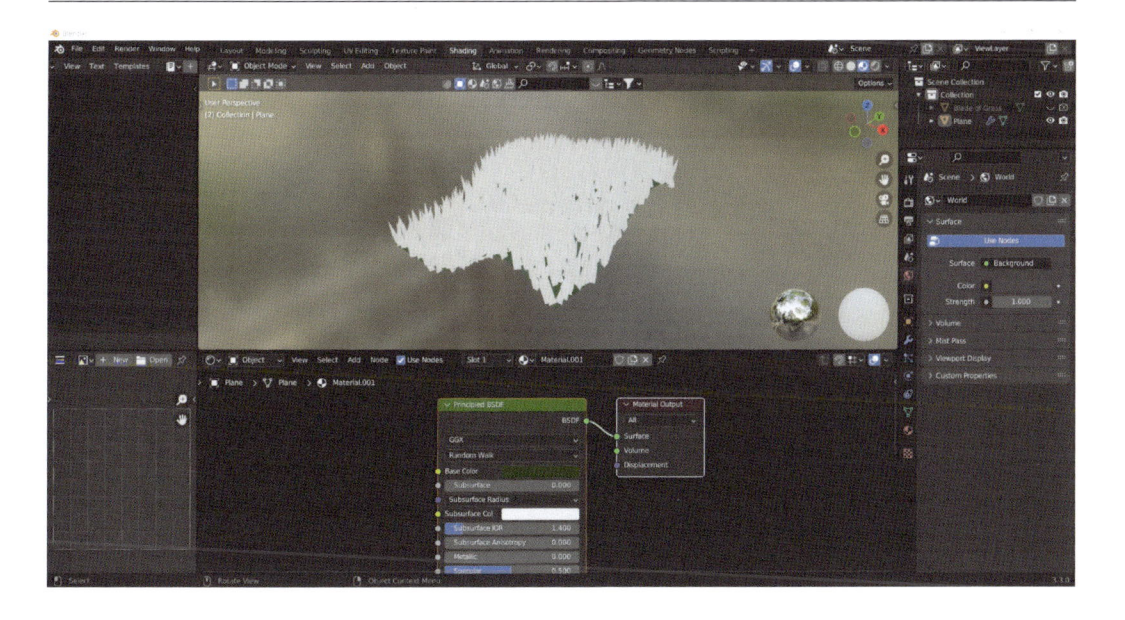

Figure 5.26: The Shading workspace

As you can see from *Figure 5.26*, the grass is not affected by the material, this is because the material has to be linked inside the Geometry Node editor. Let's head back to the Geometry Node editor to fix this.

Let's add a **Set Material** node to add the material to the blades of grass.

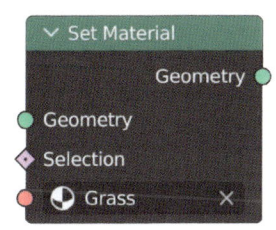

Figure 5.27: The Set Material node

Let's drop in this node at the end of your node tree to append all the mesh. Let's also select the material you created on the previous page.

If you've executed the steps successfully, this part of your node tree should look like *Figure 5.28*.

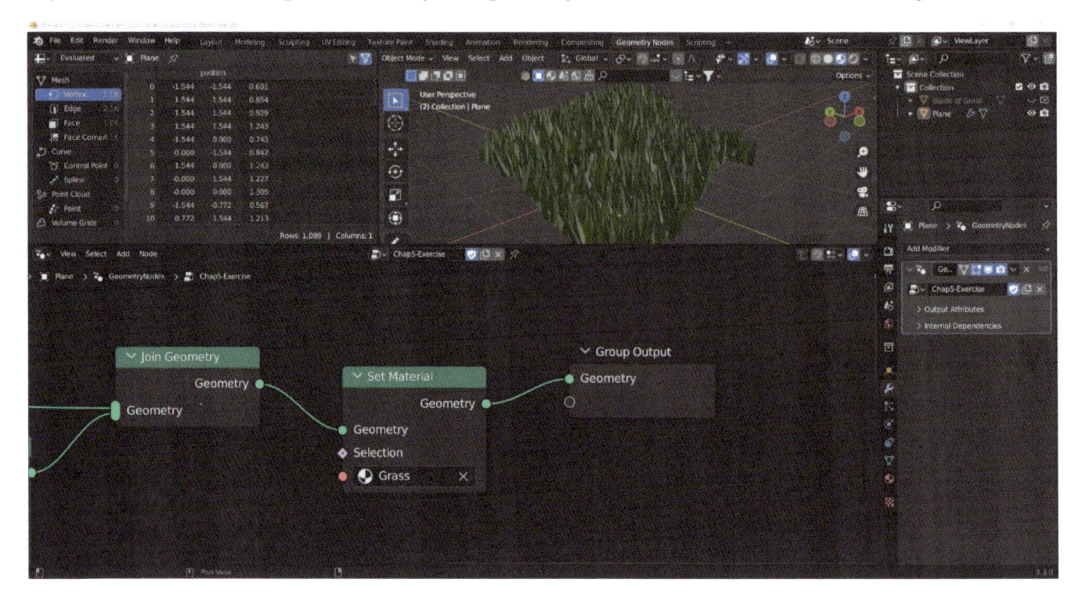

Figure 5.28: Your current node tree

Congratulations! You've now finished this node tree. In the next section, we'll be cleaning up your node tree.

Cleaning up your node tree

It's good practice to clean up your node tree after you've finished your project. We do not want to get tangled in nodes and not understand our node tree anymore.

Let's use the **Node Arrange** add-on to clean up our node tree.

When we press the **Arrange** button of the **Node Arrange** add-on, the node tree will be arranged following an algorithm.

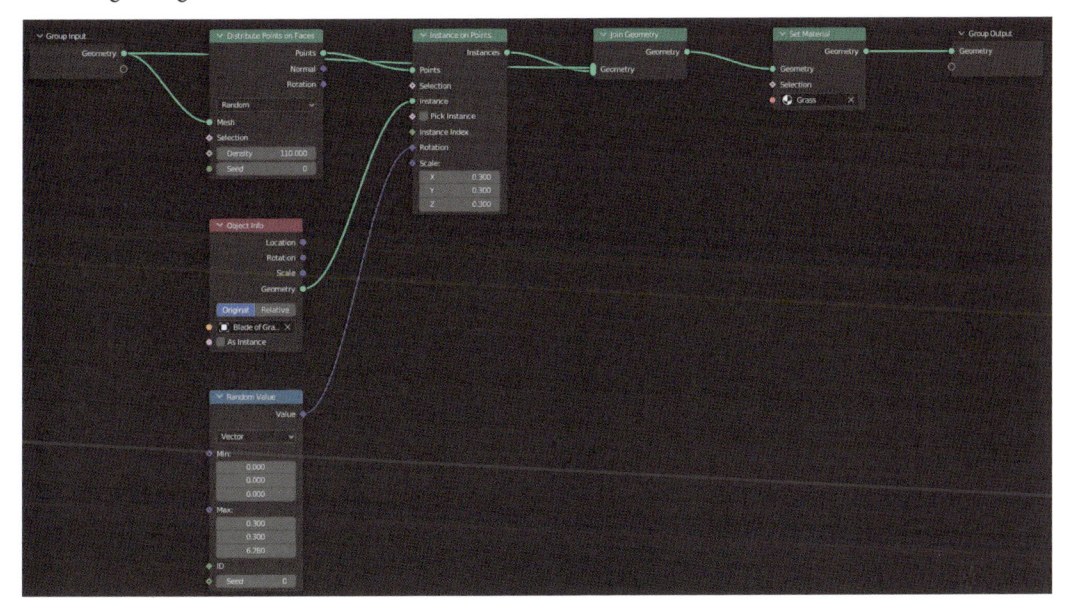

Figure 5.29: Arranged node tree

In *Figure 5.29*, you can see what the node tree looks like after arranging the nodes.

Using Group Inputs to add sliders to the modifier

To finish off this exercise, let's make it easier for end users of this node tree to control different variables.

In the *Experimenting with Group Inputs* section, we explained how to use this feature in Blender. Now, it's time to put these skills to the test.

We will add **Group Input** variables to these values:

- **Density**
- **Scale**
- **Seed**

Let's drag the gray node connection from the **Group Input** to the values that you want to be included in the modifier. That's how you add Group Inputs!

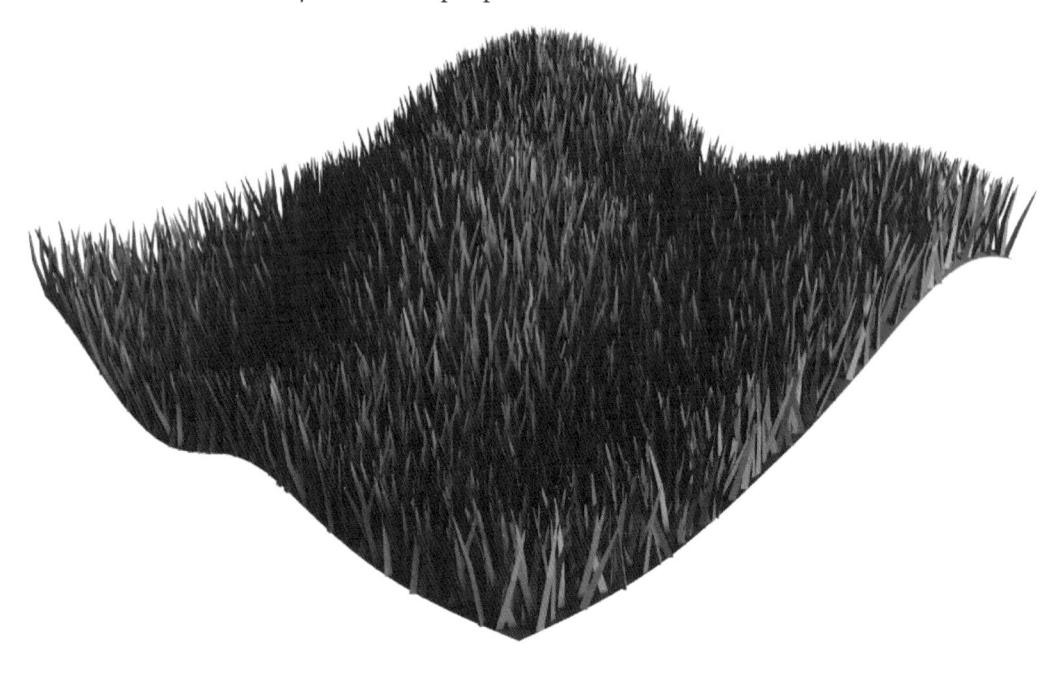

Figure 5.30: Final render of the grassy field

Finally, you can see in *Figure 5.30* what the grass looks like.

Summary

In this chapter, we discussed how to distribute points on a mesh. Following that, we talked about how to instance objects onto these distributed points, and to complete the chapter, we showed you how to randomize these objects using the **Random Value** node.

In the next chapter, we will show you how to work with the Spreadsheet.

6
Working with the Spreadsheet in Blender

In the previous chapter, you saw how to distribute points on a mesh. Now, we will teach you how to make use of the **Spreadsheet** in Blender. Just like in the previous chapter, we will also be using instances in this chapter.

While not part of the Geometry Node editor, we can make great use of the Spreadsheet when using this editor. For example, we can use the Spreadsheet to obtain information about what's going on in our Geometry Node editor.

We will cover the following topics in this chapter:

- Introduction to the Spreadsheet
- Demonstrating how the Spreadsheet can be useful
- Exercise – creating a rotated tesseract cube

Introduction to the Spreadsheet

Let's start by giving you a broad explanation of the Spreadsheet. The Spreadsheet is a list that contains information about the locations of vertices, edges, faces, and so on. We can inspect their properties and much more in this handy addition to Blender. The Spreadsheet is mainly used to inspect geometry attributes and obtain info about the geometry of your objects.

We will go over all the different datasets that we can inspect in the *Exploring the different datasets in the Spreadsheet* section.

What does the Spreadsheet do?

The Spreadsheet allows you to display the different properties of the dataset that you want to obtain information from; for example, if you want to obtain information from all the vertices in your mesh, you can use the Spreadsheet to check the positions of all the vertices in their respective x, y, and z axes.

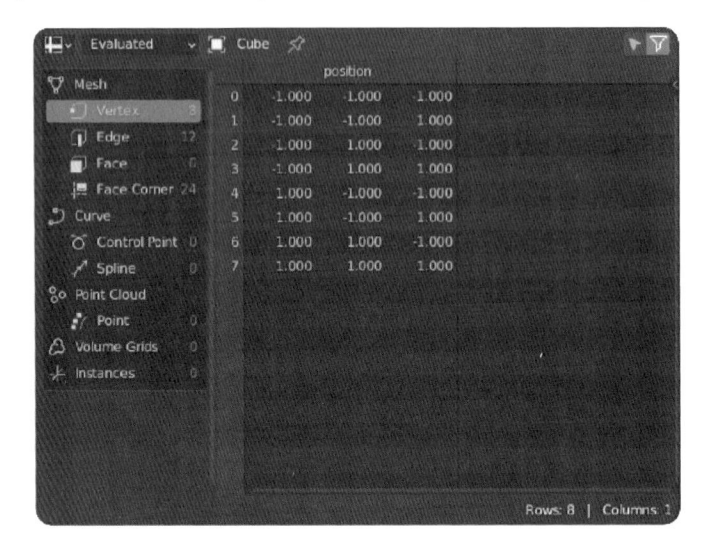

Figure 6.1: Spreadsheet

Now that you know what the Spreadsheet looks like, let's take a look at the different datasets that the Spreadsheet presents.

Exploring the different datasets in Spreadsheet

Let's quickly go over the different datasets that we see in *Figure 6.1*. Each of the following subheadings refers to a different dataset of the Spreadsheet.

Mesh

Let's first explore the different datasets we find in the **Mesh** tab of the Spreadsheet.

We're presented with four subtabs in the **Mesh** tab:

- **Vertex**
- **Edge**
- **Face**
- **Face Corner**

The **Vertex** tab defines the location of each vertex. The **Edge** tab defines how much each edge is creased. The **Face** tab defines whether the face should be shaded smooth, as well as the normal direction of these faces and the material index, which tells the object what material should be applied to each face.

You are probably familiar with **Vertex**, **Edge**, and **Face**, but **Face Corner** might be new to you. This option defines the total number of edges attached to vertices. For example, a cube has 8 vertices, and each vertex has 3 edges attached, so if we multiply 8 by 3, we get a **Face Corner** value of 24.

Curve

Let's now explore the two different subtabs that the **Curve** tab presents:

- **Control Point**
- **Spline**

The **Control Point** tab defines the tilt, radius, nurbs weight, and position of each of the control points that your curve contains.

The second option is the **Spline** tab. This tab shows how many different splines are present inside the selected object. Along with that, it also shows various variables, such as **Normal Mode**, **Nurbs order**, **Curve type**, whether the curve is cyclic or not, **Knots mode**, and the resolution of the curve, which reflects the set resolution in the **Curve Properties** tab.

Point Cloud

Here, you'll see the information that the Spreadsheet delivers about point clouds.

The **Point Cloud** tab provides information about the various points a point cloud contains. It gives the total number of points, along with the position of each point, the ID of each point, the radius, and the UV map. **UV Map** gives a vector value that can be used by the Material node editor to define the placement of textures.

Volume Grids

Let's take a look at the information the Spreadsheet offers on volume grids.

The **Volume Grids** tab defines basic info about the volume included in your geometry. If there is no volume included in your geometry, the **Volume Grids** tab will be empty.

It gives information such as the grid name, the data type, and the class of your volume.

Instances

Let's now look at what information we get on instances in the Spreadsheet.

As mentioned before in the book, an instance is a reference to the original mesh, which can be used to individually manipulate geometry, as shown in *Chapter 5, Distributing Instances onto a Mesh*. We get a lot of information about instances in the Spreadsheet. We can see the name of the instance, the position vector value, the ID of the instance, the **UV Map** vector, and the rotation and scale of each instance. Using this tab in the Spreadsheet is useful for troubleshooting problems with your instances.

Filtering items using the Spreadsheet

We can also filter the entries in the Spreadsheet. This can be done by opening the right-hand menu of the Spreadsheet.

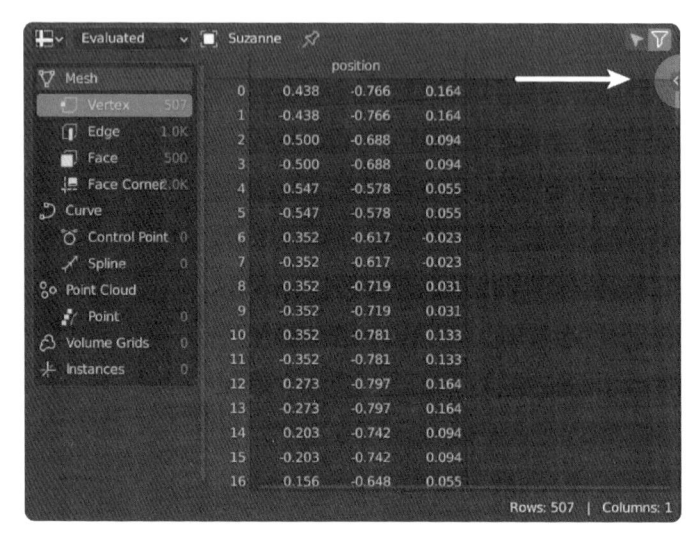

Figure 6.2: Right-hand menu of the Spreadsheet

On opening the menu, you'll be presented with a button called **Add Row Filter**.

This will add a new filter to your Spreadsheet. We can enter the column that should be filtered on. For example, you can filter by the position of each vertex.

This is what the filter looks like:

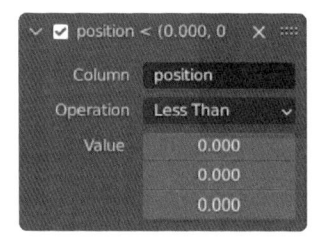

Figure 6.3: Spreadsheet filter

On filling in the parameters to your liking, you will see that entries of the Spreadsheet will start to disappear, leaving only the entries that match your filter(s).

We have multiple operations we can use when filtering entries in the Spreadsheet.

These include operations such as the following:

- **Equal to**
- **Greater Than**
- **Less Than**

Using these operations, you should find your desired entries in no time!

Now that you have been introduced to the Spreadsheet, let's demonstrate how the Spreadsheet can be useful in your Geometry Nodes workflow.

Demonstrating how the Spreadsheet can be useful

In this section, you will learn how to use the **Duplicate Elements** node to visualize how the Spreadsheet works.

Introducing the nodes you'll need

As you can see in *Figure 6.4*, these are the nodes we will be using in this demonstration:

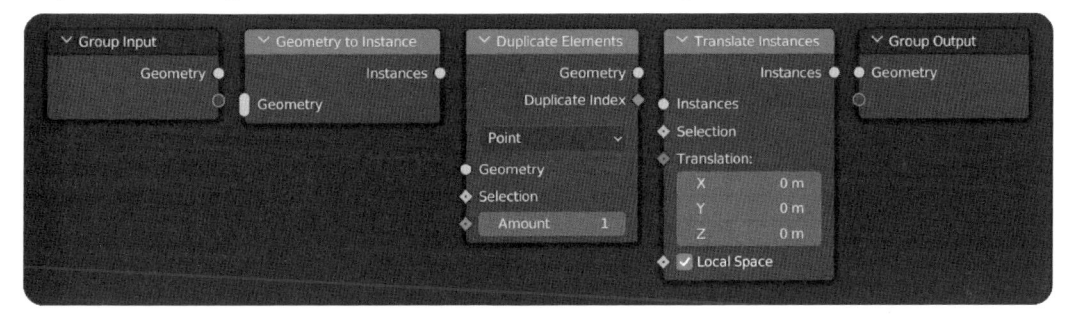

Figure 6.4: The nodes you'll need

Let's give an explanation of each of these nodes:

- **Geometry to Instance** node

    This node will be used to convert our geometry to a usable instance format. As said in previous chapters, instances are used to individually manipulate objects.

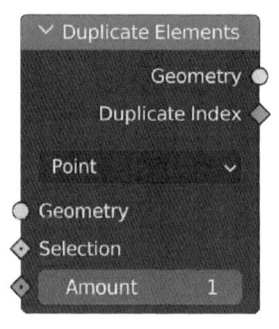

- **Duplicate Elements** node

    This node will duplicate any element that you give it. You can choose to duplicate by vertices, edges, faces, or instances. For this demonstration, we will be duplicating instances.

- **Translate Instances** node

    This node will move instances. We will need this node to move away our instances from each other using their unique ID.

As you might have guessed, we will make a custom Array modifier. We will duplicate an instance and offset each duplicate by a specific value defined by its unique ID, which we can find in the Spreadsheet. This will make the node tree function like an Array modifier. After that, we can check whether our calculations are correct using the Spreadsheet.

Building the structure of the node tree

Let's start by opening our Geometry Node editor and converting the base group input to an instance using the **Geometry to Instance** node. This will make sure we can use **Group Input** in our Geometry Node editor as an instance. This is important because to make use of the **Duplicate Elements** node, we will need to make use of instances because they allow us to edit objects separately from each other.

Now, let's add a **Duplicate Elements** node. By default, the **Duplicate Elements** node will be set to **Point**. In this case, we want to duplicate each input to an instance because we want to duplicate the inputted mesh in its entirety. So, let's put this node in **Instance** mode.

Figure 6.5: Duplicate Elements node

This node will duplicate an instance *x* number of times and output it as a single geometry output. We also get the **Duplicate Index** integer value as an output. This will be important in the next step.

Let's set the **Amount** integer to 5. This will make sure that our input will be instanced or duplicated five times.

Demonstrating how the Spreadsheet can be useful   87

When you look at the Viewport, you can see that nothing happened. We just see the object we inputted.

Figure 6.6: Your current node setup

This is normal; it is like this because the instanced duplicates are contained within each other. We will need to find a way to move the instances away from each other with a unique ID.

This is where the **Duplicate Index** value of the **Duplicate Elements** node comes into play. This value defines the unique ID of each instance. Looking at the Spreadsheet, we can see what instance gets assigned to each ID.

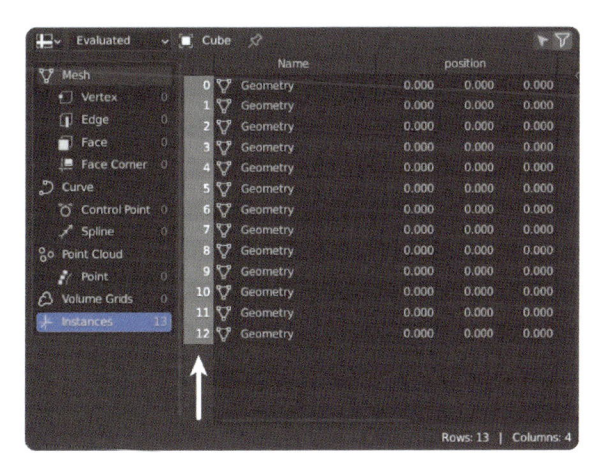

Figure 6.7: IDs in the Spreadsheet

We can multiply this ID value by a certain number so that each instance will be placed on a location that matches a multiplicate of the given ID. This will make an Array effect.

We can achieve this by using the **Translate Instances** node to move the instances.

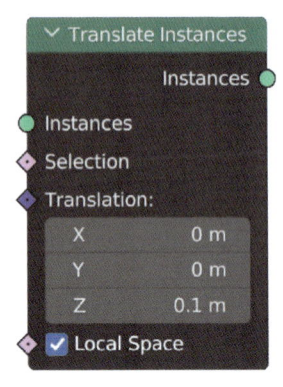

Figure 6.8: Translate Instances node

Let's feed the vector value of this node with a **Combine XYZ** node. This will make us able to use node connections on each of the three *x*, *y* and *z* values.

To make the instances move away from each other, let's multiply the ID value by how much we want each instance to move away from the others. In this demonstration, we will use a multiplication value of 3. We can multiply these values using a **Math** node, which is set to **Multiply**. Let's insert this **Math** node into the *x* axis of the **Combine XYZ** node. If you want the instances to move via the *y* axis, you can plug them into the *z* axis instead.

This is how your node tree should look.

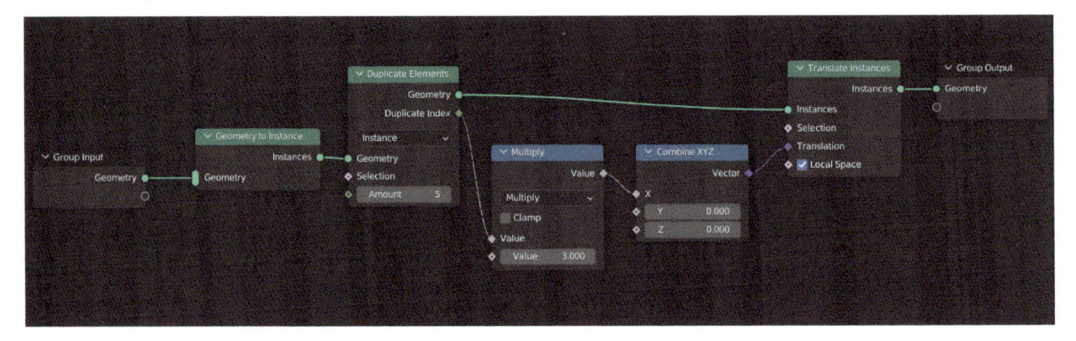

Figure 6.9: Your current node tree

If you now look at the Viewport, you can see that the instances have separated from each other (*Figure 6.10*).

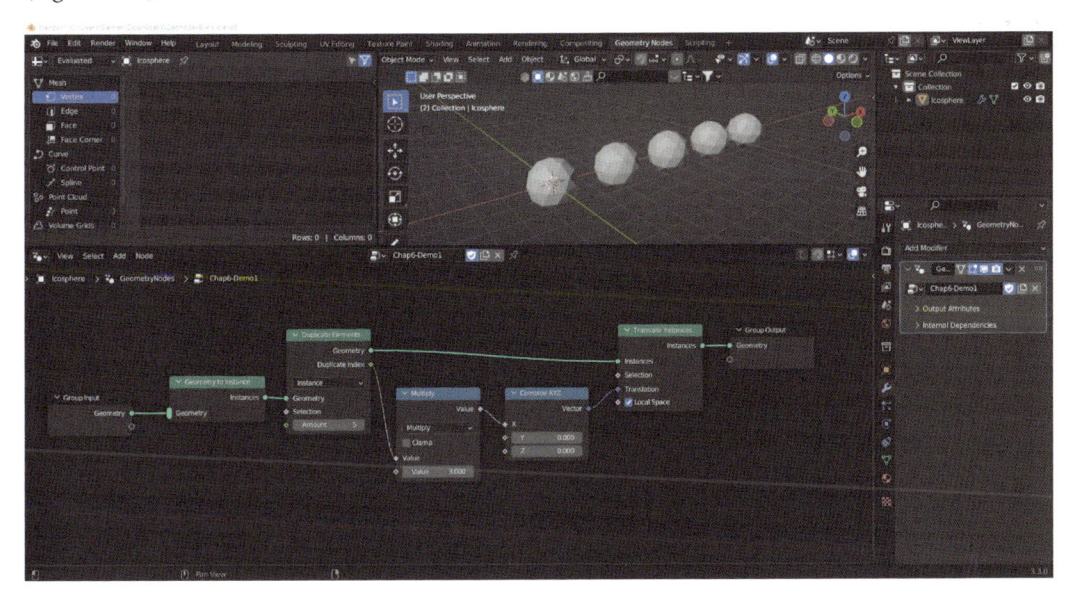

Figure 6.10: Instances separated

When we take a look at the Spreadsheet, we can see that our calculations are executed correctly.

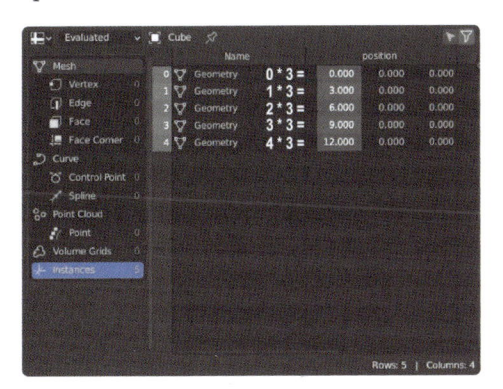

Figure 6.11: Spreadsheet of the demonstration project

And there you have it! That is how you make your very own Array modifier; we can modify the length between each instance by changing the **Math Multiply** node. We can also change the number of instances by changing the **Amount** value on the **Duplicate Elements** node. On top of that, you now know how to use the Spreadsheet to obtain information about your geometry.

To put your newly learned skill to use, let's use the **Duplicate Elements** node to create a tesseract cube.

Exercise – creating a rotated tesseract cube

In this exercise, we will teach you how to create the shape shown (a tesseract cube) in *Figure 6.12*.

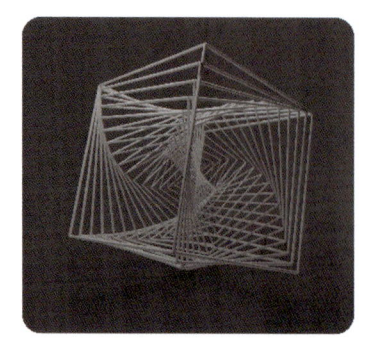

Figure 6.12: Rotated tesseract cube

Sketching the basic idea

This shape can be made by duplicating a cube while making the duplicate cubes smaller and smaller and rotating each cube by the amount of their unique ID.

We will start by adding a cube. We'll duplicate this cube, and we'll scale it in a way that they don't intersect with the other duplicates. Then, we will rotate the cube in a way that is satisfying to the end user.

To top this exercise off, we will add a wireframe effect to this shape, as seen in *Figure 6.12*.

Introducing the nodes you'll need

In *Figure 6.13*, you'll see what nodes we will use in this exercise.

Figure 6.13: The nodes you'll need

These are the nodes that we will be using in this exercise. Let's sum up each node and why we need them:

- **Cube** node

    We will need the **Cube** node as a base primitive to start our node tree. We will not make use of any existing mesh, but instead, we're going to make use of node primitives, in this case, the **Cube** node primitive.

- **Geometry to Instance** node

    It is crucial to convert this cube into an instance. If we don't convert it into an instance, we will not be able to separately manipulate the size of each cube.

- **Duplicate Elements** node

    We will need this node to duplicate the cubes as instances. This is the most important node in the whole exercise.

- **Scale Instances** node

    We will use the **Scale Instances** node to individually scale the instanced cubes separately from each other to create the desired effect seen in *Figure 6.12*.

- **Rotate Instances** node

    Just like the **Scale Instances** node, we will need a way to rotate each instance separately from each other to create a twisting effect inside of the cubes.

Building the node tree

Here's how we build the node tree.

To get started, let's add a new Geometry Nodes workspace to the default cube and delete the **Group Input** node since we won't be needing it because we're making use of a **Cube** node primitive.

Then, let's place down our first node, the **Cube** node primitive.

The current settings that the node comes with are perfect for what we need, so we won't need to change any of the properties of this node.

Let's connect this node to the **Group Output** node to visualize the cube.

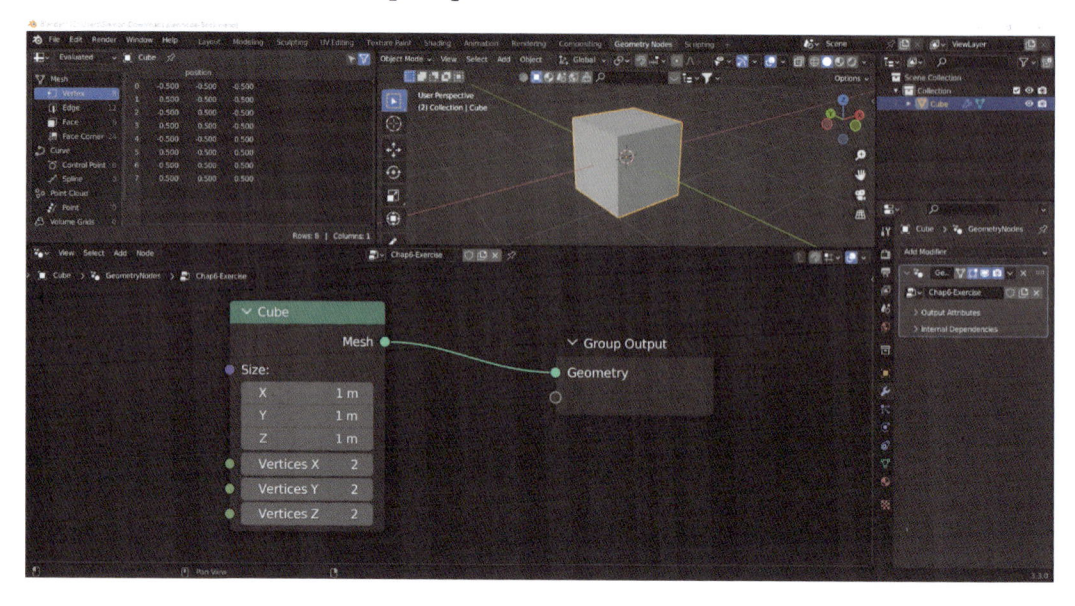

Figure 6.14: Visualizing the cube

We can see that the cube is now visible; however, we want the cube to be visible in a wireframe style. Fortunately, this can be done in the Geometry Node editor by converting your mesh into a curve and converting that cube back into a mesh.

This will turn your mesh into a wireframe because converting your mesh into a curve deletes all the faces.

Let's add in a **Mesh to Curve** node at the output of our cube, and right after the **Mesh to Curve** node, we'll add a **Curve to Mesh** node.

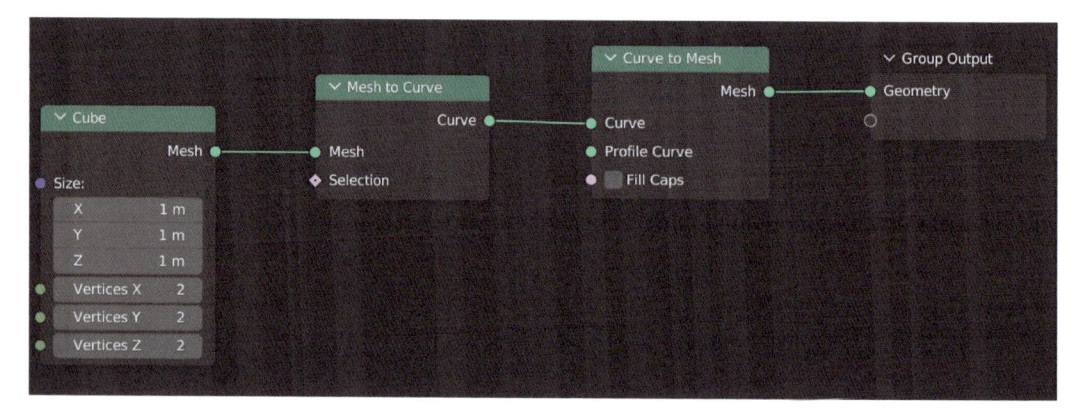

Figure 6.15: Your current node tree

You can see that nothing is visible; this is because we do not have a profile curve defined in the **Curve to Mesh** node yet. Let's add in a **Curve Circle** node and plug the output into the **Profile Curve** socket.

You will see that your wireframe appears too thick. To fix this, let's set the radius to a small value. In this exercise, we went with a value of `0.01`.

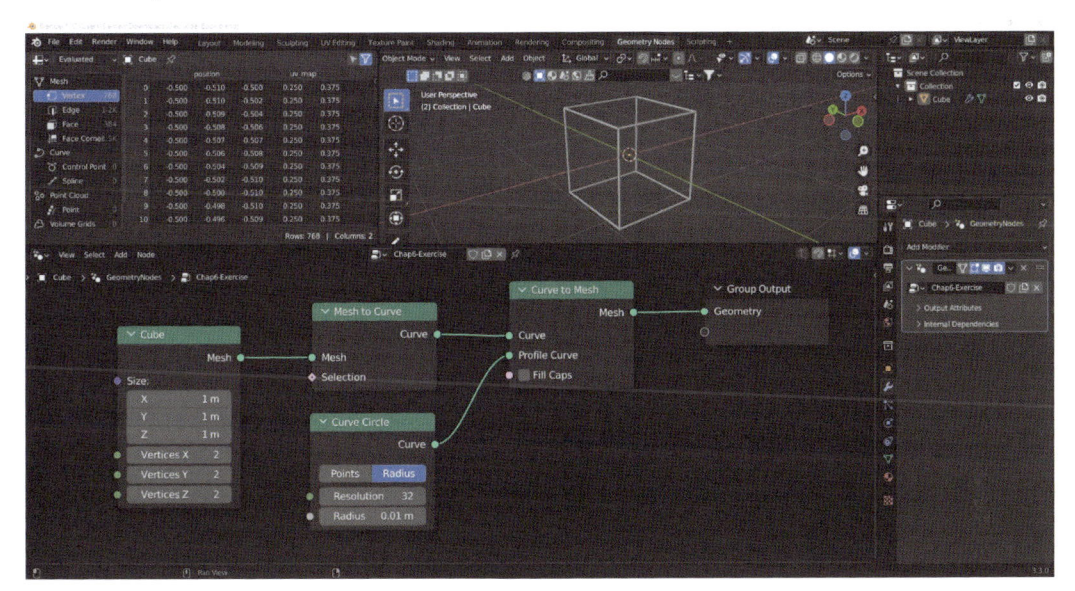

Figure 6.16: Your current node tree

Before continuing to the next part, let's put the last three nodes (the **Mesh to Curve**, **Curve to Mesh**, and **Curve Circle** nodes) in a group by selecting these three nodes and pressing *Ctrl + G*. You've now created a node group. To get out of this node group, you can press *Tab* to go back to your original node tree. You will see that we now have a simple node to convert our mesh into a wireframe. A node group will not alter the functionality of your node tree, but it will be easier to visualize your node tree.

To make this node easier to remember, we can select the node and press *F2* to rename it `Wireframe`.

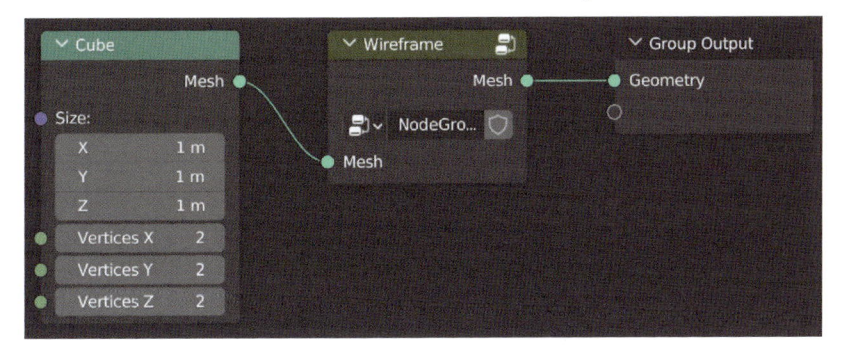

Figure 6.17: Wireframe node group

Let's convert our cube into an instance using a **Geometry to Instance** node. This will make sure our cube is seen as an instance and is ready to be duplicated. We will place this node between the **Cube** node and the **Wireframe** node group.

Now, let's add a **Duplicate Elements** node to start duplicating our instance. Let's set this node to **Instance** mode to make sure it's duplicating instances instead of points.

To begin, let's give this node an amount of 5.

If you've followed these steps correctly, your node tree should look something like this:

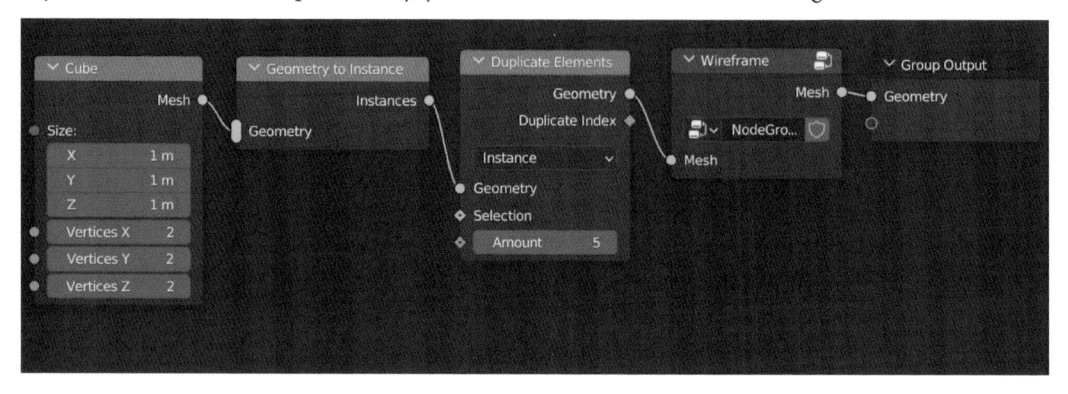

Figure 6.18: Your current node tree

We can see that nothing has happened. But as said in the previous demonstration, the cubes are duplicated inside of each other.

Let's use the **Scale Instances** node to give each duplicate a different size.

Drop in the **Scale Instances** node after the **Duplicate Elements** node and you'll see that once again, nothing happens. This is because we have to place the **ID** output into our **Scale** input. Let's connect the **Duplicate Index** output of the **Duplicate Elements** node to the **Scale** input.

Your node tree should look something like this:

Exercise – creating a rotated tesseract cube

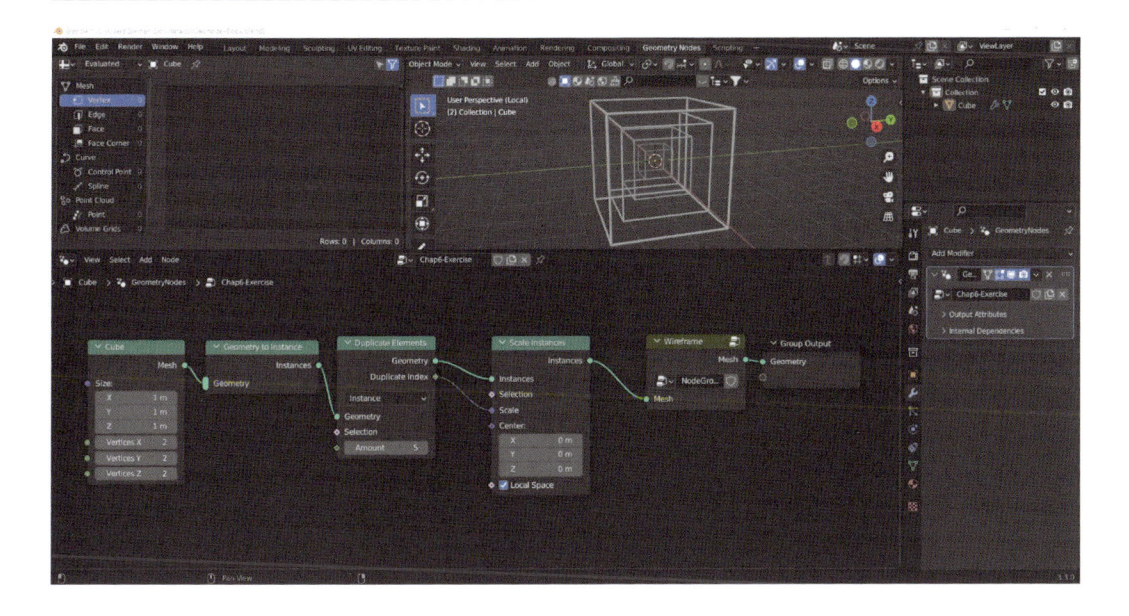

Figure 6.19: Your current node tree

To visualize the result, you might need to zoom out a little bit because we're scaling each cube by its unique ID value, which makes the cubes larger.

We can also take a look at our Spreadsheet to see the properties of our tesseract cube, including the IDs of our cubes.

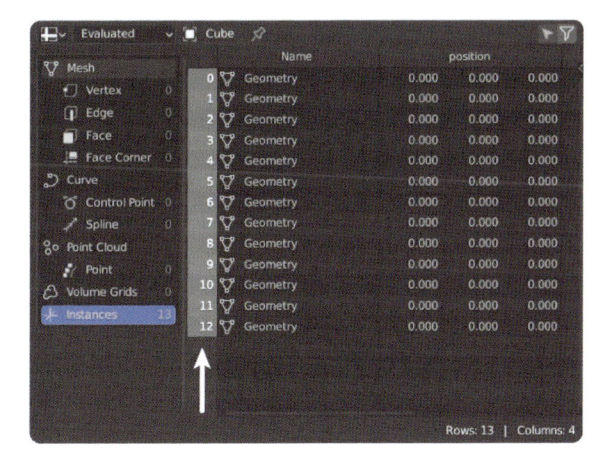

Figure 6.20: Spreadsheet

The last step of this exercise is to rotate the cubes in a way that looks pleasing to the human eye. To do that, let's add a **Rotate Instances** node after the **Scale Instances** node.

Just like we've done with the **Scale Instances** node, we'll need to rotate the cubes by their unique ID, so let's connect the **Duplicate Index** output to the **Rotation** input.

We can see that the rotation is way too aggressive. To fix this, we need to divide each of the ID values by a certain amount to decrease the rotation amount. This can be done by adding a **Math** node set to **Divide**.

Let's drop in the **Math** node between the **Duplicate Index** output and the **Rotation** input. Increase the division number until the rotation amount looks satisfying.

This is also a good moment to increase the **Amount** value on the **Duplicate Elements** node to get more cubes duplicated in the project. Pick a number that you think looks good. We went with 19.

This is how your current node tree should look:

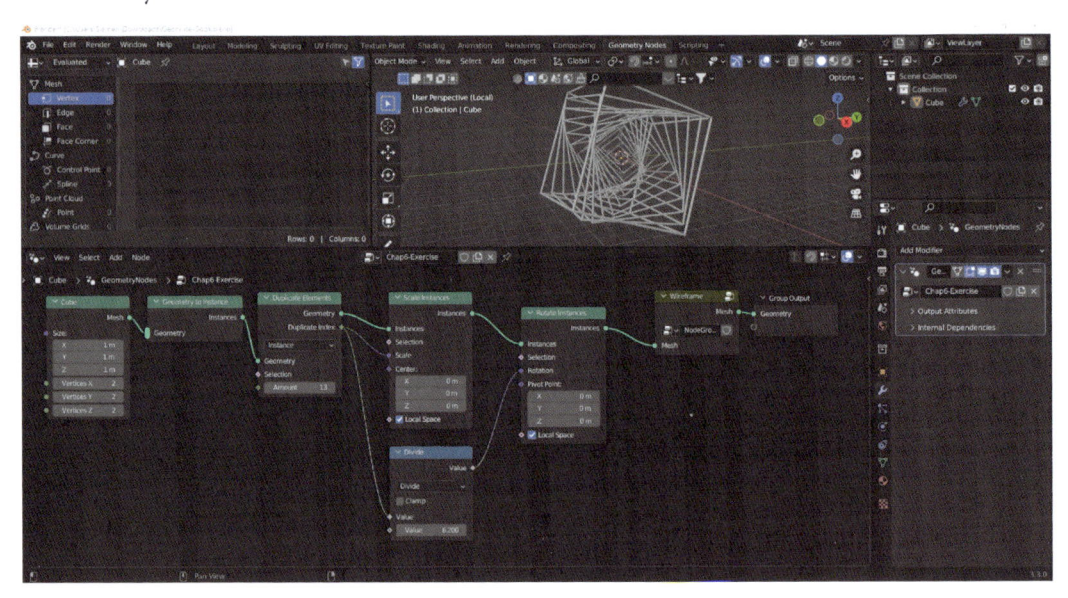

Figure 6.21: Your current node tree

Adding a material to your tesseract cube

You can add a material to your tesseract cube, but it is completely optional. This is how you do it:

1. Make a material in the material editor.
2. Head back to the Geometry Node editor and add a **Set Material** node.
3. Drop in this **Set Material** node at the end of your node tree.
4. Select your material from the dropdown on the **Set Material** node.

And there you have it! That's how you make a rotated tesseract cube in the Geometry Node editor.

This is how the finished render will look:

Figure 6.22: Final render

In this exercise, we reiterated how to use the **Duplicate Elements** node to make the effect in *Figure 6.22* where we rotate and scale a cube by its unique ID.

Summary

In this chapter, you've learned how to use the **Duplicate Elements** node to duplicate instances. In the demonstration in the *Demonstrating how the Spreadsheet can be useful* section, you learned how to make a custom Array modifier, and in the exercise, you learned how to use the **Duplicate Elements** node to make a rotated tesseract cube.

In the next chapter, you'll be introduced to the String system inside the Geometry Node editor.

7
Creating and Modifying Text in the Geometry Node Editor

In the previous chapter, we introduced you to the Spreadsheet. In this chapter, we will introduce you to another important part of the Geometry Nodes world, the String system. This is also referred to as the text system of the Geometry Node editor. You will learn about how strings work and function in the Geometry Nodes editor. Along with that, you will also learn how to modify, create, and convert strings on your own.

In this chapter, we'll cover the following topics:

- Introducing strings
- The various nodes we will use in this chapter
- Converting strings to a usable mesh
- Exercise – making a procedural countdown

Introducing strings

In this section, we will give you an introduction to the String system of the Geometry Node editor inside Blender.

In the Geometry Node editor, we have various nodes at our disposal to modify and create text procedurally.

As we discussed in *Chapter 1, An Introduction to Geometry Nodes*, String node connections can be found using a blue-colored socket. This socket works as an input/output and will carry over string datatypes.

As you can see in the following figure, this is what the String node connection looks like.

Figure 7.1: The String node connection

The strings in the Geometry Node editor work via underlying Curves. This is also the case when adding a normal text object to your Blender project. The upside of this is that we can modify these Curves like any other Curve object in the Geometry Node editor, such as modifying the shape of the curve, adding noise to a curve, or instancing points on a curve.

Just like the other parts of the Geometry Node editor, we can also procedurally generate strings using the various String nodes we have in Blender, which we will demonstrate in the exercise at the end of this chapter.

In this section, we've learned how the String system works in the Geometry Node editor and how we can recognize its node connection. In the next section, you'll learn about the nodes you'll use in this chapter.

The various nodes we will use in this chapter

In this section, we will be introducing you to the various nodes that we can use to create, manipulate, and convert strings in the Geometry Node editor. But first, let's talk about where to find String nodes.

Where can you find String nodes?

Like any other node in the Geometry Node editor, this set of nodes can be found by pressing the **Add** button in your Geometry Node editor or by pressing *Shift + A*. Pressing either of those will bring up the menu you can see in *Figure 7.2*.

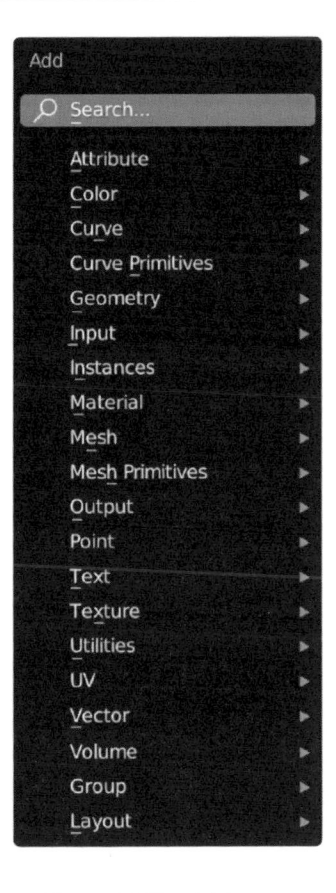

Figure 7.2: The Add menu

In this menu, you can hover your mouse over the **Text** entry on the list, and once you do so, you will see this menu appear.

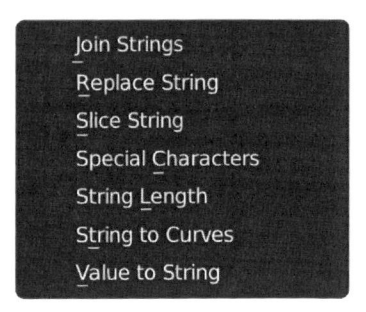

Figure 7.3: Text entry

The nodes you see in *Figure 7.3* are the String nodes we'll cover in this chapter.

Introducing you to the different String nodes

Now, we will be introducing you to all the different nodes that we will be familiarizing you with in this chapter. These can be divided into three categories: the nodes that are used to create strings, the nodes to modify strings, and the nodes that are used to convert strings into geometry. Let's go over each category.

Nodes to create strings

The nodes that will be introduced to you below are nodes that are designed to help you create and procedurally generate strings.

The String node

The **String** node is used to convert an input box into a String node connection.

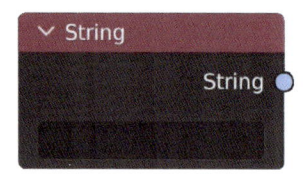

Figure 7.4: The String node

This node allows you to put any text into the textbox, and it will output the text as a String node connection; it's pretty straightforward.

The Value to String node

In the following screenshot, you can see the **Value to String** node. As the title of this node suggests, this node converts a value into a string.

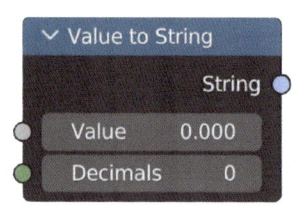

Figure 7.5: The Value to String node

As you can see in *Figure 7.5*, we can provide a **Value** input and a **Decimals** input. The **Decimals** input allows you to change the location of the decimal point in your value. If the decimal point is at the lower end, your value might be rounded to the floor or ceiling.

This node will output the values you've provided in a string format.

Nodes to modify strings

The following nodes that are introduced are used to modify existing strings by performing word processing on your inputted string. The output of these nodes will be the processed string.

The Join Strings node

Here, you see the **Join Strings** node. This node allows you to combine multiple strings together into one string.

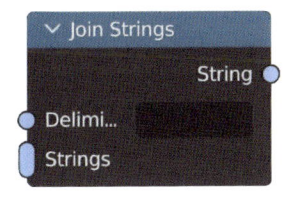

Figure 7.6: The Join Strings node

This node presents two inputs; the first input is the **Delimiter** input. This input allows you to put characters between the different strings you process in this node.

The second value, the multi-connection **Strings** input, allows you to connect as many strings as you want to join into one big string.

The String Length node

Now, we'll talk about the **String Length** node. This allows you to output the length of your inputted string as an integer value.

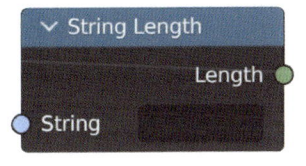

Figure 7.7: The String Length node

This node presents us with a **String** input node connection, but we can also make use of the convenient input box right next to it.

The length of the inputted string will be outputted as an integer value called **Length**.

The Replace String node

Next, the **Replace String** node. This node performs searches and replaces within your string according to your inputs.

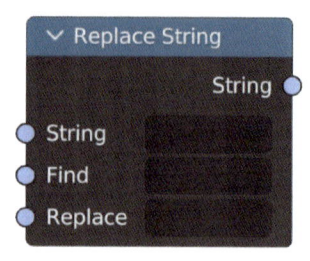

Figure 7.8: The Replace String node

The first input in this node is the **String** input, this is your base string or text. The next input, the **Find** input, allows you to input a string to search for, and after that, you can use the **Replace** input to replace the string you've searched for in the **Find** input.

The Slice String node

In *Figure 7.9* you see the **Slice String** node. This node allows you to cut off certain parts of your inputted string.

Figure 7.9: The Slice String node

The first input, the **String** input, requires your base string. The **Position** integer value then defines at what character from the left the string should be cut off. After that, the **Length** integer value defines how long the final string should be after being cut off from the right side.

Nodes to convert strings into geometry

The following nodes introduced here are the nodes used to convert your String node connection to a Geometry node connection, in other words, Curves.

The String to Curves node

The **String to Curves** node is very important when working with strings in the Geometry Node editor.

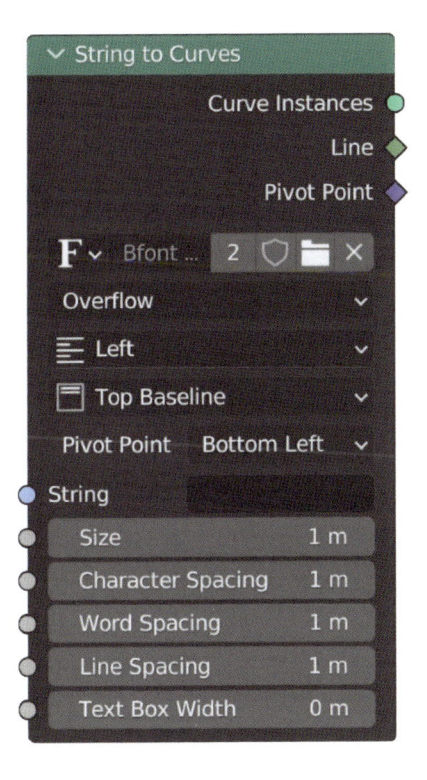

Figure 7.10: The String to Curves node

This node allows you to output your strings to a viewable format; in other words, it converts your strings to curve instances, which can be viewed in the Viewport.

As you can see from *Figure 7.10*, lots of these options resemble the text properties we see when we add a text object in Blender. The only difference is that these values are controllable via the Geometry Nodes editor, which gives lots of flexibility to your projects.

It is notable to mention that the curve this node outputs won't be filled in. So, it will just output an outline of your string. To fix that, let's take a look at the next node.

The Fill Curve node

As the title of this node suggests, this node allows you to fill Curves, including the outlines of string Curves. We can use this after the **String to Curves** node to fill in our text.

Figure 7.11: The Fill Curve node

We are only presented with two buttons on this node: the **Triangles** button and the **N-gons** button. In *Figure 7.12* you can see the difference in topology for each of the two options.

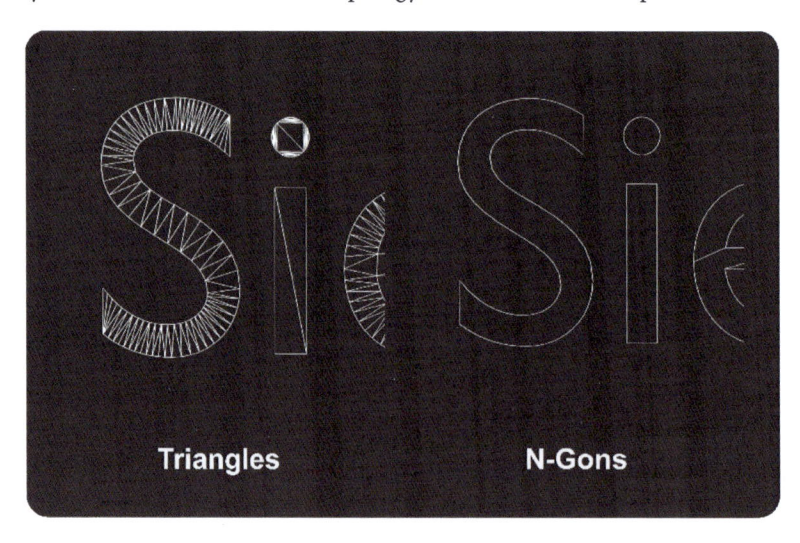

Figure 7.12: Difference in topology

Using the **Triangles** mode, the top faces of the string will be filled in using triangles. You should use this method most of the time since Blender is not optimized to work with **N-gons**. You should only use **N-gons** if you specifically need them.

In this section, you've learned about the various nodes we will be using in this chapter, along with the functions of the nodes. In the following section, we will demonstrate to you how to convert strings into a usable mesh.

Converting strings into a usable mesh

In this section, you'll learn a step-by-step approach to how to make your strings visible in the Geometry Node editor. Learning this is crucial to using strings in the Geometry Node editor because, without these nodes, you won't be able to visualize the text you're generating. Let's get started with the most important node, the **String to Curves** node.

The String to Curves node

As explained in the previous heading, this node will convert your string into a series of Curves to make the string visible in the Viewport. Let's demonstrate this by adding a **String** node and a **Group Output** node.

Drop in the **String to Curves** node between these two nodes, wire the nodes up to each input and output, and append the settings to your liking.

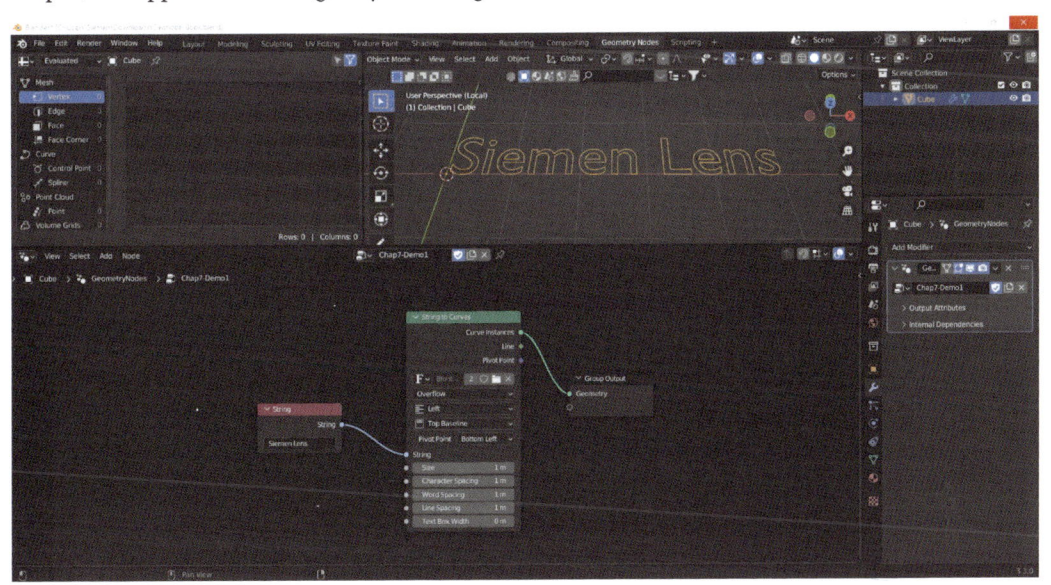

Figure 7.13: String to Curves demonstration

You will notice that the text is now visible - everything apart from the filling of the text. To fix that, let's take a look at the next step.

The Fill Curve node

To make the filling of the text visible, we will make use of the **Fill Curve** node. Let's drop in this node between the **String to Curves** node and the **Group Output** node.

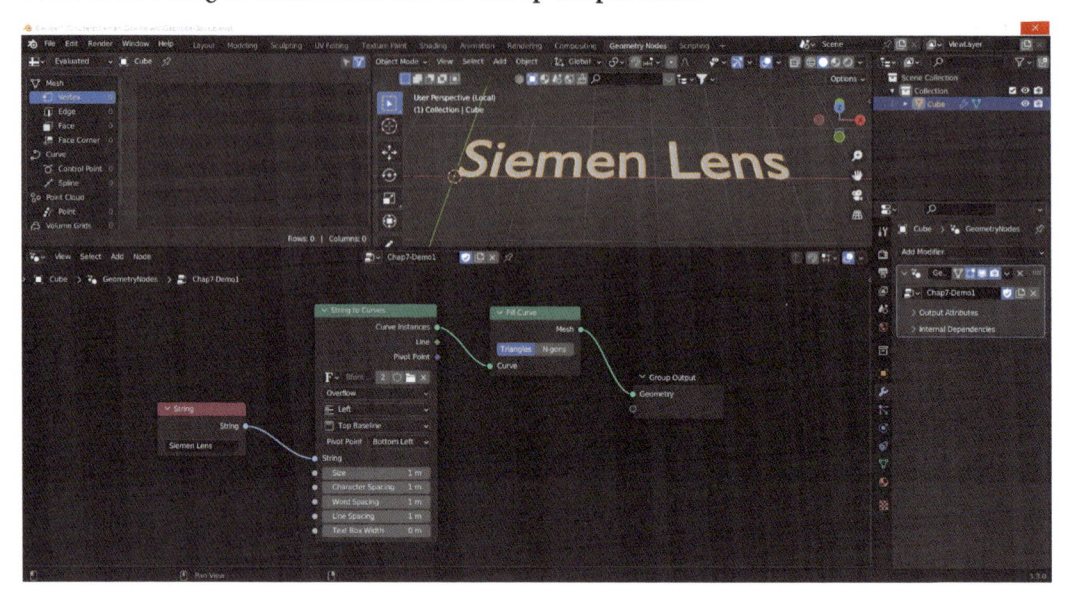

Figure 7.14: Fill Curve demonstration

We can see that the string we've written is now easy to read in the Viewport.

The Extrude Mesh node

This last step is completely up to you. If you want to extrude your text after doing all these steps, we can use an **Extrude Mesh** node to extrude the current geometry.

To extrude this geometry, let's drop in an **Extrude Mesh** node between the **Fill Curve** and **Group Output** nodes.

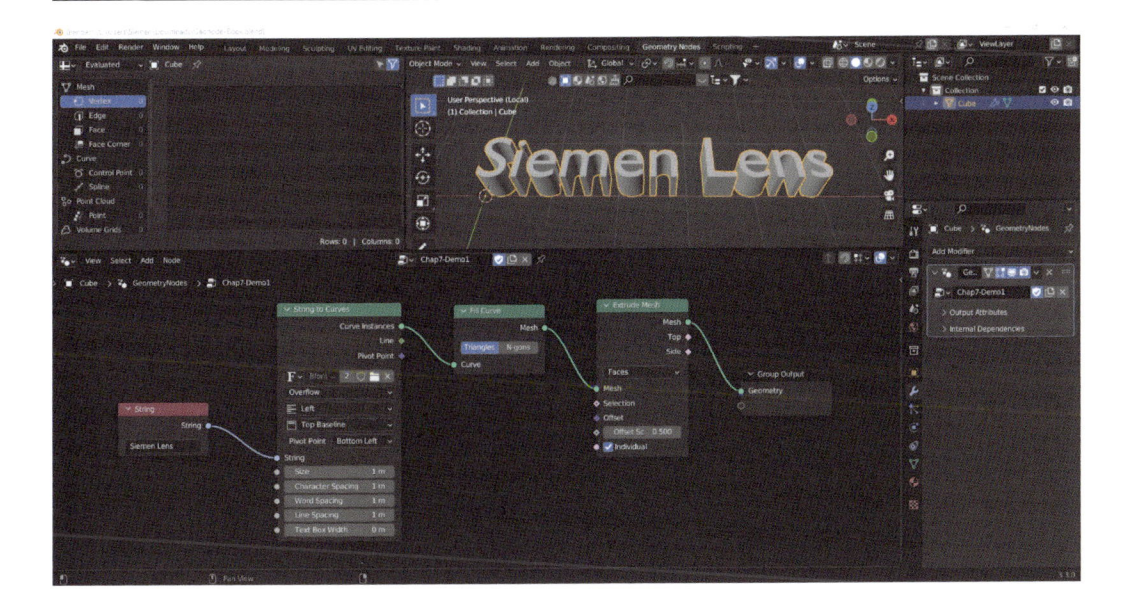

Figure 7.15: The Extrude Mesh node demonstration

After we have dropped in this node, we can see that the effect is immediately noticeable. The text is no longer flat, as seen in *Figure 7.15*.

In this section, you've learned how to visualize your text by converting your strings to Curves, filling your Curves, and extruding these Curves.

You now know the basics of the String system in the Geometry Node editor, and you are ready to move on to this chapter's exercise, where you will make a procedural countdown.

Exercise – making a procedural countdown

In this exercise, we will be making a procedural countdown using the Strings system inside the Geometry Node editor. All the knowledge you gained in this chapter will be put to use in this fun exercise.

Sketching the basic idea

To achieve this goal of creating a procedural countdown, we will have to make use of some **Math** nodes. The first step is to obtain our seconds count. We can do this by dividing the frame count by 24 to obtain our seconds count. Subtracting our seconds count from 10 will give us a countdown of 10 seconds. After that, we will use a **Value to String** node to convert our countdown to a string. And lastly, we will convert this string to a curve to visualize our countdown.

Exploring the nodes required to make a procedural countdown

In this section, we will go over the nodes that are required to make this procedural countdown. You can see the required nodes in *Figure 7.16*.

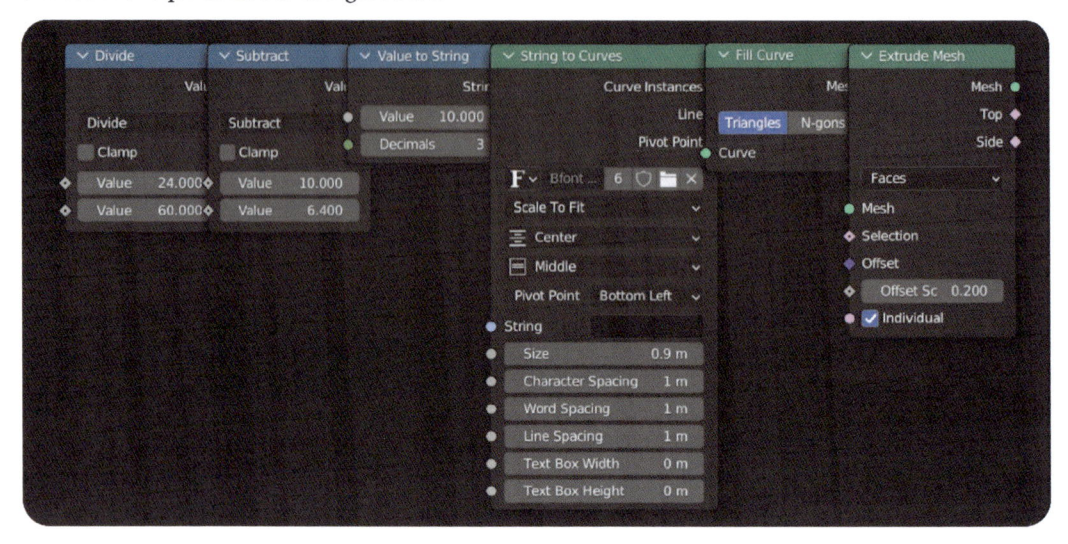

Figure 7.16: The nodes you'll need for this exercise

Let's go over each of these nodes and why we need them in this exercise:

- The **Math** nodes (**Divide** and **Subtract**): We will need these nodes to execute the math explained in the previous *Sketching the basic idea* section. These will make sure our countdown is calculated correctly.

- The **Value to String** node: This node will be used to convert our calculated countdown value to a string.

- The **String to Curves** node: This node will allow us to convert the string we obtained directly into a curve geometry, so it is visible in the Viewport for us to see.

- The **Fill Curve** node: This will allow us to fill in the outlines of the Curves so that our text is easier to read.

- The **Extrude Mesh** node: The last node we will need is the **Extrude Mesh** node. This will allow us to extrude our mesh into the third dimension.

Building the node tree

Let's start by making the countdown calculation. For this, you will need to duplicate two **Math** nodes to create a **Subtract** node and a **Divide** node.

We want to divide the frame count of our animation by our frame rate to get our seconds count. After that, we can subtract our seconds count from 10 to get our final countdown value.

To get our frame count, enter `#frame` into the top value of your **Divide** node. If executed correctly, the value should become purple.

In the bottom value, you will fill in the current frame rate of the project. By default, Blender uses a frame rate of 24 frames per second.

This is how your **Divide** node should now look.

Figure 7.17: The Divide node configuration

This, as explained before, will divide the frame count with our frame rate to get our seconds count.

The next step is to subtract our countdown length by this **Divide** node. In this case, we will go with a countdown length of 10 because the standard Blender project is about 10 seconds long when using 24 frames per second.

Let's subtract our current **Divide** node from 10. In other words, let's plug the output of our **Divide** node into the bottom socket of the **Subtract** node. The top value will contain the length of our countdown, which is 10 seconds.

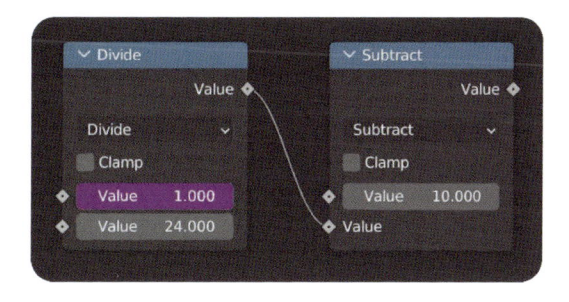

Figure 7.18: Countdown value calculation

Now that we are done calculating our countdown, it's time to begin coding the strings part of your node tree.

Creating and Modifying Text in the Geometry Node Editor

To begin, let's add a **Value to String** node to convert our countdown value to a usable string.

We will connect the output from the **Subtract** node to the input of the **Value to String** node. Let's set the **Decimals** value to 2.

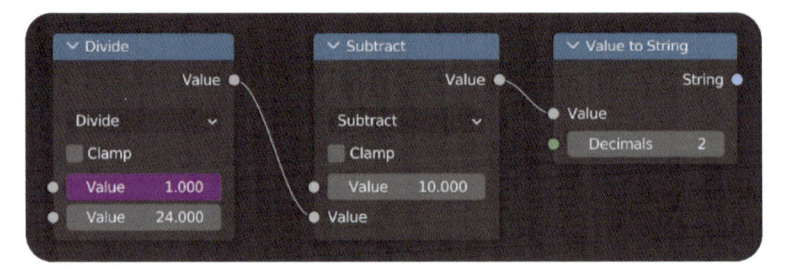

Figure 7.19: Converting our countdown value to a string

Now that we finally have a string output, we can start visualizing our string. To do this, let's add a **String to Curves** node after the **Value to String** node.

Let's center our text and put our text in the middle, then connect your string output to the string input of the **String to Curves** node.

Nothing is visible yet, but that is because we do not have a **Group Output** node yet. Let's drop in a **Group Output** node to visualize what we have so far.

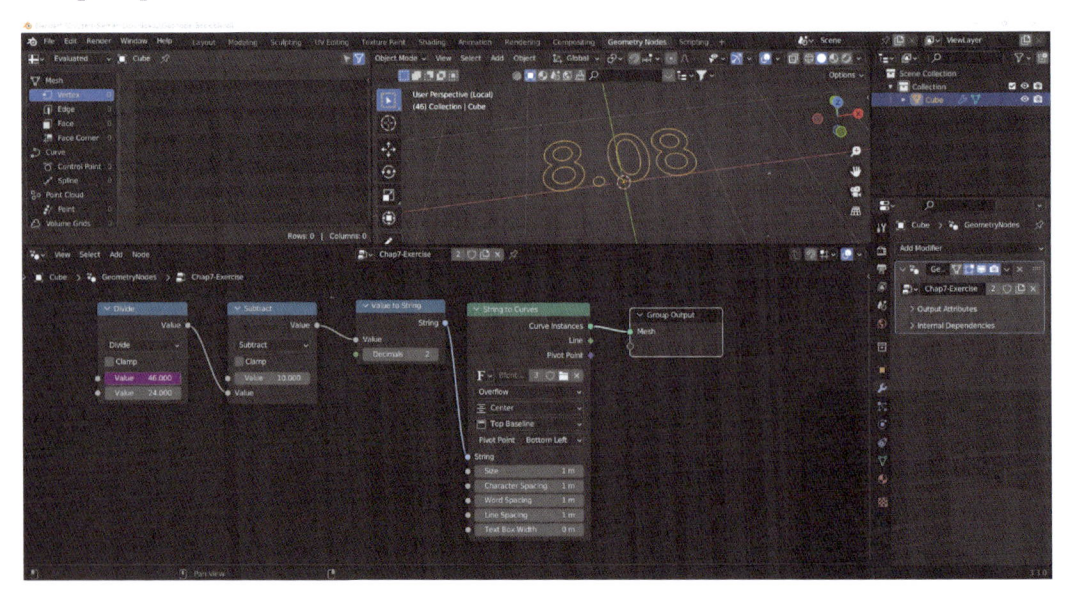

Figure 7.20: Your current node tree

Exercise – making a procedural countdown 113

We can already see the countdown. The only problem is that it's not filled in yet. Let's solve this with a **Fill Curve** node after the **String to Curves** node.

After you've dropped this node in at the correct place, we can see the countdown more clearly. You can hit the space bar to play your countdown.

The last step is to extrude the text into the third dimension. At the end, add an **Extrude Mesh** node. Let's use an **Offset Scale** of 0.2.

You will see that our countdown is now in 3D and works as we intended.

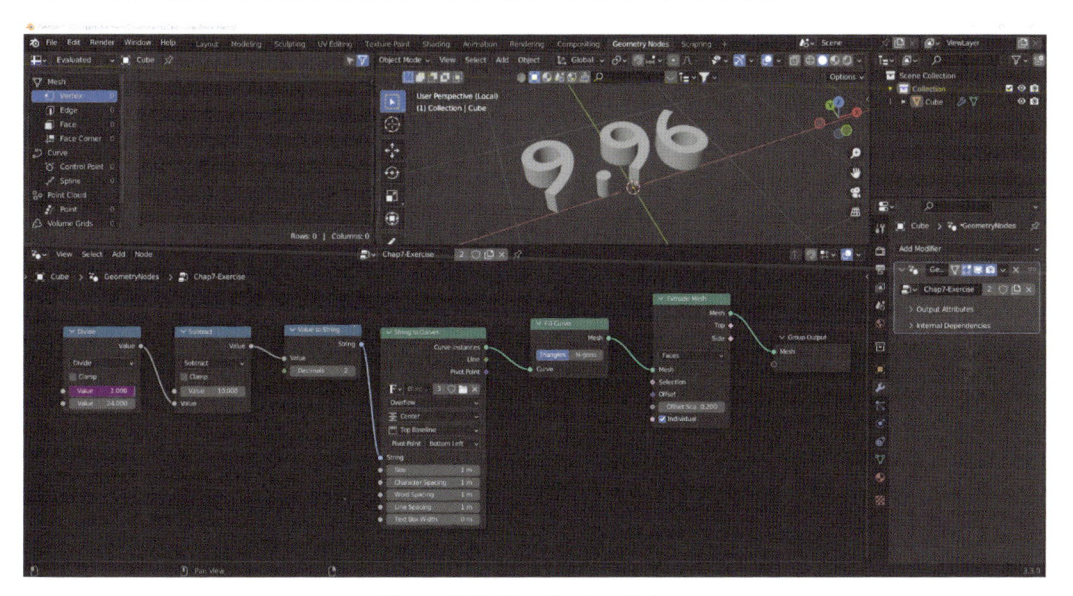

Figure 7.21: Your final node tree

And now, you can see the final render.

Figure 7.22: The final render

And with that, this is the end of this exercise and the end of this chapter.

Summary

In this chapter, you've learned about the various nodes we can use to create, manipulate, calculate, and convert strings. We have also explained the important String nodes in detail. This will help you build a more calculative and analytical mindset, a very helpful tool for the coming chapter.

Lastly, you've learned how to make a procedural countdown using these String nodes.

In the next chapter, we will teach you how to edit Curves with nodes.

Part 3 – Modifying Meshes and Curves in the Geometry Node System

In the third part of this book, you will learn about editing curves and manipulating meshes using the powerful tools provided by the Geometry Node system in Blender. You'll learn how to add noise to your geometry, along with how to give thickness to curves and make use of Booleans.

This section comprises the following chapters:

- *Chapter 8, Editing Curves with Nodes*
- *Chapter 9, Manipulating Mesh Using Geometry Nodes*

8
Editing Curves with Nodes

In the previous chapter, we went over the string system inside the Geometry Node editor. Those strings were converted into Curves to visualize them in the viewport. In this chapter, we will be taking a closer look at some fun things we can do with the Curve system in the Geometry Node editor, such as adding noise to Curves and adding thickness to these Curves.

We will discuss the following topics in this chapter:

- Adding noise to your Curves
- Giving thickness to your Curves
- Exercise – making a simple lightning bolt

Adding noise to your Curves

In this section, we will show you how to manipulate your Curves by adding a noise pattern to them. This will be handy if you're making anything that involves a curved line of some sort, for example, a lightning bolt or a tree trunk.

In the following figure, you can see the nodes that we will be using in this section.

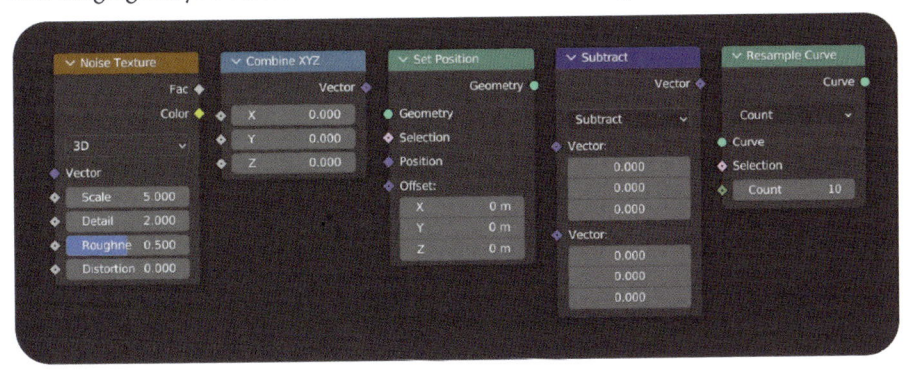

Figure 8.1: The nodes you'll need

Let us take a quick look at the individual nodes:

- The **Noise Texture** node – We will need the **Noise Texture** node to add noise randomization to our Curve.
- The **Combine XYZ** node – This node will be used to combine the *x*, *y*, and *z* values into a vector value that we can use in the **Offset** input of the next node that we will need to add noise to our Curve.
- The **Set Position** node – This is the most important node in this section because it is responsible for modifying our Curve. The task of this node is to set the position of different points in your geometry. For example, this can be used to add some randomization to your Curve by plugging in a noise map into the **Offset** socket.
- The **Vector Math** node – We will make use of the **Vector Math** node. By default, Blender's noise textures aren't normalized to average out to 0. This means that your midlevel will be off by 0.5. To counteract this, we will need a **Vector Math** node to subtract the midlevel value to 0.
- The **Resample Curve** node – Lastly, this node will interpolate geometry into your curve. In the case of this demonstration, we will be using this node to get more geometry into our Curve with the help of a higher resampling count to get a better-looking noise pattern. A higher resampling count means a higher resolution of your Curve and more geometry in your Curve.

Now that you know the nodes we'll be using in this section, let's get started with this demonstration.

Offset by Random values

Let's start by teaching you how to randomize your Curve by making use of the **Random Value** node:

1. Firstly, go ahead and make a Curve in **Edit** mode. This can be any shape you want.

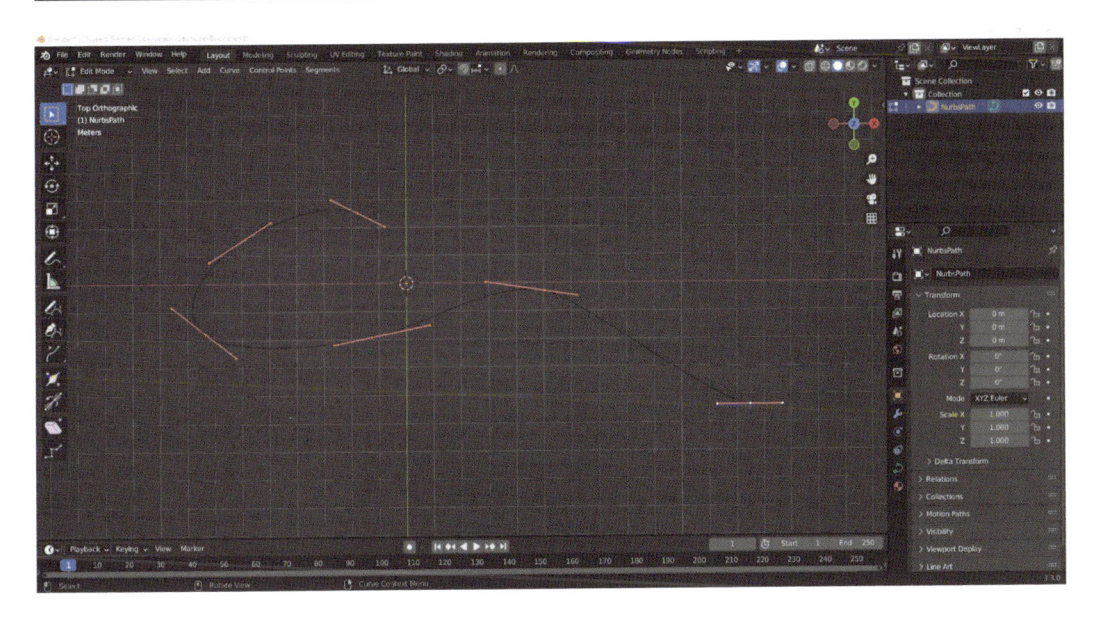

Figure 8.2: Draw a curve

2. After that, we can open the Geometry Node editor. Let's add a new node tree to this Curve object.
3. Now, it's time to make use of the **Set Position** node.

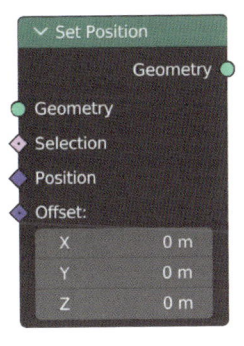

Figure 8.3: The Set Position node

This node will offset the position of geometry by using either the **Position** input or the **Offset** input. In this demonstration, we will make use of the **Offset** input because we want to offset the geometry by a random value.

4. Let's start by adding this **Set Position** node in between **Group Input** and **Group Output**.

5. At first, you'll notice that nothing happens. This is because we have not modified the geometry in any way. Let's start modifying this Curve by adding a **Random Value** node set to **Vector**. We'll put the **Min** value to -1.000 on all axes. This will ensure that our midlevel value sits at zero. This is crucial when you want your geometry to shift evenly.

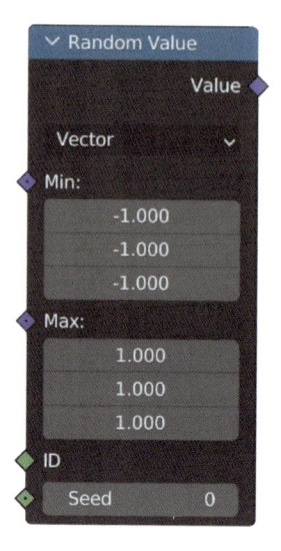

Figure 8.4: The Random Value node set to Vector

6. Let's plug in the output vector socket into the vector **Offset** input of the **Set Position** node.

   We can see that, depending on how much geometry we have in our Curve, the Curve moved a bit. If we want to get more detail in our randomization, the Curve needs to be resampled.

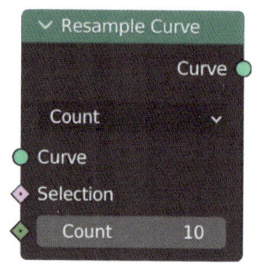

Figure 8.5: The Resample Curve node

Resampling is the process where we interpolate more geometry into the Curve to have more control points to work with. This can be useful for tasks such as distributing points or, in this case, randomizing a Curve by offsetting each control point.

7. To achieve this, we can add a **Resample Curve** node in between the **Group Input** node and the **Set Position** node. Let's give this node a **Count** value of 50.

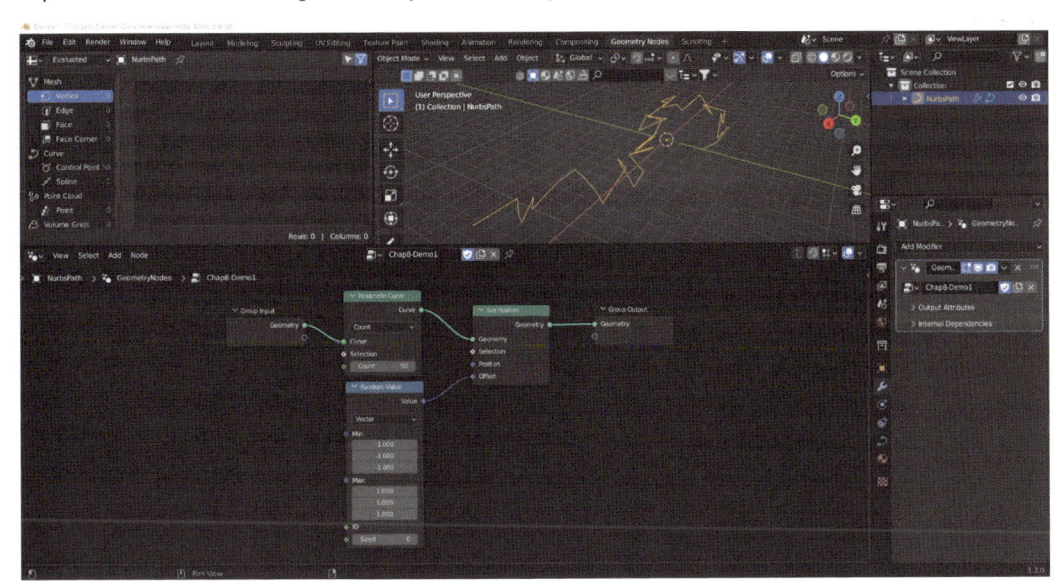

If you've executed these steps correctly, this is how your node tree should look:

Figure 8.6: Your current node tree

You can tweak the **Random Value** node to your liking, just keep in mind that the **Min** value should be the negative of the **Max** value. Doing this will ensure that your midlevel value will be equal to 0.

Offset by Noise Textures

Let's now base our **offset** on **Noise Texture**:

1. To do this, let's disconnect the **Random Value** node that we added in the previous section. As you do this, you will see that your Curve turns back to its normal shape.

    To use noise textures, we will need to make use of a **Combine XYZ** node to pull apart the **X**, **Y**, and **Z** values, respectively. Each of these axes will need to use a different noise pattern. Otherwise, we will have diagonal moving lines, and we don't want that!

2. Let's drop in a **Combine XYZ** node on the same spot that we dropped in the **Random Value** node before. Let's also add in a **Noise Texture** node and duplicate it twice so that we've got three **Noise Texture** nodes. If you'd like to use any other **Texture** node, feel free to experiment with it.

3. Let's plug in all of these **Noise Texture** nodes in each of the three **X**, **Y**, and **Z** axes.

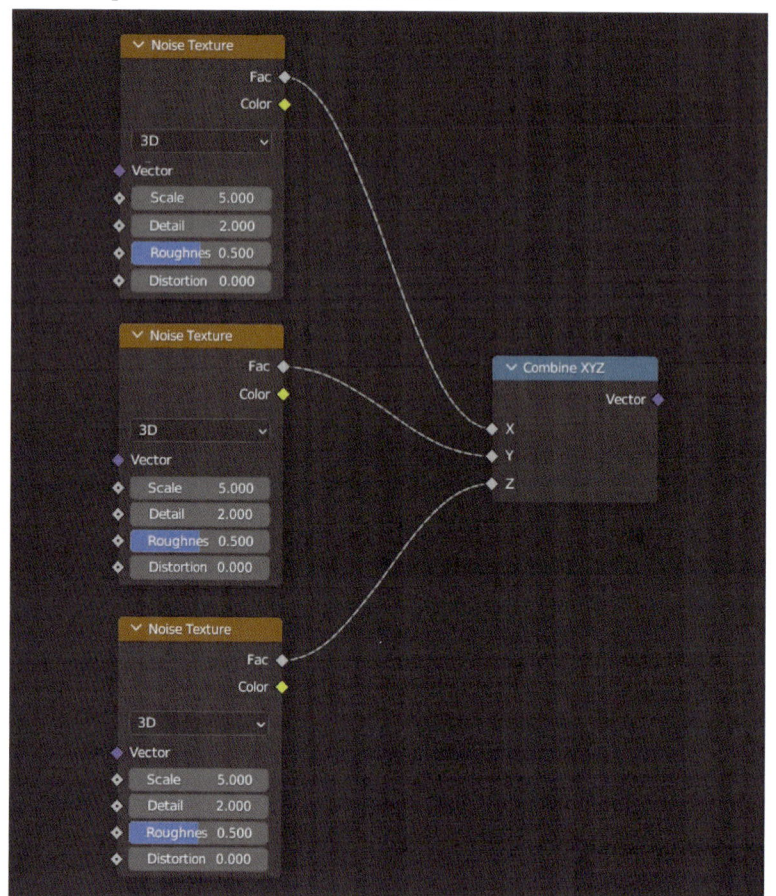

This is how this part of the node tree should look:

Figure 8.7: Noise Texture to vector

After doing this, we can see that our Curve gets some noise randomization. The only problem is that the noise happens equally on all three axes. This causes a diagonal effect, where the noise pattern appears to shift diagonally. We can solve this by giving each of the three **Texture** nodes a different seed.

4. To add a seed to the Texture nodes, put the Texture node in 4D mode. This will add a new value called **W**.

    These **W** values don't have to mean much. Just make sure that the values are far enough so we don't have any repeating patterns. This is also a good moment to play around with the **Count** value of the **Resample Curve** node.

Adding noise to your Curves   123

This is how your node tree should look if you've executed the steps correctly:

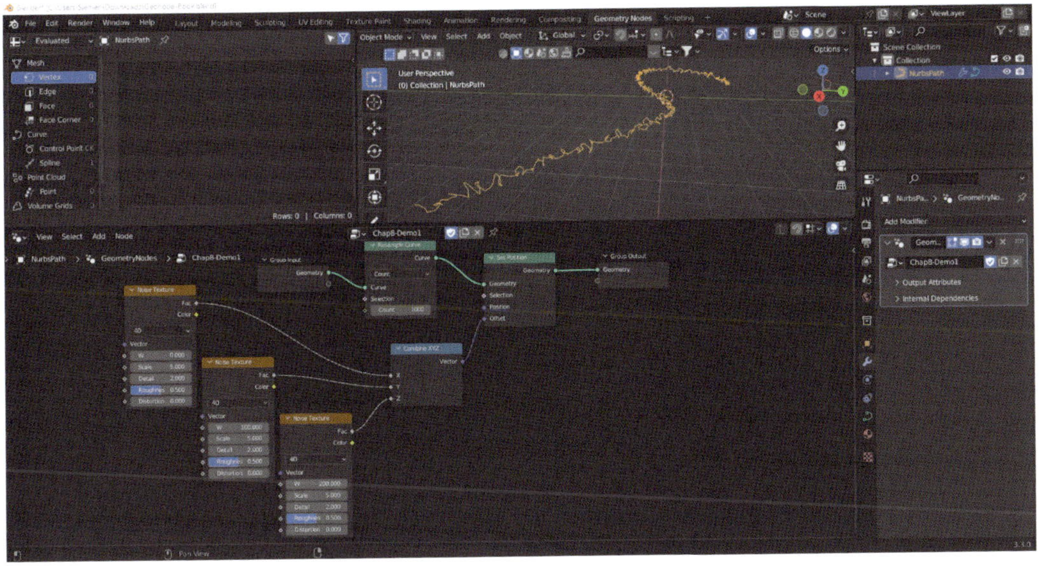

Figure 8.8: Your current node tree

5. You might've noticed that our Curve has shifted away from its origin a little bit. This is because, as explained before, the midlevel value of our **Noise Texture** node is not 0; it's closer to 0.5. To fix this, let's subtract 0.5 from our vector to get the midlevel to equal 0.

   To do this, add a **Vector Math** node set to **Subtract** and use 0.5 as the subtraction value. This will subtract 0.5 from all the *x*, *y*, and *z* axes. We can drop in this node between the **Combine XYZ** node and the **Set Position** node.

6. As the last step of this section, we can intensify the scale of this randomization. To do this, add another **Vector Math** node set to **Multiply** after the **Vector Subtract** node. Let's choose a value of 5 but be sure to play around with different values.

This is how your node tree should look after following these steps correctly.

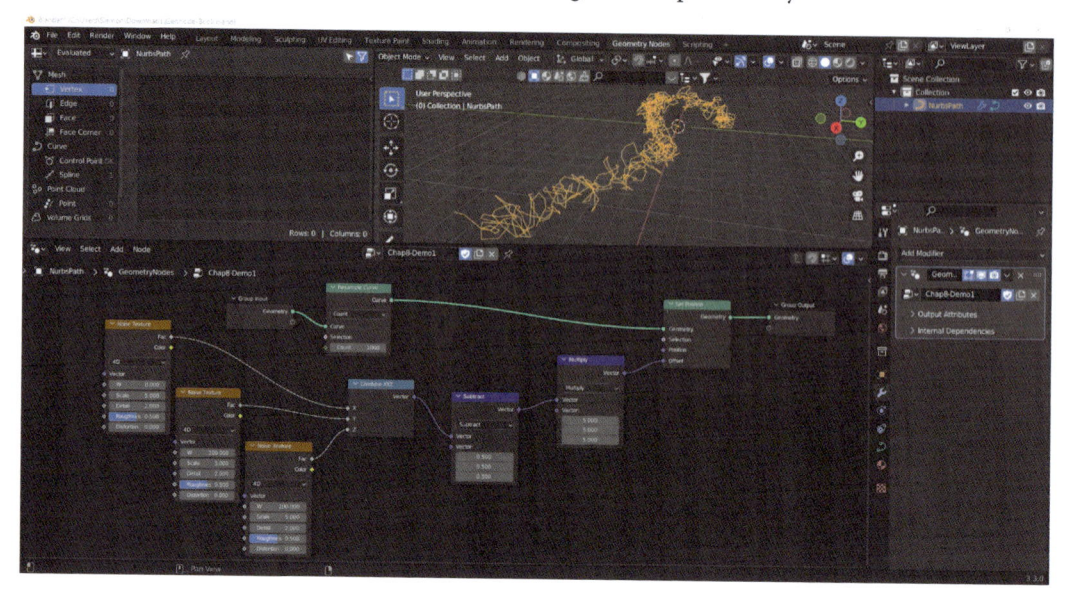

Figure 8.9: Your current node tree

There you have it! That's how you add noise to your Curve by using a **Noise Texture** node.

We can also see that if we want to edit our Curve, the noise pattern will extend procedurally, which is very cool.

Giving thickness to your Curves

In this section, we'll show you how to give your Curves thickness, along with some handy nodes to use in the Geometry Node editor.

In the following figure, you can see all the nodes that we will use in this section.

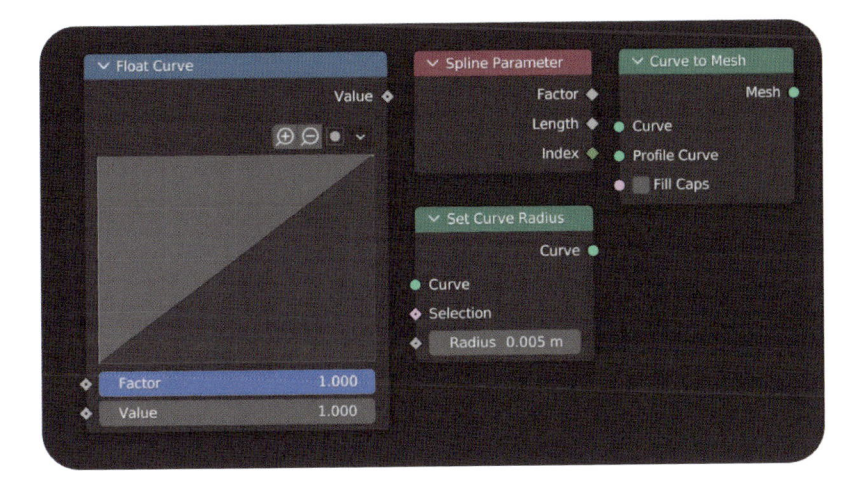

Figure 8.10: The nodes you'll need

Let's take a quick peek at them individually:

- The **Float Curve** node – This node works by mapping an input float to a Curve and then outputting this as another float value. It processes values from 0 to 1 and the Curve editor seen on this node also represents 0 to 1. This will be explained in depth in the *Advanced thickness control* section.

  The **Spline Parameter** node – This node will output info about your Curve if your base object (the object you've made in **Edit** mode) is a Curve:

  - The **Factor** value will return the progress of the Curve in a value from 0 to 1. The beginning of the Curve means 0 and the end of the Curve means 1.
  - The **Length** value will return the length of the Curve.
  - The **Index** integer value will return the unique identifier of each Curve that the object contains.

- The **Set Curve Radius** node – This node will allow you to set the radius of your inputted Curve. This can be connected to the **Spline Parameter** node's **Factor** output to create a pointy spike, which will be explained in the *Advanced thickness control* section. This radius will not be visible unless you use a **Curve to Mesh** node.

- The **Curve to Mesh** node – This node will convert a Curve, like the one we're working with in this chapter, into a mesh that we can use to display geometry. The **Profile Curve** input of this node will define the profile that this Curve will use based on whatever you plug into this input. Keep in mind that the **Profile Curve** input only accepts other Curves.

Now that we have a fair idea of the nodes required to control the thickness of Curves, let's see how we can do it.

Basic thickness control

Let's get started by learning how to add thickness to our Curves:

1. Start by drawing a Curve in **Edit** mode. This can be any shape you want.

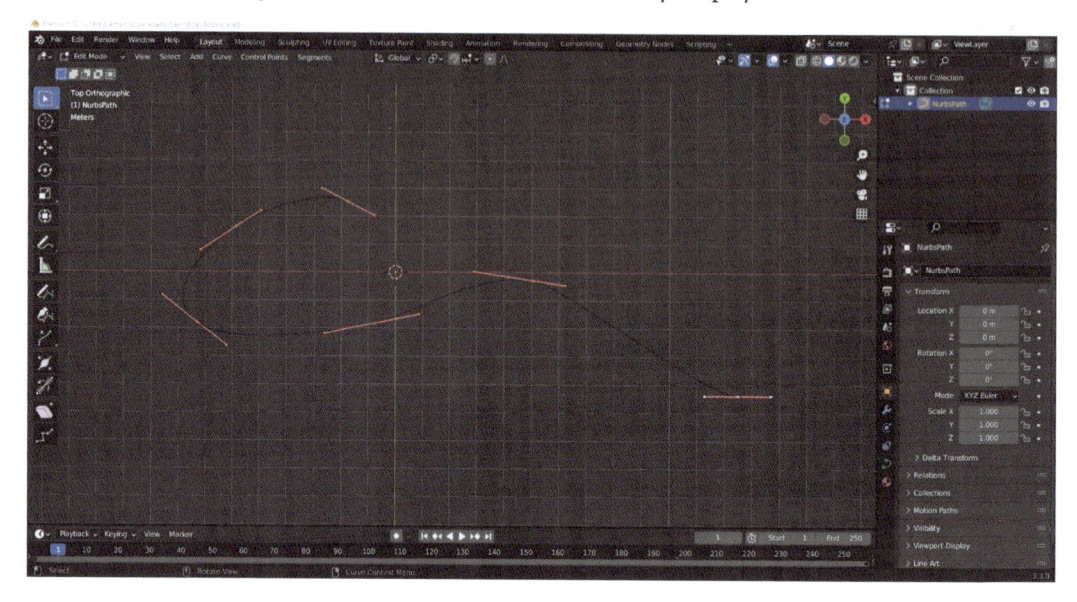

Figure 8.11: Draw a Curve

2. Next, we'll open the Geometry Node editor to add a new node tree to this Curve.
3. To get started with controlling the thickness of this Curve, we will need to drop in a **Curve to Mesh** node to convert our Curve into a mesh.

Giving thickness to your Curves   127

4. You will see that nothing happens because we do not have a **Profile Curve** yet. Let's use a **Curve Circle** as our **Profile Curve**. You can change the **Radius** input of your **Curve Circle** to your liking.

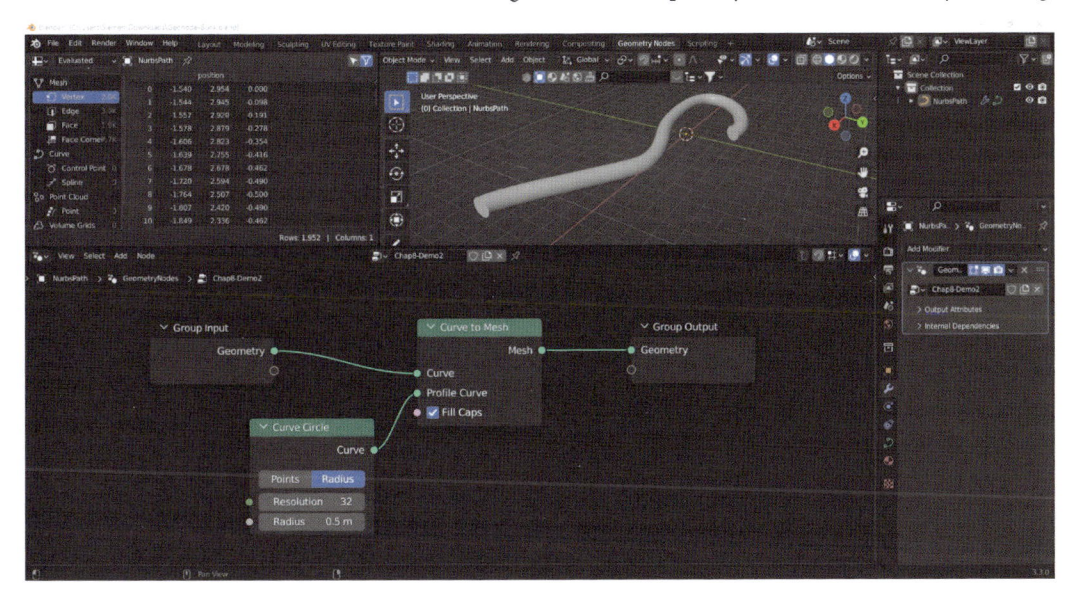

Figure 8.12: Your current node tree

5. Let's now add the **Set Curve Radius** node to start controlling the thickness of our Curve.

You will drop in this node between **Group Input** and the **Curve to Mesh** node because we want to modify the original Curve.

After you've done that, you should be able to control the thickness of your Curve!

Advanced thickness control

Let's make it so that we have finer control over where the thickness occurs in our Curve. This can be done by making use of the multi-valued node connection that the Set Curve Radius node uses.

Let's start simply:

1. We will add a **Spline Parameter** node to obtain the **Factor** value of our Curve. As said before, the factor value returns the progress of our Curve.

2. Let's drop in a **Spline Parameter** node and connect the **Factor** output to the **Radius** input of the **Set Curve Radius** node.

128 Editing Curves with Nodes

As you can see, the beginning of our Curve is thick and the end of our Curve is thin because the **Factor** represents the beginning and end of our Curve in a number. So, if we use that number to reflect our thickness, we get this specific result.

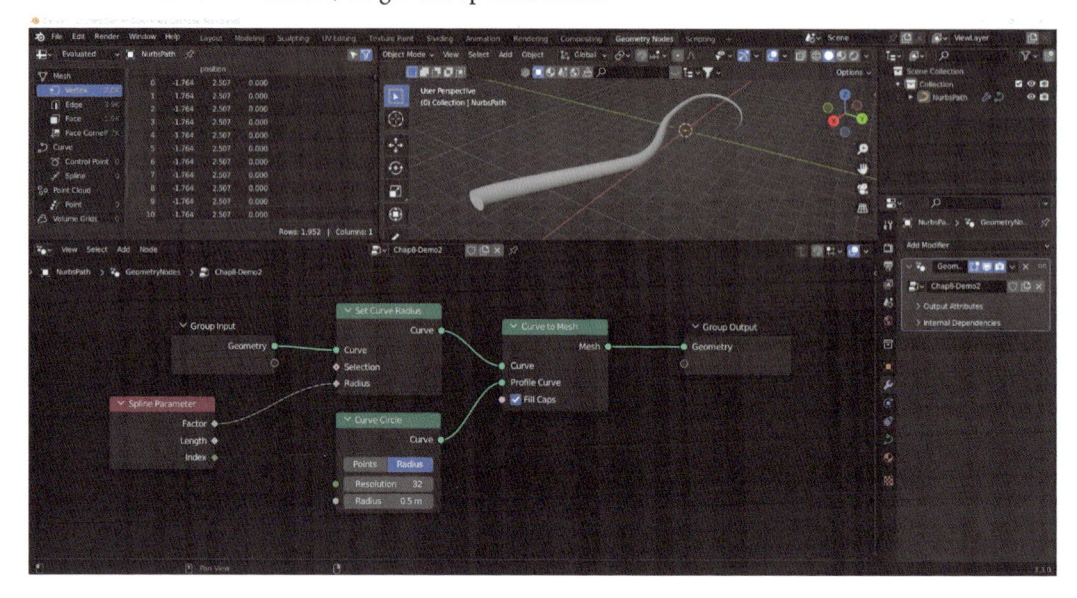

Figure 8.13: Your current node tree

3. Let's take this a bit further, we can define a custom thickness gradient by adding in **Float Curve**, which will convert this 0 to 1 value into any gradient that we want.

   For example, let's add **Float Curve** in between the **Spline Parameter** node and the **Set Curve Radius** node and modify the Curve to look like the following figure.

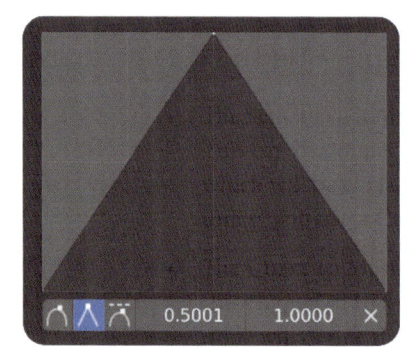

Figure 8.14: The Float Curve editor

As the Curve editor shows, the beginning and end of the Curve will be thin, but the middle of the Curve will be thick. When we look at our viewport, we can see that this is exactly the case.

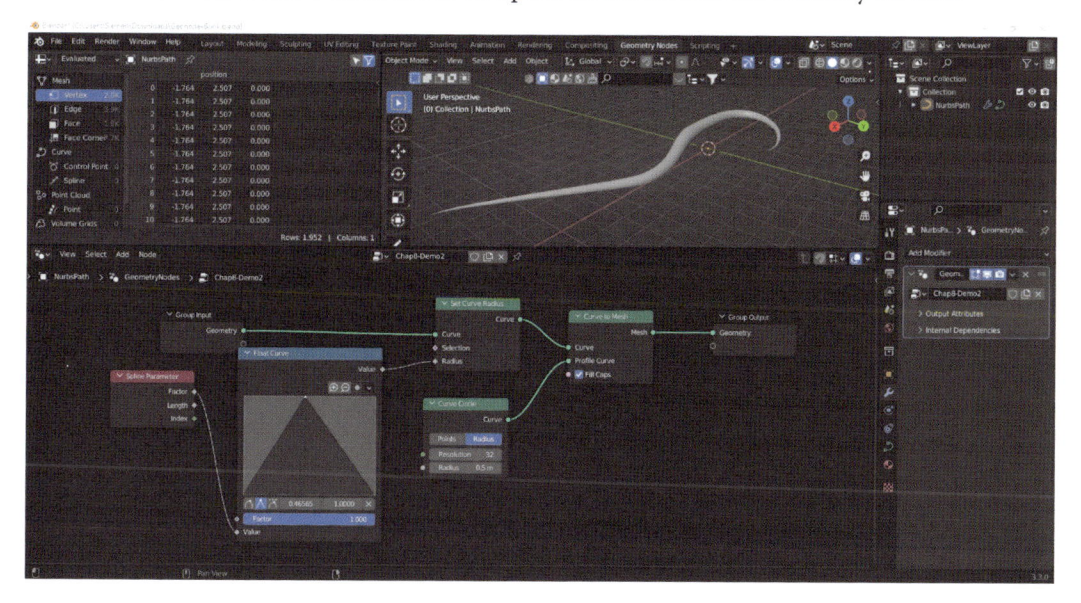

Figure 8.15: The viewport

With that, we've come to the end of this demonstration. You now possess the skills to start working on the exercise in the next section!

Exercise – making a simple lightning bolt

In this exercise, you will be making a lightning bolt by giving a curve line some randomized offset.

Sketching the basic idea

We will add a **Curve Line** node. After that, we will add a randomized offset to this **Curve Line** node using a **Set Position** node and a **Random Value** node. We will also add thickness to the Curve so that it is thick at the top and thin at the bottom. To finish it all off, we'll add an emissive material to the lightning bolt.

Making the node tree

Let's get started with a **Curve Line** node.

This will be plugged straight into **Group Output**. We will not need the **Group Input** node yet:

1. The first step is to add some randomization to this Curve. As seen in the previous sections, this can be done using a **Set Position** node. Let's drop in this node between the **Curve Line** node and the **Group Output** node.
2. To define the offset, let's use a **Random Value** node set to **Vector**.
3. We do have to change the parameters a bit though since we don't want any randomization happening on the Z axis. So, you can leave **Z min** and **Z max** at zero. We also want **X min** and **Y min** to start at **-1.000** since that will equal out the midlevel.
4. Once you have done these steps, you can plug this node into the **Offset** input of the **Set Position** node.

This is how your current node tree should look:

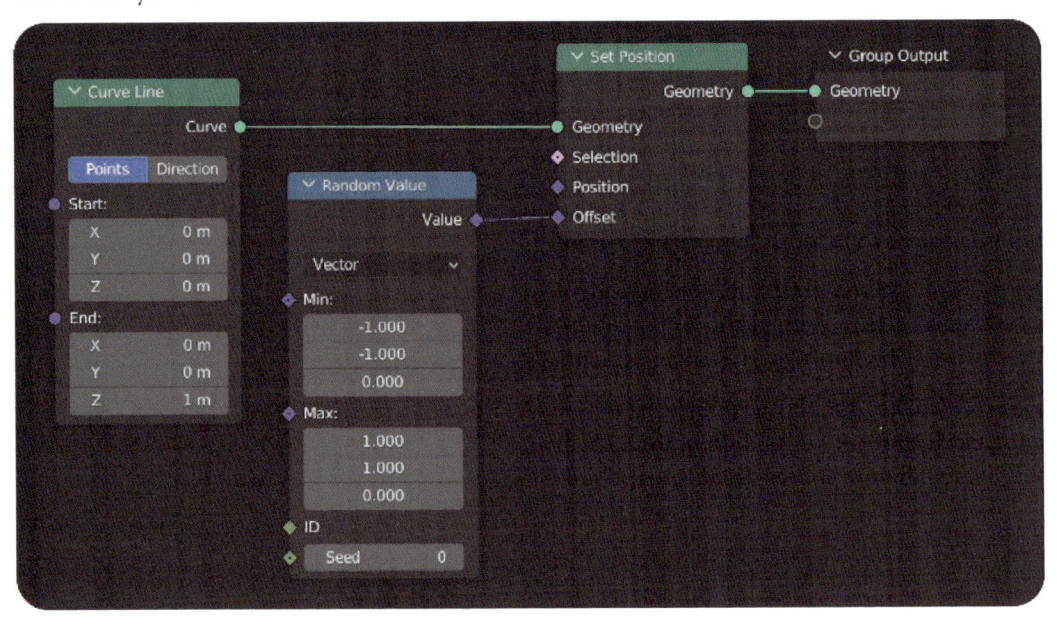

Figure 8.16: Your current node tree

If you take a look at the viewport, you can see that not much is happening. This is because our curve line does not have enough geometry to work with:

1. To fix this, let's use a **Resample Curve** node to add more geometry.

2. Drop in the **Resample Curve** node between the **Curve Line** node and the **Set Position** node. Let's give it a **Count** value of 5. This means that our lightning bolt will have 5 points. In the following figure you can see what different **Count** values look like in the final render:

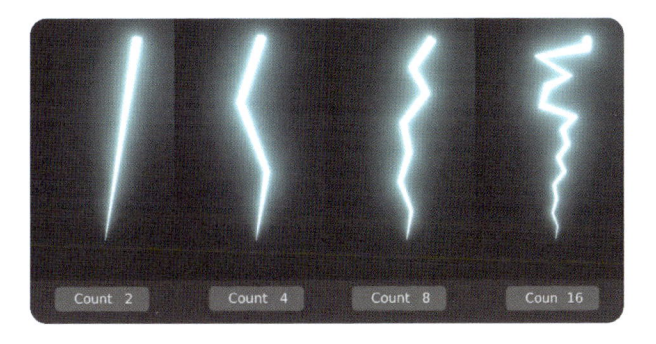

Figure 8.17: The different Count values in the final render

3. Once you drop in this **Resample Curve** node, you will see that your Curve now has 5 points.

4. There is still a problem though, a lightning bolt gradually gets less chaotic when it's nearing the ground. To mimic this, let's take two nodes: a **Vector Math** node set to **Multiply** and a **Spline Parameter** node.

   The idea is that we will multiply the **Random Value** vector by the **Spline Parameter** node. The closer it gets to the ground, the less chaotic the Curve will be since it will be multiplied by a smaller number.

5. Let's plug these two nodes in like this:

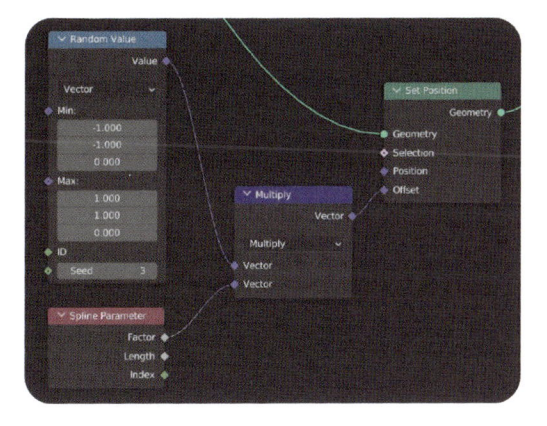

Figure 8.18: Multiply by Factor

When we look at the viewport, we can already see our Curve starting to look like a lightning bolt! Let's move on to the next step, where we will be converting the Curve to a mesh.

6. Let's add a **Curve to Mesh** node after the **Set Position** node. As our **Profile Curve** input, we'll use a **Curve Circle** node.

   If your lightning bolt looks a bit too large, you can scale down the **Radius** input of your **Curve Circle** node. A value such as 0.1 meters should match.

   This is also a good moment to play around with the curve line's length to increase the length of your lightning bolt.

If you've followed all these steps correctly, this is how your node tree should look:

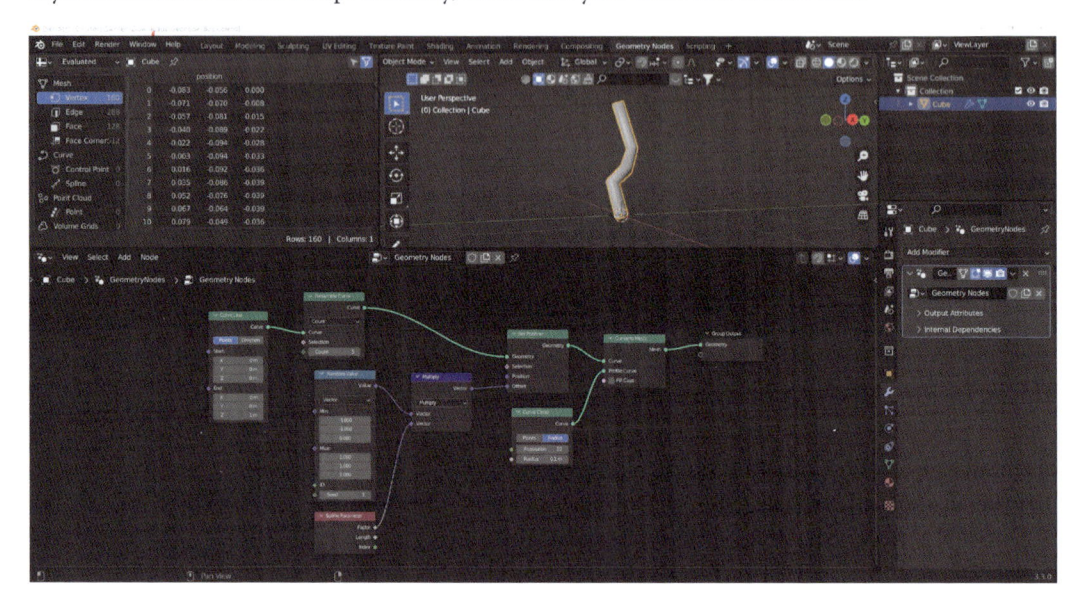

Figure 8.19: Lightning bolt so far

There is a problem though, the thickness of our lightning bolt is consistent. Real lightning bolts are thicker at the beginning and thinner at the end. Let's mimic that!

1. To do this, add a **Set Curve Radius** node in between the **Set Position** node and the **Curve to Mesh** node.

Exercise – making a simple lightning bolt   133

2. As seen in the *Advanced thickness control* section, we can plug in the **Spline Parameter** node's **Factor** into the **Radius** input of the **Set Curve Radius** node to get the desired effect.

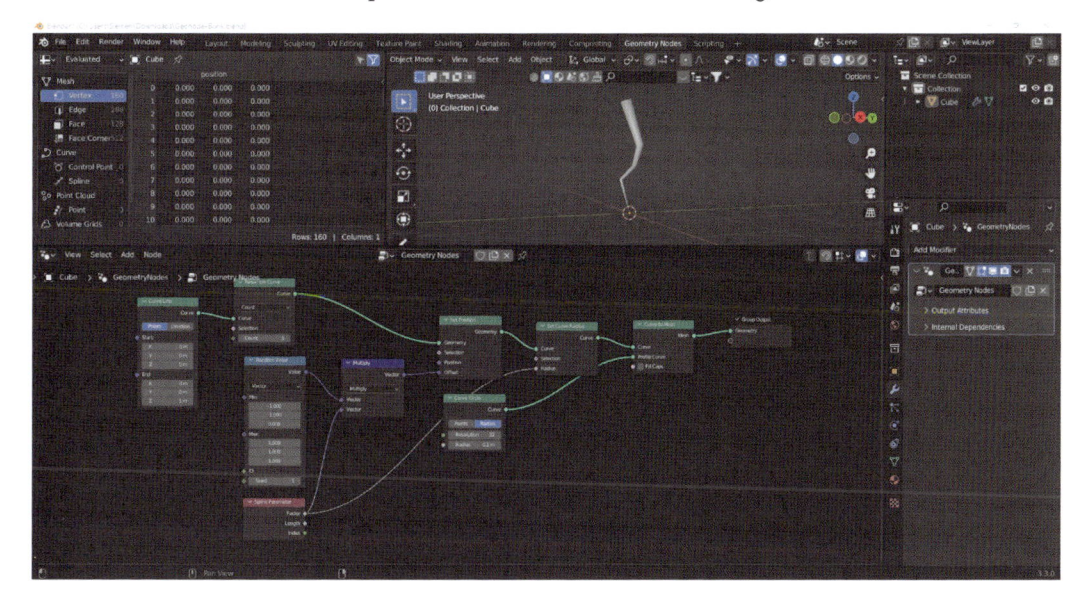

Figure 8.20: Lightning bolt goes from thick to thin

3. If you are not happy with the shape that the lightning bolt has, you can add a **Float Curve** node to give the lightning bolt a custom thickness profile. I found the following thickness profile works great for a lightning bolt.

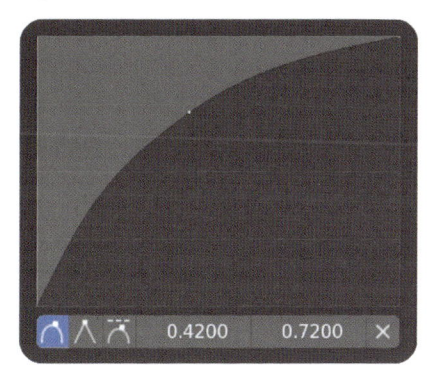

Figure 8.21: Thickness profile in Float Curve

134　　Editing Curves with Nodes

4. Let's add this **Float Curve** node in between the **Spline Parameter** node's **Factor** output and the **Radius** input of the **Set Curve Radius** node.

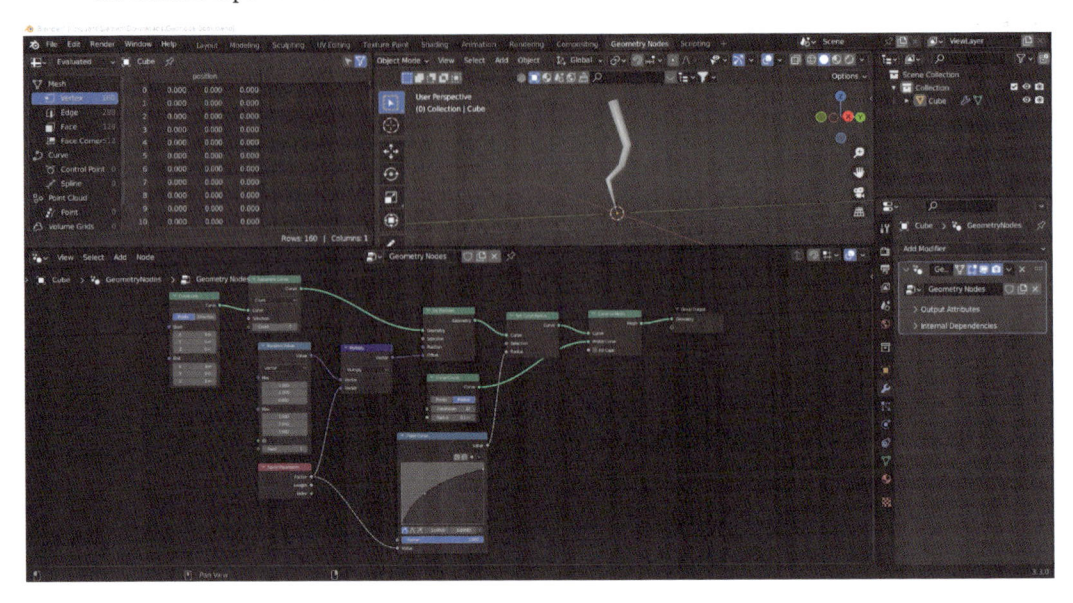

Figure 8.22: Final shape of the lightning bolt

The last thing we have to complete is adding a material to our lightning bolt. A lightning bolt is not a lightning bolt without an emissive material:

1. In the **Shading** tab, make a simple emissive material in light blue, as shown in the following figure:

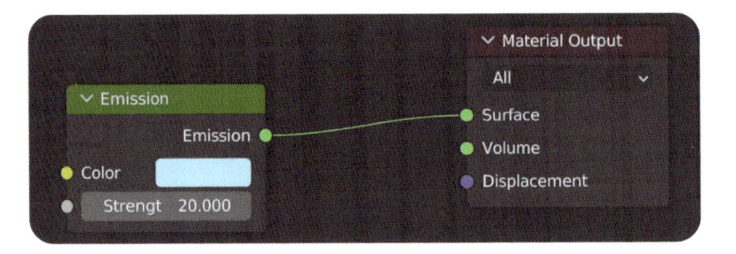

Figure 8.23: Emissive material

2. We can see that the material does not reflect on the lightning bolt we made. To fix that, let's go back to the Geometry Nodes workspace, add a **Set Material** node, and select the material you've just made. Drop this in at the end of your node tree.

Figure 8.24: The Set Material node

Now, you can see the final render in *Figure 8.25*:

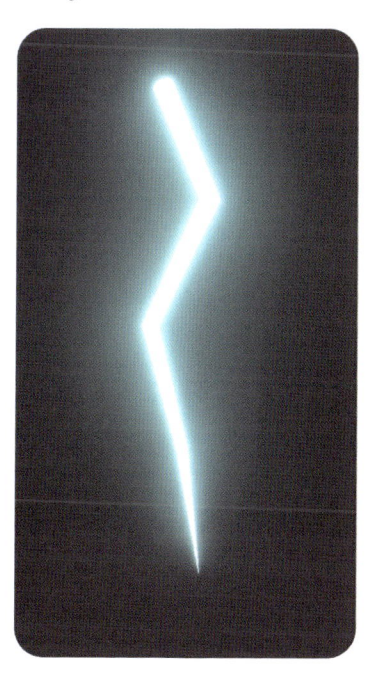

Figure 8.25: Final render

That's all you need to do to make an easy-to-modify, procedural lightning bolt! In this exercise, you've reiterated the brand-new skills you've learned in this chapter, such as adding a thickness profile to your Curve, adding noise to your Curve, and giving materials to your Curves. We also learned how to use the **Float Curve** node in a practical situation.

Summary

In this chapter, you learned how to manipulate Curves in the Geometry Node editor by adding noise to them and giving them thickness. You also learned how to use various nodes, such as the **Noise Texture** node, the **Combine XYZ** node, the **Set Position** node, the **Vector Math** node, and the **Resample Curve** node, to achieve these effects. In addition, you learned how to create a simple lightning bolt using these techniques.

These skills are useful for creating various types of curved objects and shapes in Blender, such as lightning bolts, tree trunks, and other organic shapes. Adding noise to your Curves will allow you to add variation between models, which makes your scene look more realistic. Being able to manipulate Curves in this way can allow for greater flexibility and creativity in your projects.

The next chapter will delve into the exciting topic of using Geometry Nodes to modify meshes. With this powerful tool at your disposal, you will have the ability to transform the geometry of your meshes in a variety of ways.

9
Manipulating a Mesh Using Geometry Nodes

In the previous chapter, we showed you how to edit and manipulate Curves in the Geometry Node editor. This will benefit your workflow when you want to align or modify a mesh using a Curve. To take you further, in this chapter, we will teach you how to manipulate a mesh using the Geometry Node editor. This will help you create all sorts of shapes, from landscapes to tree trunks. To aid you in achieving that goal (of manipulating meshes), we will cover how to extrude meshes, how to use Booleans, and how to add noise to your meshes, and at the end of the chapter, we'll combine these skills into an exercise.

In this chapter, we will cover the following subjects:

- Extruding your mesh
- Using Booleans on your mesh
- Adding noise to your mesh
- Exercise – make a procedural tree

First, let's see how to extrude a mesh.

Extruding your mesh

Extruding a mesh is a very handy function in Blender. It can help you create extra faces in your mesh. It allows you to pull faces, edges, or vertices out of the original mesh. An example of extrusion can be seen in *Figure 9.1*.

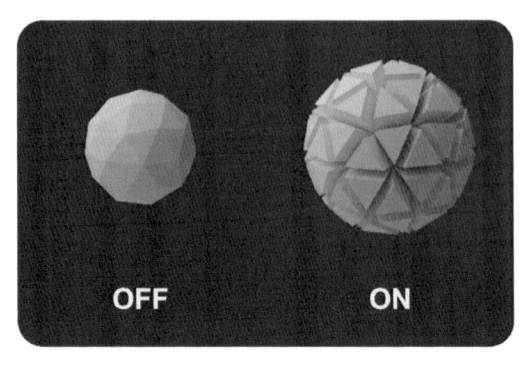

Figure 9.1: An example of extrusion

The node that we will use to achieve this effect is the **Extrude Mesh** node, which can be seen in the following figure:

Figure 9.2: The Extrude Mesh node

Let's start off this chapter by giving you a demonstration of this node.

Demonstrating the Extrude Mesh node

We will begin by adding an Ico Sphere to your Blender project and adding a new node tree to this Ico Sphere.

Luckily, the **Extrude Mesh** node is quite easy to use. All we need to do is to drop the **Extrude Mesh** node between the **Group Input** node and the **Group Output** node. As you do this, you will see that our **Extrude Mesh** node works as intended!

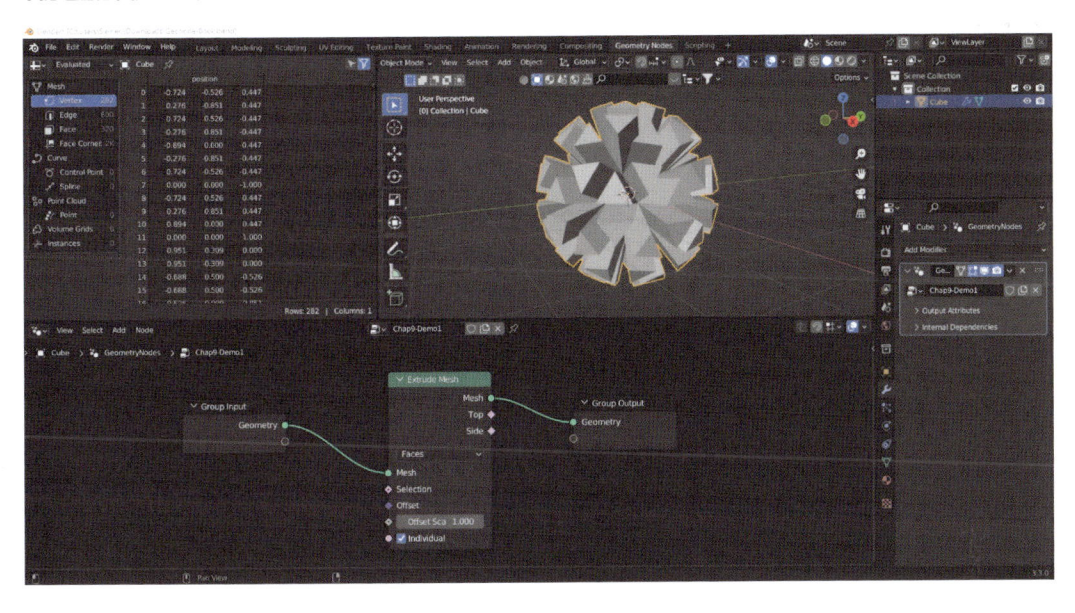

Figure 9.3: Extrusion in the Geometry Node editor

Using the **Offset Scale** input of our **Extrude Mesh** node, we can decide how much each face should be extruded. We can also choose whether the faces should be individually extruded or whether the extruded mesh should be connected to each other. You can see the difference between these two options in the following figure:

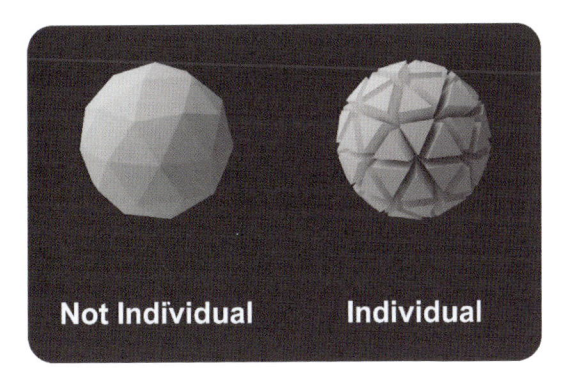

Figure 9.4: Not individual versus individual

As you can see in *Figure 9.4*, this option will add additional faces between the gaps of the extrusion poles.

Using random values with the Extrude Mesh node

As we've seen throughout the previous chapters, we can use the **Random Value** node to randomize different aspects of our geometry in the Geometry Node editor. This can also be done with the **Extrude Mesh** node.

To do this, let's add in a **Random Value** node and connect the output to the **Offset Scale** input of the **Extrude Mesh** node. As you can see, you get the following result:

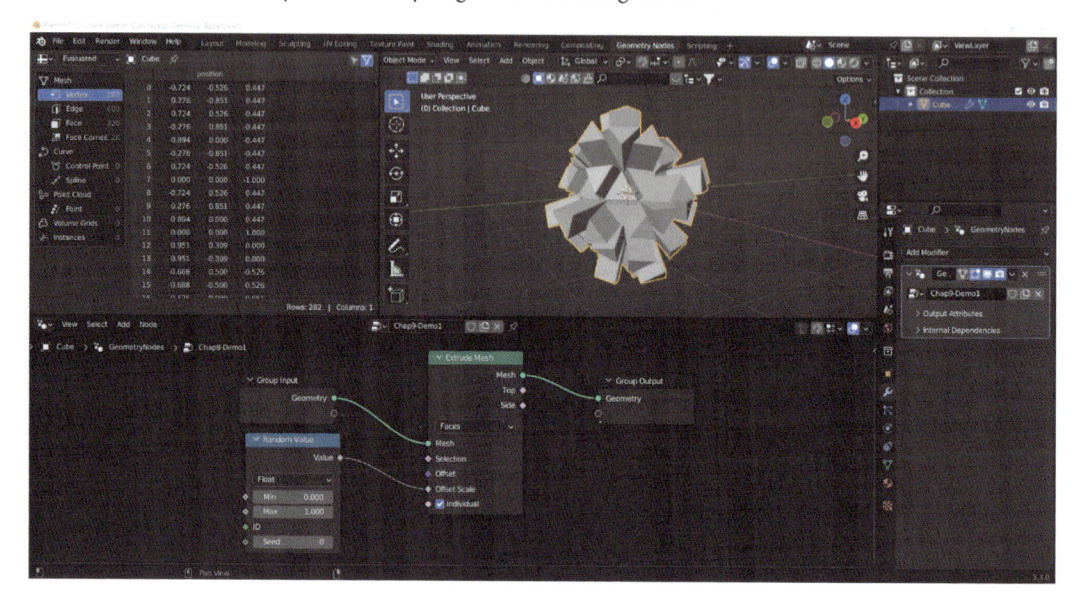

Figure 9.5: Random extrusion

As you can see in *Figure 9.5*, the extrusion poles have been randomized and now vary in length. We can set the length by editing the **Random Value** node's parameters to anything you like.

As you might have noticed, the **Extrude Mesh** node has various modes of extrusion, and we have the option to extrude **Faces**, **Edges,** and **Vertices**. You can see what each option does in the following screenshot:

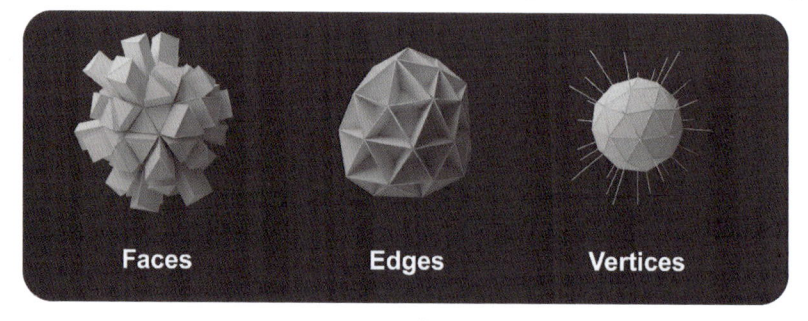

Figure 9.6: Extrusion modes

As you can see in *Figure 9.6*, the first option, **Faces**, will extrude the faces of your mesh, which you'll use the most. The second option, **Edges**, will extrude the edges of your mesh, which can be useful to create walls on a plane. The last option, **Vertices**, will only extrude each vertex separately. You won't see this effect rendered unless you use additional nodes to visualize it.

Using Booleans in your mesh

In this section, we will show you how to use Booleans in the Geometry Node editor.

You might have worked with the **Boolean Modifier** before in Blender. This modifier performs operations on meshes such as cutting, combining, or intersecting two meshes.

The Boolean system in the Geometry Node editor works in much the same way. In the following figure, you'll see the node that we will be using to perform these actions:

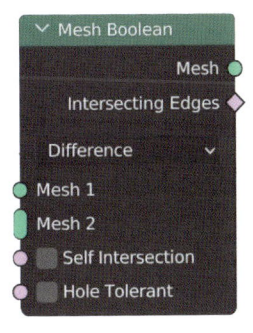

Figure 9.7: The Mesh Boolean node

As you can see, at the top of the node, we see the mode selection of this node. Let's go over each mode that this node presents:

- **Intersect**: As the title of this mode suggests, this mode will detect the intersection of multiple (two or more) meshes. If a mesh is present at a given point on every input, a mesh will be generated on the output. *Figure 9.8* is an example of an intersection:

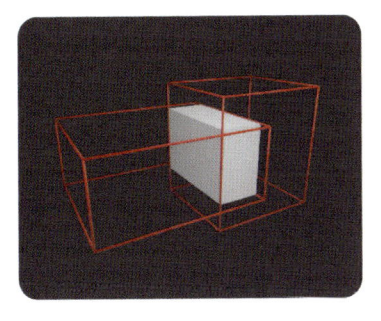

Figure 9.8: Example of an intersection

The red lines in the figure are there to show you where the two cubes are and are not visible in your Blender projects. They are shown here for illustrative purposes.

- **Union**: The **Union** mode combines various meshes into one big mesh.

    You might think: *Wait, doesn't the Join Geometry node do that already?*

    The answer is *No*. The **Join Geometry** node joins the multiple objects together into one geometry, but the meshes will still be separate. On the other hand, the **Union** mode performs calculations to make sure that the mesh is welded to the other mesh. In the following wireframe screenshot, you can see the difference between these two functions:

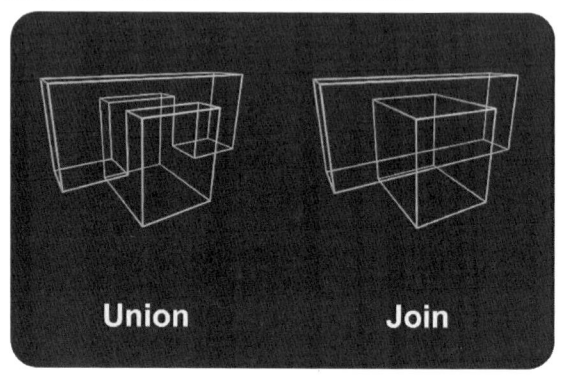

Figure 9.9: Union versus Join Geometry

- **Difference**: The last node that we will be covering is the **Difference** mode. This is probably the most classical use of a **Boolean** function. You can use the **Difference** mode to cut away parts of your base mesh by utilizing objects as your Boolean.

As you can see in *Figure 9.7*, we have two mesh inputs. The first input is called **Mesh 1**. This is where your base mesh should be input. The second input is **Mesh 2**. This is where your cutting mesh should be input.

Let's demonstrate the **Difference** mode, the classic mode, using the following demonstration.

Demonstrating the Difference mode

Let's begin our demonstration with the following steps:

1. Start by adding two **Cube** nodes into your Geometry Node editor. We will give them both a size of 1 by 1 by 1 meter.

2. The second **Cube** node should be followed by a **Transform** node to move the cube 0.4 meters on the X and Z axes. This is how your node tree should look:

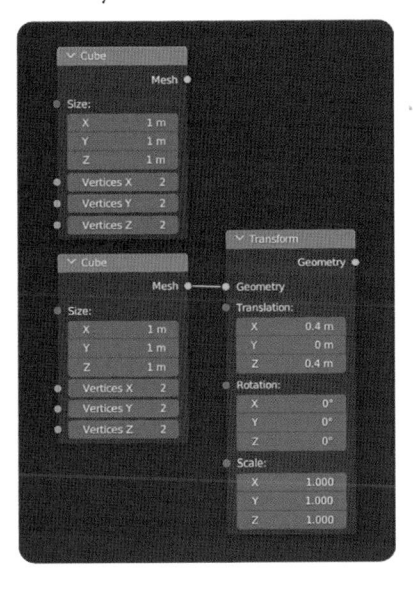

Figure 9.10: Your current node tree

3. Once you've done that, it's time to make use of the **Mesh Boolean** node. Let's plug the top **Cube** node into **Mesh 1** and the **Transform** node into **Mesh 2**.

In other words, we're taking the first **Cube** node and we're cutting it away with a second **Cube** node that we've moved 0.4 meters on the X and Z axes.

This is how your current node tree should look:

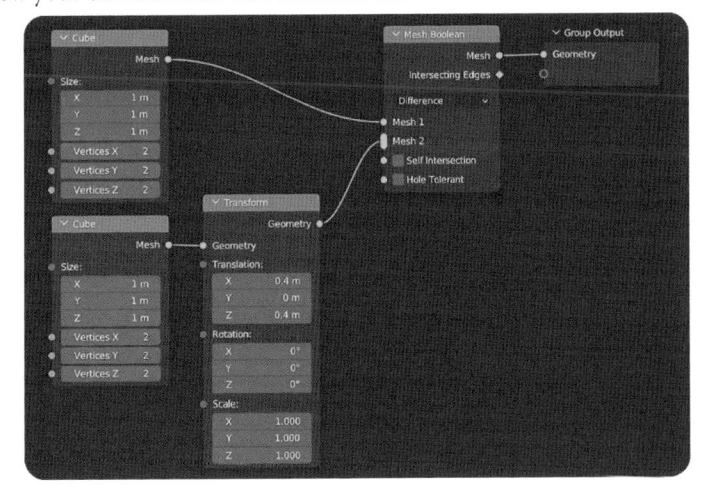

Figure 9.11: Your current node tree

If you look at your viewport now, you can see that it worked. We see **Mesh 1** with **Mesh 2** cut away. The red lines on the figure are for illustrative purposes and are not visible in Blender; these represent **Mesh 2**.

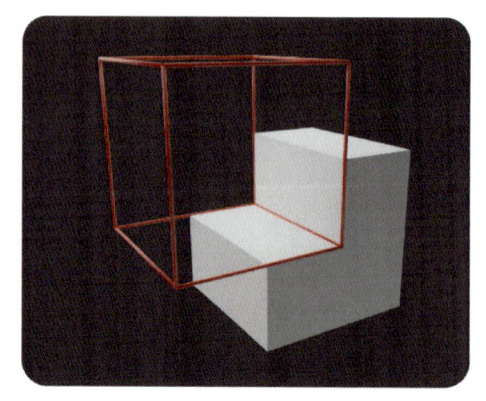

Figure 9.12: Difference Boolean example

Now we know how to use the **Mesh Boolean** node in the Geometry Node editor. Next, let's learn how to add noise to your mesh, as we learned in *Chapter 8, Editing Curves with Nodes*.

Adding noise to your mesh

Let's begin our journey into adding noise to mesh.

We will add a plane (**Grid**), and we'll use a **Set Position** node to add displacement to our mesh using **Noise Texture**, just like we executed in the previous chapter. The difference now is that we'll be performing it on a mesh instead of a Curve.

Demonstrating how to add noise to your mesh

Doing this is straightforward Let's start by following these steps:

1. Add a **Grid** node and give it enough resolution. Let's give it a resolution of 50 vertices on both the *X* and *Y* axes.
2. After the **Grid** node, let's add a **Set Position** node to start modifying the grid.
3. Before we start adding a **Noise Texture** node to the **Offset** input, we need to be able to convert the **Offset** input value to its separate **X**, **Y**, and **Z** values. This can be done using a **Combine XYZ** node.

Adding noise to your mesh   145

This is how your current node tree should look:

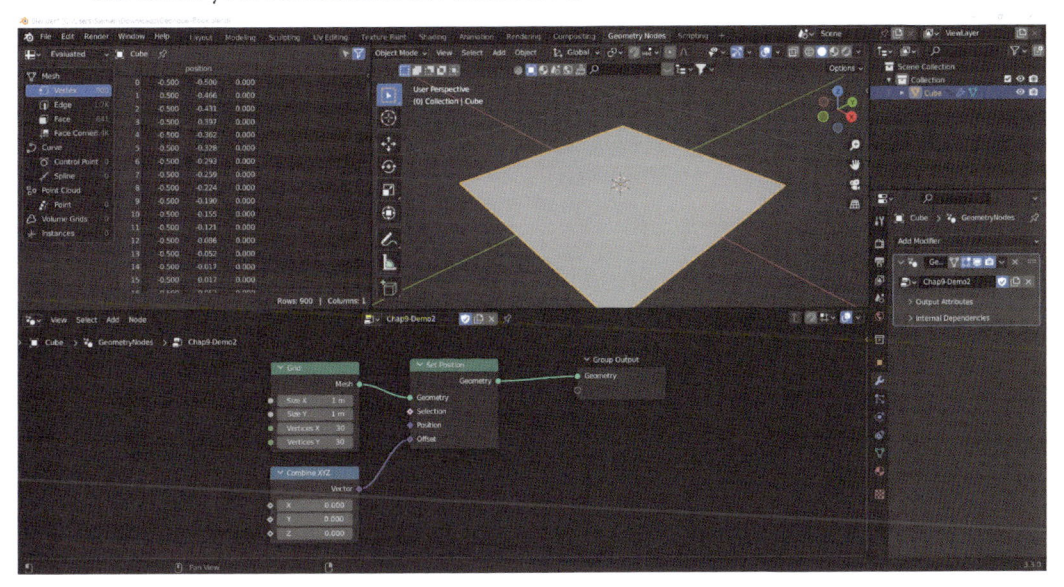

Figure 9.13: Your current node tree

4. Now, it's time to start modifying our grid. Let's add in any **Texture** node of your choice. In this demonstration, we will be using a **Noise Texture** node.

Let's add a **Noise Texture** node and connect the **Fac** (factor) output to the **Z** input of the **Combine XYZ** node. This will make sure that our offset happens on the z axis. If you want the displacement to happen on the x axis or y axis, you can connect it to the needed axis.

Once you connect the node, you can see that our grid starts to deform:

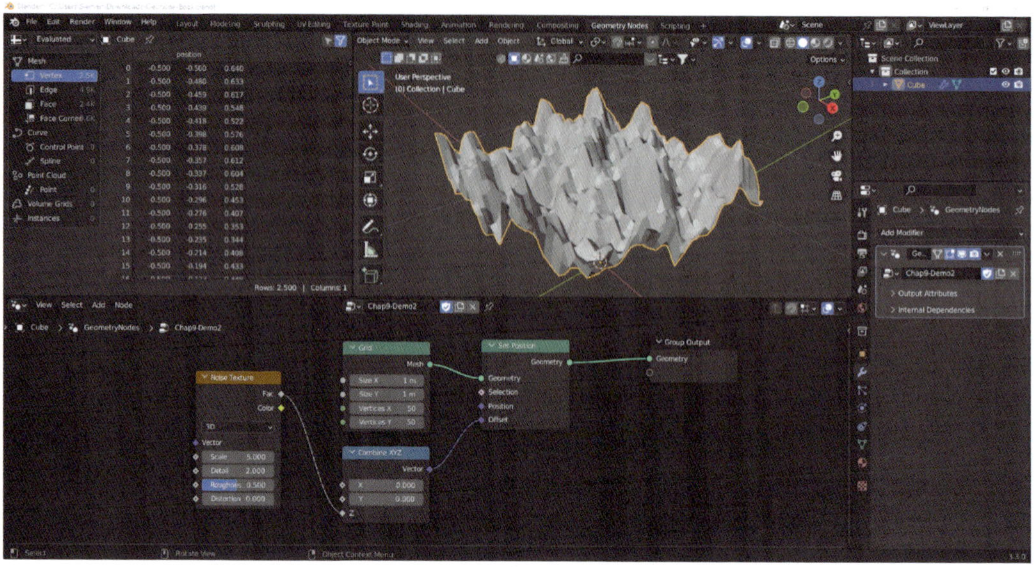

Figure 9.14: Your current node tree

5. As you might be able to see, our mesh is not on the ground anymore, and in terms of displacement, this means that our midlevel is not zero. To correct this, add a **Math** node set to **Subtract**, and drop it between the **Noise Texture** and the **Combine XYZ** nodes. Let's give it a subtraction value of 0.5.

Once you do that, you'll see that our grid is now on the ground.

Now that you know all these new functions of the Geometry Node editor, it's time to prove your new skills in the following exercise, where you will be making a procedural tree.

Exercise – making a procedural tree

In this exercise, we will show you how to make a procedural tree, which includes two items, the leaves and the trunk of the tree. Let's get started with this exercise!

We will start by creating a line, which we will thicken into the shape of a tree trunk. After that, we will randomize the mesh to create the illusion of tree bark. Then, we will create some Ico Spheres and place them around the tree trunk. To finalize the project, we will merge all these objects into one mesh.

Making the node tree

Let's start by making the tree trunk; this is the first step we will be taking to make this procedural tree.

Exercise – making a procedural tree   147

Making the tree trunk

The idea of the tree trunk is that we will take a **Curve Line** node and modify the radius of this **Curve Line** node using a **Spline Parameter** node and a **Float Curve** node to appear like a tree trunk. Then, we will use the **Set Position** node to add more detail to our tree trunk:

1. Let's start by adding in our first node, the **Curve Line** node. The only thing we will need to modify on this node is the **End Z** vector. We will put this to 25. This will make our tree trunk 25 meters high.

2. Let's connect this **Curve Line** node to the **Group Output** to visualize what it looks like.

    Now, we will need to convert this **Curve Line** node to a mesh. This can be done using the **Curve to Mesh** node.

3. Let's drop a **Curve to Mesh** node after the **Curve Line** node. For **Profile Curve**, we will use a **Curve Circle** node.

    This is how your current node tree should look:

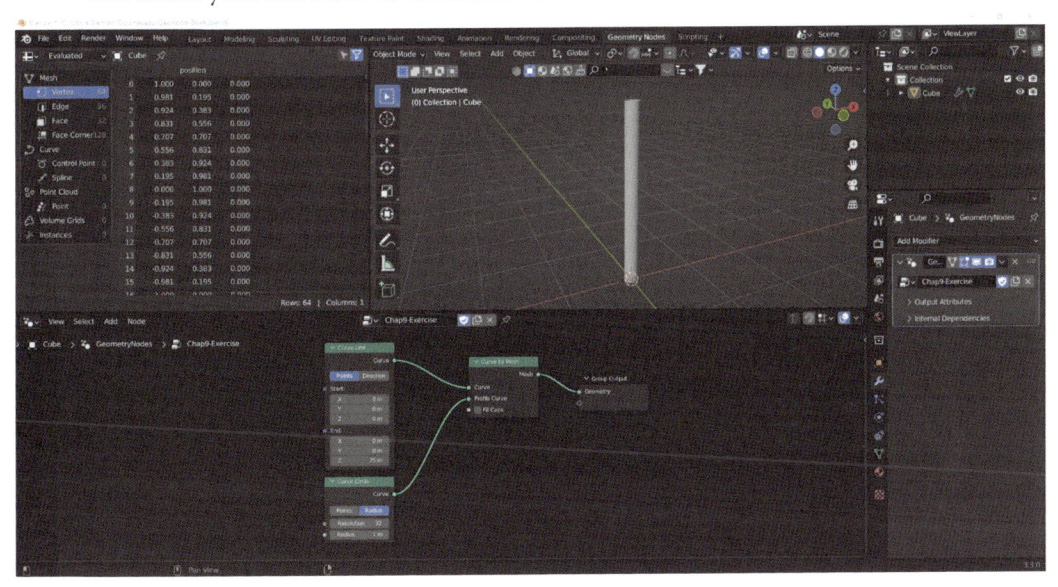

Figure 9.15: Your current node tree

4. Next, we will determine the radius of the tree trunk. This will be done by using a **Set Curve Radius** node as we saw in the previous chapter.

148   Manipulating a Mesh Using Geometry Nodes

5. Let's drop a **Set Curve Radius** node between the **Curve Line** node and the **Curve to Mesh** node.

6. After that, let's add a **Spline Parameter** node to read the info on our **Curve Line** node. Connect **Factor** of the **Spline Parameter** node to **Radius** of the **Set Curve Radius** node. Your node tree should look like this:

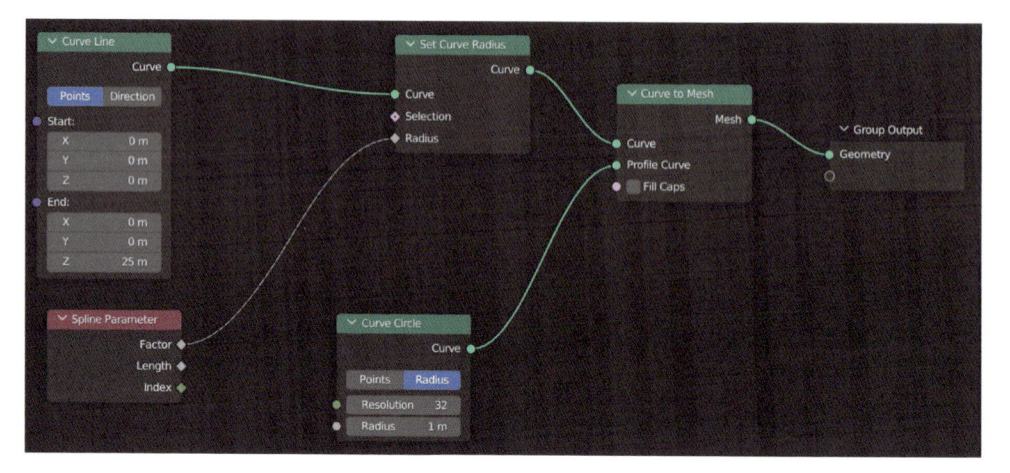

Figure 9.16: Your current node tree

You will see that your Curve should now look something like an upside-down spike.

7. Before we start editing this Curve, we will have to resample it as we did in the previous chapter.

   Let's drop a **Resample Curve** node between the **Curve Line** and **Set Curve Radius** nodes. This will make sure our Curve has enough geometry to start applying a custom thickness. The standard **Count** value of 10 should be enough.

8. Now that we have enough geometry, we can start applying a custom thickness effect using the **Float Curve** node.

   Let's add a **Float Curve** node between the **Spline Parameter** node and the **Set Curve Radius** node and apply the following profile:

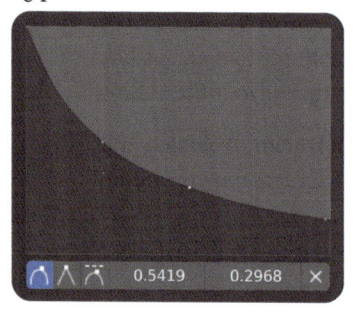

Figure 9.17: Your current node tree

This profile will determine the shape of your tree trunk. Once you've completed that, you'll see that you now have the shape of a tree trunk in your viewport.

If your tree trunk appears a bit thin, you can always increase the **Radius** value of the **Curve Circle** node.

This is how your current node tree should look:

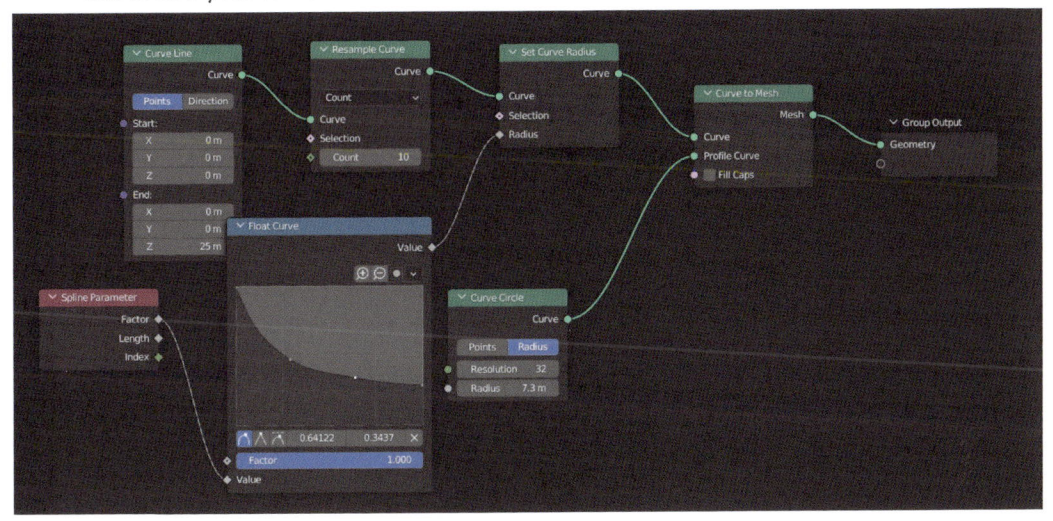

Figure 9.18: Your current node tree

Now that we have the rough shape of our tree trunk, let's move on to the next step!

Randomization of the tree trunk

In this section, we will randomize the tree trunk to give it some texture. This will make the trunk look more like a trunk. We will do this using a **Set Position** node:

1. Let's add a **Set Position** node between the **Curve to Mesh** node and the **Group Output** node.
2. After that, we will add a **Combine XYZ** node to be able to add Noise Textures in the respective **X**, **Y**, and **Z** values.
3. Connect this **Combine XYZ** node to the **Offset** input of the **Set Position** node.
4. After that, we can add a texture to our node tree. Let's add two **Musgrave Texture** nodes to our node tree. Set these to **4D** because we will need to change the **W** value to get two different Musgrave textures. Let's give the second texture a **W** value of 10.
5. Connect one of these Musgrave Textures to the **X** input of the **Combine XYZ** node and one to the **Y** input of the **Combine XYZ** node.

You will see that you have now added randomization to your tree trunk:

Figure 9.19: Your current node tree

6. You might notice that we have some shading issues at the top of our tree trunk. To fix this, we will need to add more geometry to our tree trunk. To do this, let's add a **Subdivision Surface** node at the end of our node tree and give it a **Level** value of 2.

7. You might also notice that our tree trunk has a hole; we don't want that. To fix that, we need to go back to the **Curve to Mesh** node and tick the box called **Fill Caps**:

Figure 9.20: The Fill Caps option

Now, we have a randomized tree trunk. With this step completed, it's time to move on to making the bushes.

Making the bushes of the tree

The next step for our tree is to make the bushes. These will consist of three simple Ico Spheres. Let's get into it:

1. Disconnect the **Subdivision Surface** node from the **Group Output** node; we will connect this back later.

2. Now, let's add an **Ico Sphere** node and connect it to the **Group Output** node instead. Let's give this **Ico Sphere** node a **Radius** of 8 meters and a **Subdivisions** count of 4.

   The idea is that we will transform this Ico Sphere three times to appear like a stylized bush.

   To do this, let's add three **Transform** nodes and join them all together with a **Mesh Boolean** node set to **Union**.

   It should look like this:

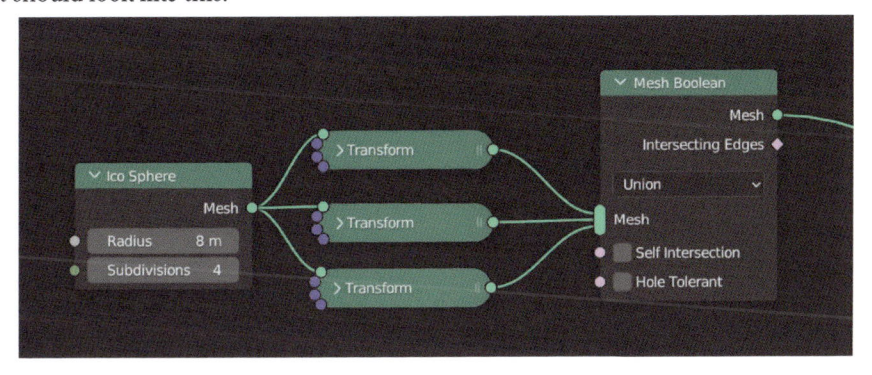

   Figure 9.21: A collapsed view of the Transform nodes

3. To make visualizing this node tree easier, the **Transform** nodes have been collapsed. Now, give each **Transform** node a random location value so that they are spaced out but still intersecting, like this:

   Figure 9.22: Bush

Now we have the bushes of our tree.

Finalizing the tree

The last step to finalize our tree is combining the bush and trunk geometry into one object. We will do this by adding a **Join Geometry** node to the end of our node tree:

1. Connect the **Subdivision Surface** node from earlier to the **Geometry** input of the **Join Geometry** node.
2. Let's also connect the **Mesh** output of the **Mesh Boolean** node to the **Geometry** input.
3. If your bushes appear too low on the ground, raise the **Z** location of each of the **Transform** nodes to 20 meters since our bushes should be at the height of 20 meters.
4. To end this exercise, let's add a **Set Shade Smooth** node to smooth out everything in our final tree. You can drop this node at the end of your node tree.

This is how your final node tree should look:

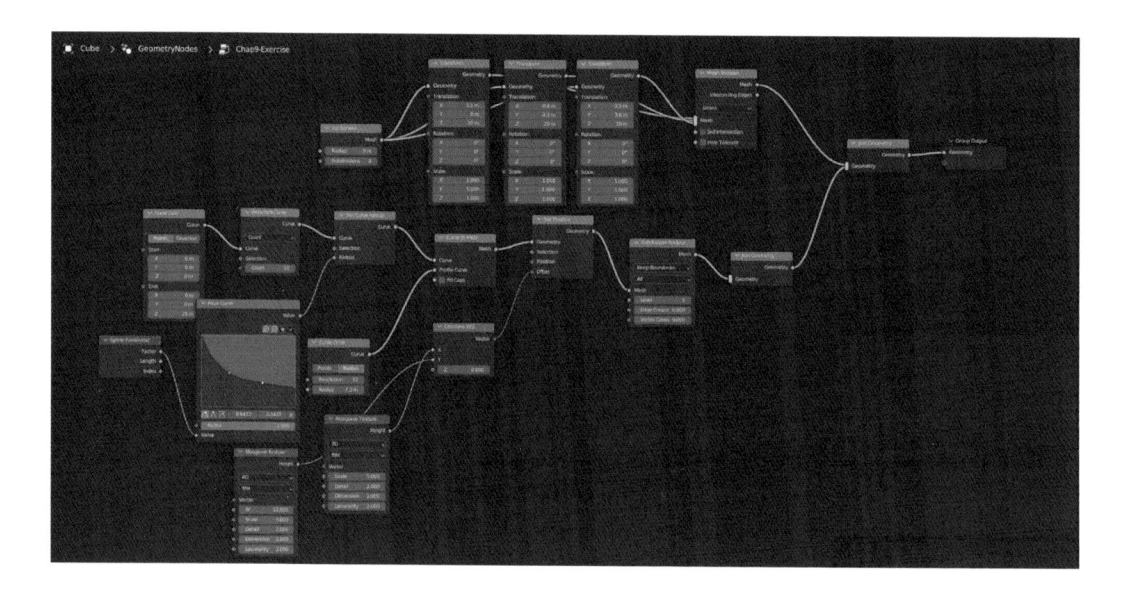

Figure 9.23: Your final node tree

> **Tip**
> To get more color in your final render, you can add the **Set Material** before the **Boolean Mesh** node.

Now we've come to the end of the exercise, and our final render looks like this:

Figure 9.24: Final render

This brings us to the end of the chapter. We've created a procedural tree using a Curve as our trunk and using three Ico Spheres as our leaves.

Summary

In this chapter, we learned how to work with the mesh manipulation nodes of the Geometry Nodes workspace; these include the **Extrude** node, the **Mesh Boolean** node, and the **Set Position** node. You also learned how to utilize these with other nodes, such as a **Random Value** node.

In the next chapter, you'll put your skills to use, where you will be creating a procedural plant generator.

Part 4 – Hands-On Projects Involving Advanced Workflow Techniques

In the fourth part of this book, you will delve into hands-on projects that involve advanced workflow techniques. This section includes chapters on creating a procedural plant generator, developing a procedural spiderweb generator, and constructing a procedural LED panel. These projects will help you enhance your skills and improve your workflow.

This section comprises the following chapters:

- *Chapter 10, Creating a Procedural Plant Generator*
- *Chapter 11, Creating a Procedural Spiderweb Generator*
- *Chapter 12, Constructing a Procedural LED Panel*

10
Creating a Procedural Plant Generator

Congratulations! You've now mastered the basics of Geometry Nodes in Blender! Now, it's time to get started on the more advanced projects. One of these advanced projects includes making a procedural plant generator. Let's get into it!

We will start this chapter off by adding a **Curve Line** node, to which we will add some noise using a **Set Position** node. After that, we will create a stem using a **Curve to Mesh** node and a **Spline Parameter** node to define the thickness. We will also be creating the leaves on our plant using instancing. We will rotate these leaves in a way that looks realistic. To finish off this node tree, we will be making a pot using the **Mesh Boolean** node and joining it with our leaves and stem.

To end the chapter, we will also teach you how to add **Group Inputs** to your node tree. This will be done to give end users easy access to the key variables of your node tree, such as height, leaf count, and resolution inputs.

We will cover the following topics in this chapter:

- Creating a curve with a custom thickness
- Distributing leaves on the curve
- Creating a pot using Geometry Nodes

Creating the node tree

Open a new Geometry Node editor on the default cube. Once you've done that, you're ready to start the exercise. The first step is to create the stem of the plant. Let's begin.

Creating the stem

In this section, we will add a **Curve Line** node, to which we will add some noise displacement using a **Set Position** node. After that, we will give this curve some thickness using a **Set Curve Radius** node:

1. Let's start by adding a **Curve Line** node to our Geometry Node editor. This will be the base of our stem.
2. To visualize this node, connect it to the **Group Output** node.
3. After that, add a **Set Position** node after the **Curve Line** node to start giving displacement to the curve.
4. We will also need a **Combine XYZ** node to split the **Offset** vector value into its respective **X**, **Y**, and **Z** components. Drop this **Combine XYZ** node into the **Offset** input of the **Set Position** node.

If you've followed these steps correctly, this is how your node tree should look:

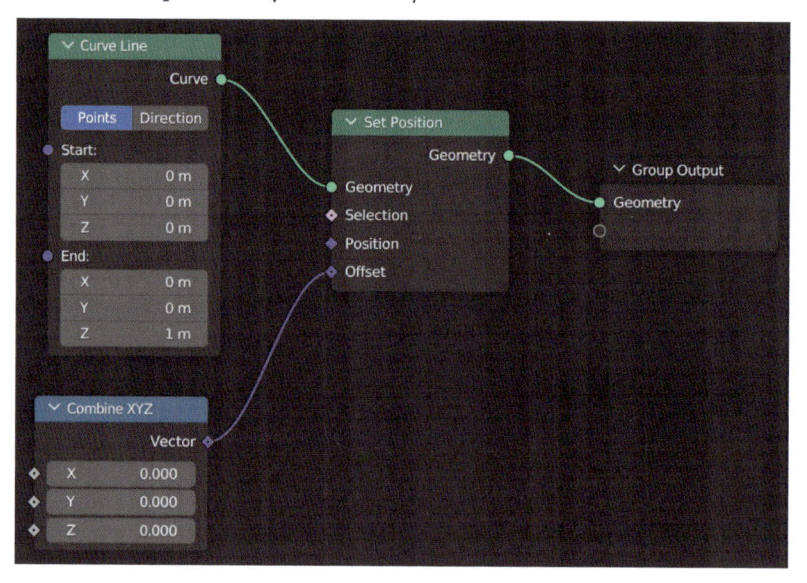

Figure 10.1: Your current node tree

Now, it's time to add **Noise Texture** nodes to start randomizing our curve:

1. Let's add two **Noise Texture** nodes with the given parameters shown in *Figure 10.2*.

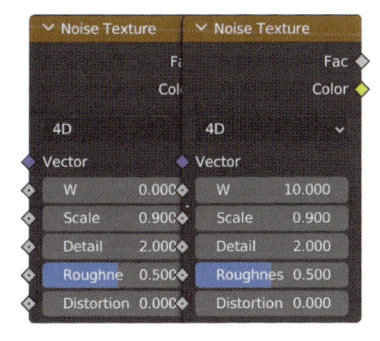

Figure 10.2: Noise Texture parameters

Make sure that both **Noise Texture** nodes have **W** values different from each other. This is to ensure that we have enough randomization in our displacement.

2. Let's plug in these **Noise Texture** nodes in their respective **X** and **Y** inputs in the **Combine XYZ** node. Use the **Fac** output as your input for this node.

3. We can see that not much happens when you do this. The reason for this, as covered in *Chapter 8, Editing Curves with Nodes*, is that we need to resample our curve first. Let's add a **Resample Curve** node between the **Curve Line** node and the **Set Position** node. Give this a **Count** value of 20.

4. You might have noticed that our curve is offset from our origin point. To fix this, add a **Vector Math** node, set it to **Subtract**, and subtract 0.5 from the **X** and **Y** axes. You can drop this node after the **Combine XYZ** node. This will set the median of our **Noise Texture** nodes to 0, as explained in the previous chapters. This is how your node tree should look after executing these steps correctly:

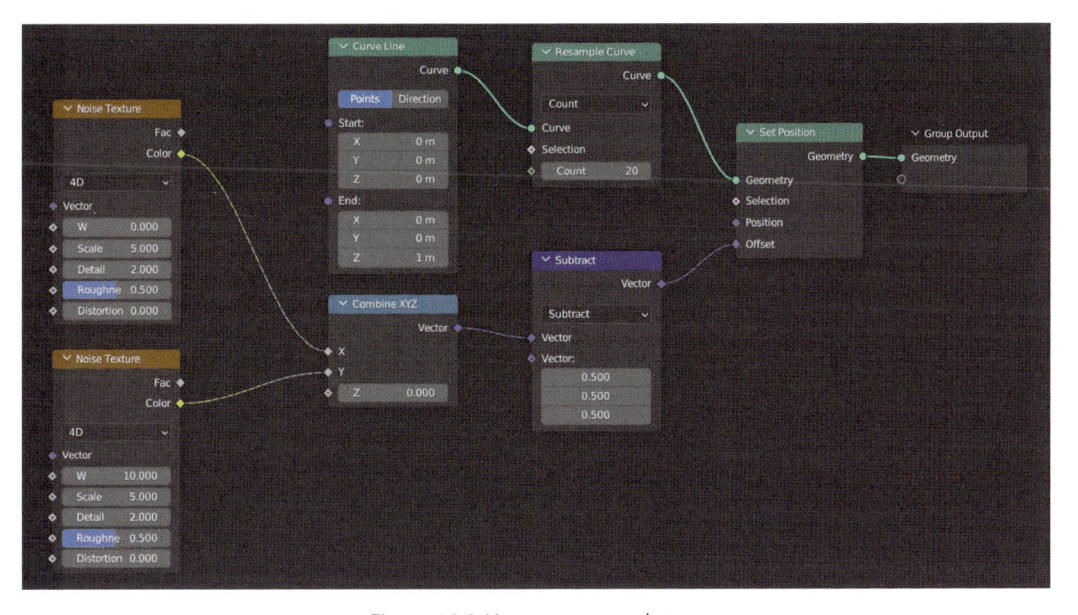

Figure 10.3: Your current node tree

Now, it's time to give our stem some thickness:

1. We can do this by adding a **Curve to Mesh** node at the end of our node tree. Let's tick **Fill Caps** because we want the ends of our stem to be filled.
2. Let's also add a **Curve Circle** node as our **Profile Curve**. Give this circle a **Radius** value of `0.05`; we can always tweak this afterward if our stem appears too thick.
3. Now, we will give the curve a custom radius profile; to do this, add a **Set Curve Radius** node behind the **Curve to Mesh** node. This will give us fine control over the thickness of our stem.

    As seen in *Chapter 8, Editing Curves with Nodes*, we can use a **Spline Parameter** node along with a **Float Curve** node to create a custom thickness profile. Let's execute this.

4. Add in a **Spline Parameter** node and a **Float Curve** node, and then connect the **Factor** output of the **Spline Parameter** node to the **Value** input of the **Float Curve** node.
5. Lastly, connect the **Value** output of the **Float Curve** node to the **Radius** input of the **Set Curve Radius** node. Let's give the **Float Curve** node the profile detailed in *Figure 10.4*.

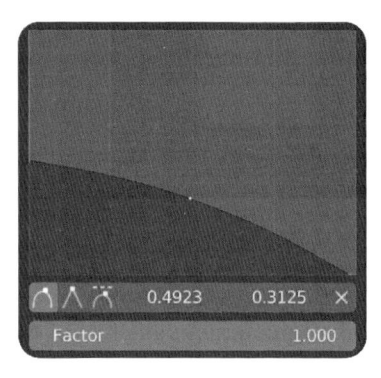

Figure 10.4: The Float Curve node profile

Of course, you can always tweak these nodes to your liking. If you executed all these steps correctly, this is how your node tree should look:

Creating the node tree 161

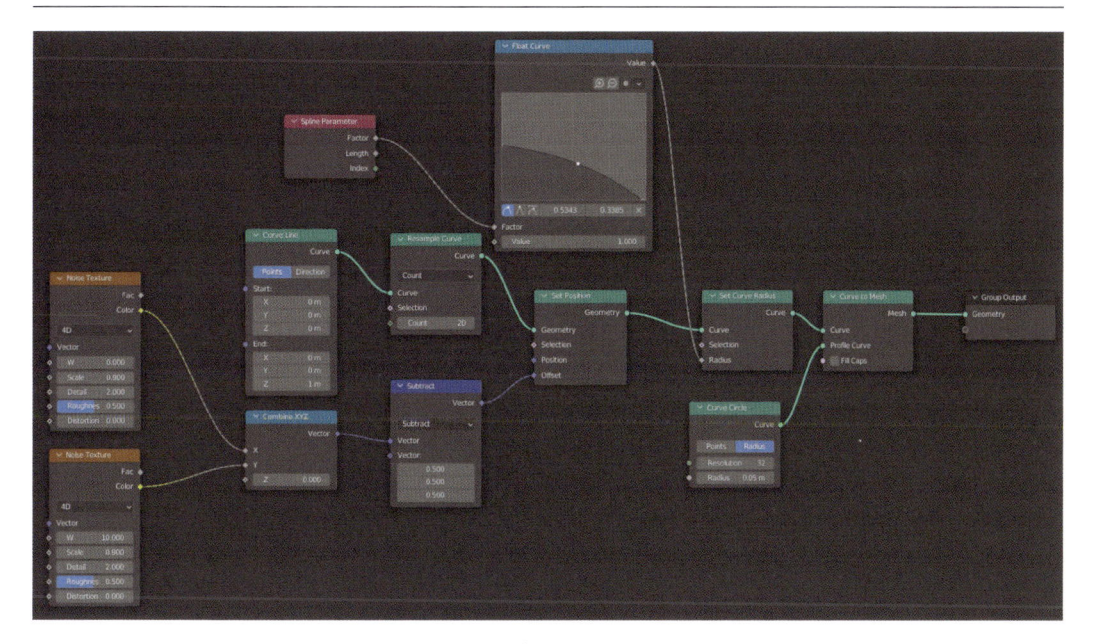

Figure 10.5: Your current node tree

This is how your current model should look:

Figure 10.6: The stem

Congratulations! You've now completed the stem. Let's move on to the leaves of our plant!

Creating the leaves

Now, we will be creating the leaves of our plant. We will do this by instancing some self-modeled leaves on our stem and rotating them around, using a **Random Value** node.

Before we start instancing leaves on our curve, let's resample it again; this will determine how many leaves we will put on our plant.

Add in a **Resample Curve** node with a **Count** of 10. This count means we will instance 10 leaves on our stem. You can connect this node after the **Set Position** node as highlighted in *Figure 10.7*. In other words, we're branching off from the previous part of the node tree.

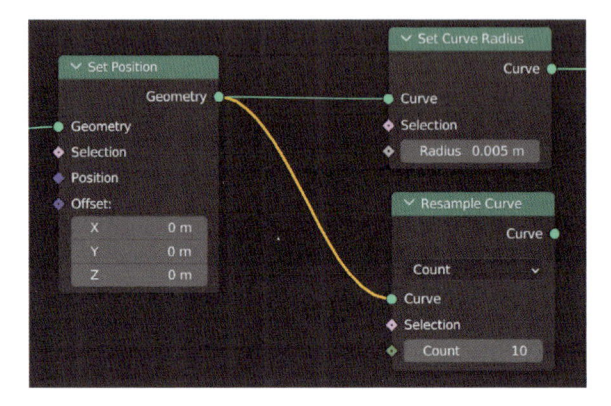

Figure 10.7: The Set Position and Resample Curve nodes

This will give our Curve node more resolution to work with, which is what we need if we want to add noise to our stem:

1. Now, let's go back to the Viewport editor to model a leaf. This can be really basic.

Figure 10.8: A basic leaf model

> **Important note**
> Make sure that your origin point is at the stem of your leaf! This will be important in the next step. You can also give some downward curvature to your leaf for extra realism!

2. The next step is to start instancing this leaf in our Geometry Node editor. Let's go back to the editor and select our stem to go back to the node tree.

   To drop in the leaf in our Geometry Nodes workspace, a simple trick we can execute is to drag our leaf from the Outliner to the editor, as shown in the following figure.

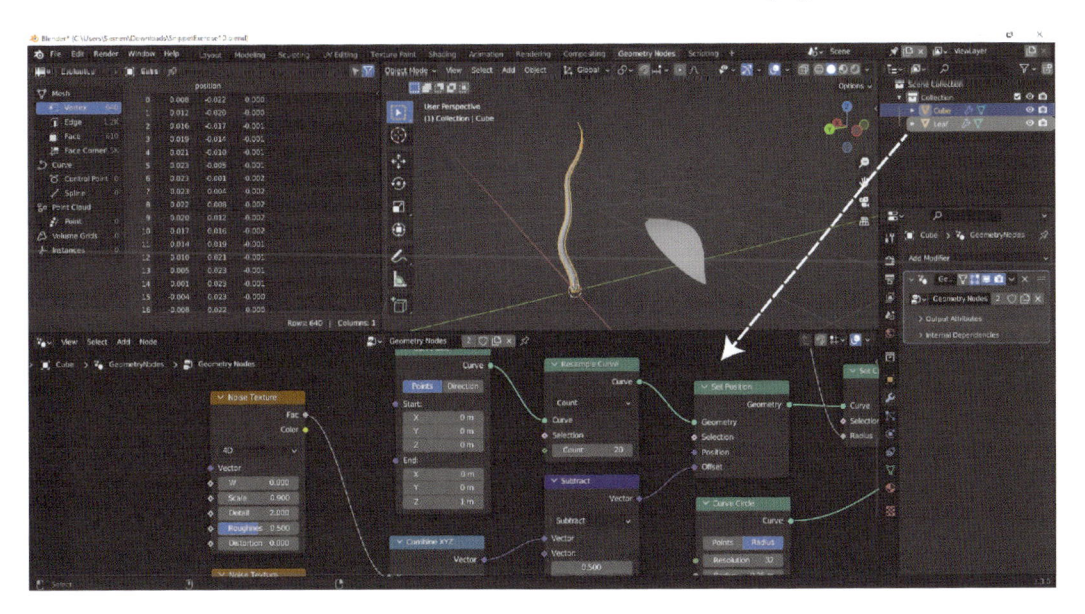

Figure 10.9: Drag your leaf to the editor

You will see that this will create an **Object Info** node in the Geometry Node editor.

3. To start instancing this leaf on our curve, let's add an **Instance on Points** node.

4. Let's connect the **Resample Curve** node to the **Points** input of the **Instance on Points** node. As you might have guessed, we can also use the **Instance on Points** node on any mesh; in that scenario, Blender will read all the vertices the mesh contains as points.

5. To add our leaf as the instance object, let's also connect the **Object Info** node's **Geometry** output to the **Instance** input of the **Instance on Points** node.

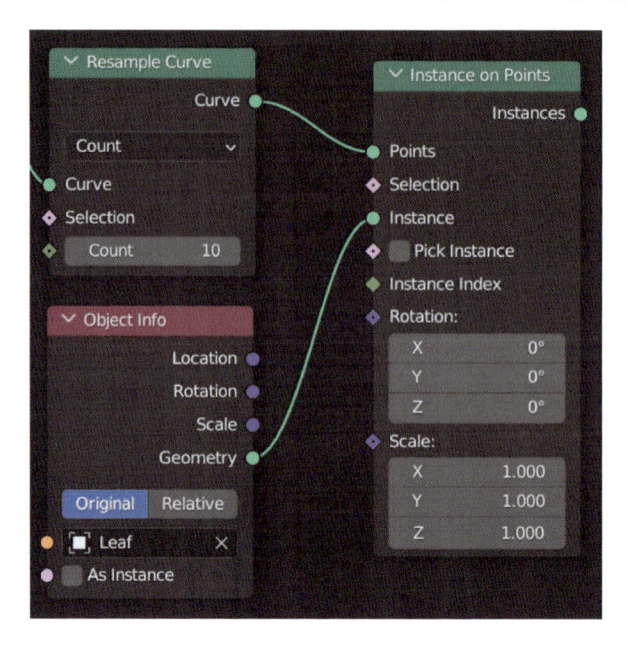

Figure 10.10: A node tree snippet

6. We can see that nothing happens yet because the **Instance on Points** node is not being outputted to the **Group Output** node. To fix this, add a **Join Geometry** node at the end of the node tree to join the stem and the leaves together.

7. At first, you can see that our leaves are way too big. To fix this, use the **Scale** input to scale your leaves to the correct size. The value you use for this really depends on how you modeled your leaves.

> **Tip**
> You can hide the original leaf from the Viewport without hiding the instances.

8. There is a problem though – all our leaves are on the same side of our plant, and this is not realistic. To fix this, add a **Random Value** node, set to **Vector**. Let's enter the parameters as shown in the following figure.

Figure 10.11: The Random Value node

To explain these values easily, we're basically rotating a bit on the **X** and **Y** axes, but we're making a full rotation on the **Z** axis.

9. We can drop the output of this node straight into the **Rotation** input of the **Instance on Points** node.

When you now take a look at your Viewport, you can see that the leaves have spun around! We're getting closer!

166   Creating a Procedural Plant Generator

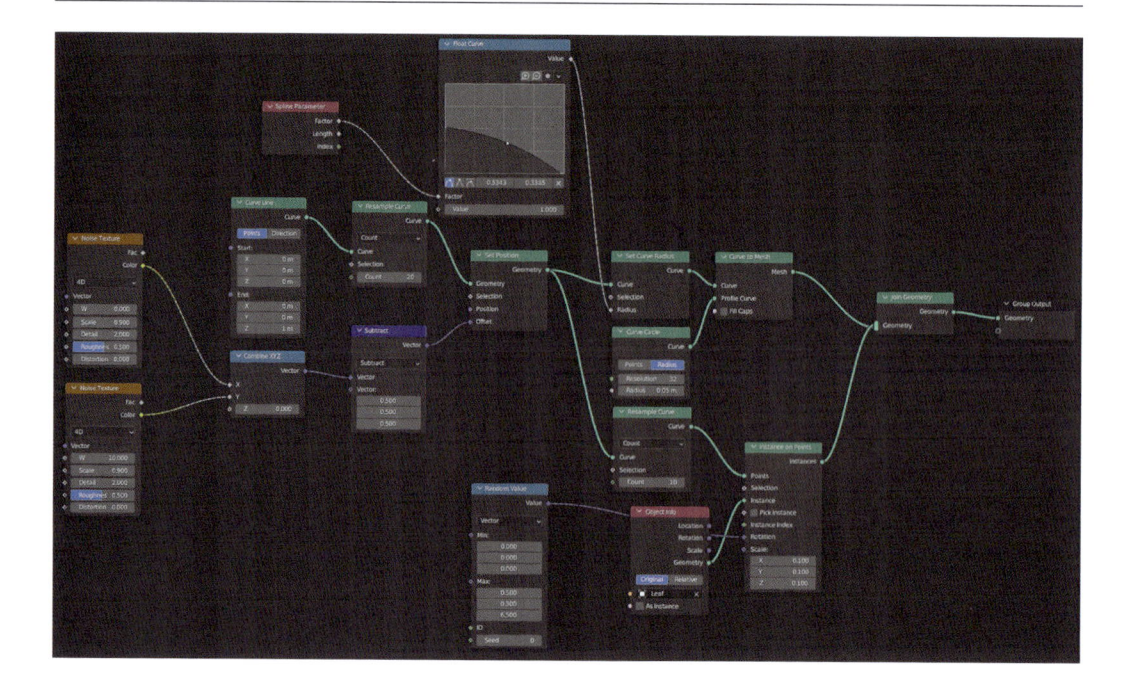

Figure 10.12: Your current node tree

Figure 10.12 is what your node tree should look like by now.

Creating the pot

This is the last step in creating our plant. In this section, we will take two cylinders and use a **Mesh Boolean** node to cut away the insides of this pot. Let's get into it:

1. Add a **Cylinder** node to the existing **Join Geometry** node at the end of the node tree.

2. Give it a **Radius** value big enough so that it covers all the leaves perfectly. Let's also give it a **Depth** value of about 0.8 meters.

3. After that, use the **Transform** node to move the cylinder down to the bottom, and pick a **Z Location** value that you think is suitable.

4. Let's now add a **Mesh Boolean** node to cut away the middle of our pot. We can drop this node after the **Transform** node.

   We can see that nothing happens; this is because we have not entered a **Mesh 2** input yet.

5. To fix this, let's add in another **Transform** node that is slightly smaller and slightly higher than our original cylinder, which will cut out the top of our **Mesh 1** input. We went with a **Z** location of 0.1 and a **Scale** value of 0.8 on all axes, but be sure to experiment with different values.

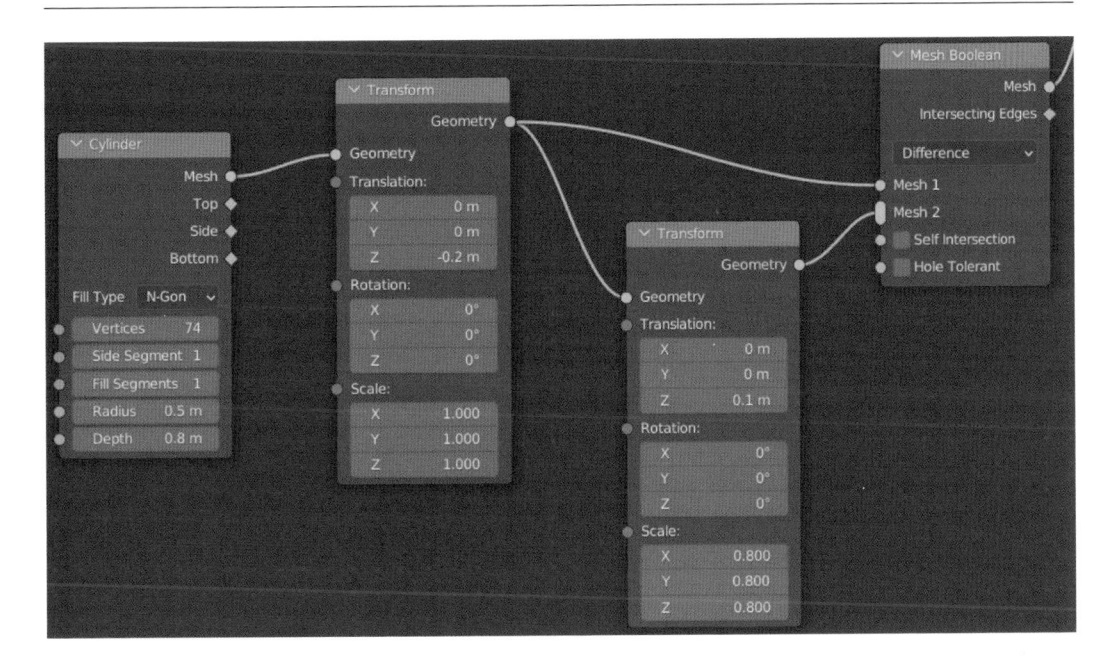

Figure 10.13: The pot node tree

If you now take a look at the viewport, you can see that the plant is finished!

Figure 10.14: Your final model

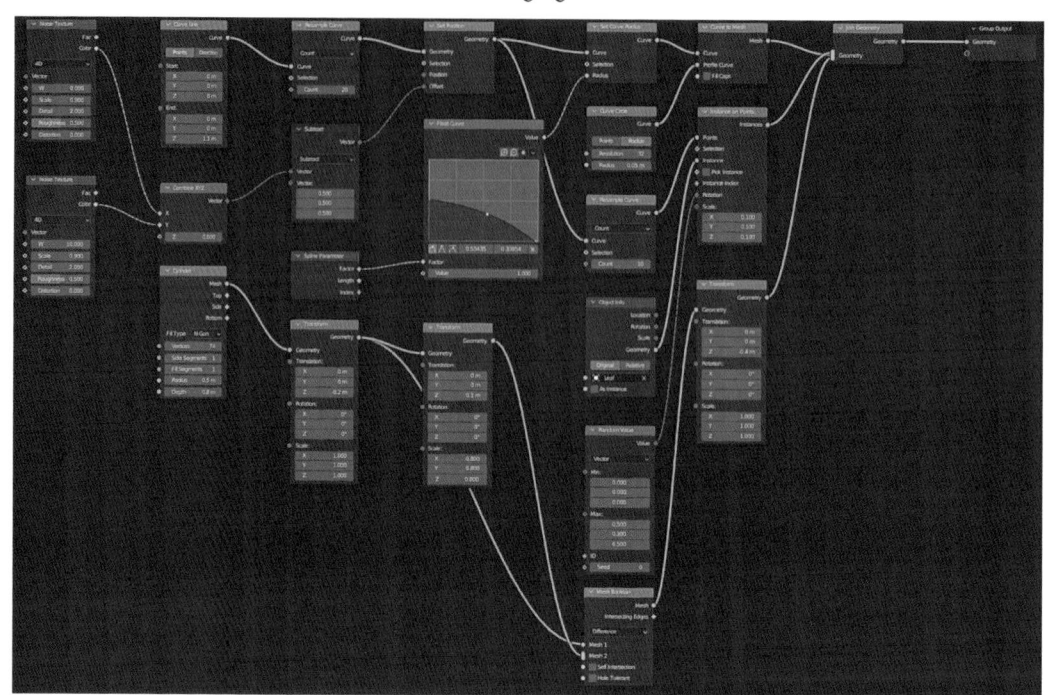

You can see the finished node tree in the following figure:

Figure 10.15: The final node tree

Keep in mind that you can still try out different parameters for leaf count, resolutions, noise patterns, and so on.

This brings us to the end of this node tree-building exercise! In this section, you've learned how to create a stem for a plant using Blender's Geometry Nodes. Specifically, you've learned how to do the following:

- Create a **Curve Line** node and add noise displacement to it using a **Set Position** node and some noise textures
- Give the stem some thickness by using a **Set Curve Radius** node and a **Spline Parameter** node
- Add leaves to the stem using instancing and rotation
- Create a pot using the **Mesh Boolean** node and join it with the leaves and stem to complete the node tree

Utilizing group inputs

In this section, we will add group inputs to our node tree. These can be handy when you want to distribute the node tree to other users so that they can easily access your variables. We'll be adding group inputs to the most important variables in the node tree.

What inputs will we include?

The inputs that we will include are as follows:

- The **End Z** value of the **Curve Line** node, which we'll call `Plant Height`
- The **Count** value of the second **Resample Curve** node, which we'll call `Leaf Count`
- The **Max** value of the **Random Value** node, which we'll call `Leaf Rotation`
- The **Count** value of the first **Resample Curve** node, which we'll call `Stem Resolution`

Let's start implementing these group inputs!

Plant Height

First, let's implement the Plant Height group input:

1. To implement the Plant Height group input, we first need to utilize a **Combine XYZ** node to split the **X**, **Y**, and **Z** values of the **Curve Line** node's **End** input.

2. After that, let's add a **Group Input** node and drag the gray node connection to the **Z** value of the **Combine XYZ** node.

    Once you have done this, you can see that a new value called **Z** appears.

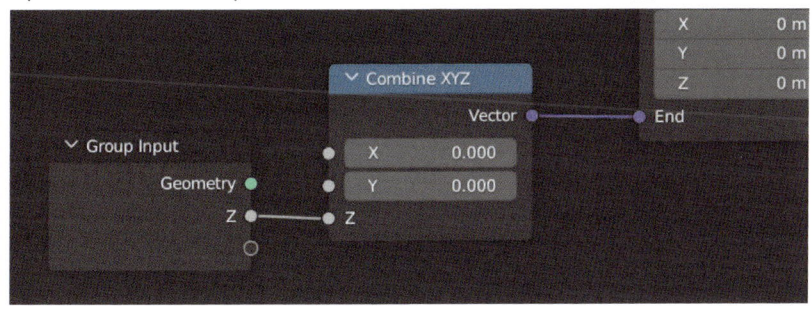

Figure 10.16: The Plant Height group input

In *Figure 10.16*, you can see the node tree for this specific part.

Leaf Count

Let's now implement the Leaf Count group.

Luckily, this is really easy. All we need to do is drag the gray node connection to the **Count** input of the second **Resample Curve** node. When you do this, you'll see that a **Count** value has been made on the **Group Input** node.

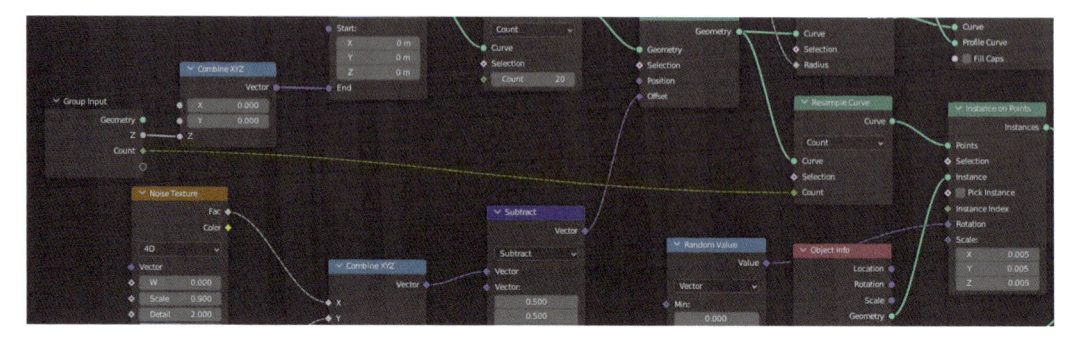

Figure 10.17: The Leaf Count group input

Do this for the rest of the group inputs we mentioned until you have the following result:

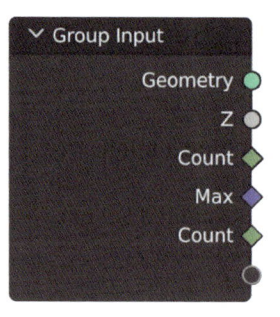

Figure 10.18: The group inputs

Now, let's start renaming all of these variables.

Renaming the group inputs

Right now, it's not that easy to remember all the different names that Blender assigned to these group inputs. Fortunately, we can choose to rename these:

1. If we want to rename the group inputs, open the right-hand menu of the Geometry Node editor, which can be seen in *Figure 10.19*, and head to the **Group** tab.

Figure 10.19: The right-hand menu button

2. Once you are in the **Group** menu, look at the **Inputs** section, which is shown in *Figure 10.20*.

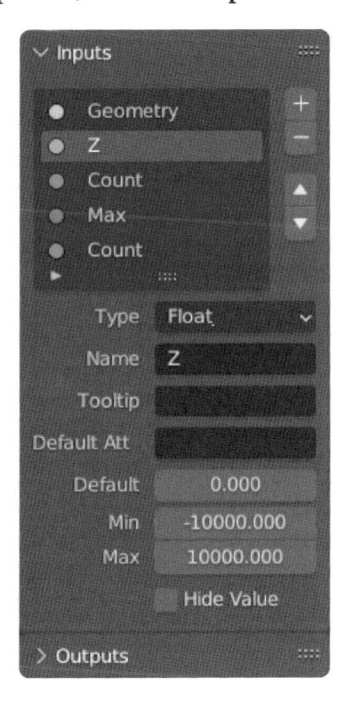

Figure 10.20: The group inputs list

3. When you click on one of the entries, we are presented with the option to change the datatype, give a name to the group input, add a tooltip to the input, add a default value, and give a value range.

   Let's rename each of the entries as follows:
   - `Plant Height`
   - `Leaf Count`
   - `Leaf Rotation`
   - `Stem Resolution`

4. Once you've done this, we can head to the Modifier stack to take a look at our finished **Group Input** control panel.

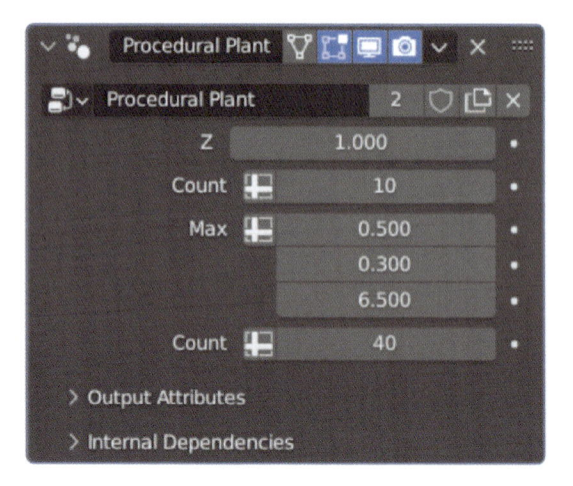

Figure 10.21: The Geometry Nodes Modifier

And there you have it! That's how you make a procedural plant generator, complete with group inputs.

Figure 10.22: The final render

In *Figure 10.22*, you can see the final render of what we made in this chapter.

And that's how you add group inputs to your node tree, which can be useful for the end users of your node tree so that they can easily access important variables from the Modifier stack.

Summary

In this chapter, you've learned how to utilize Geometry Nodes to create a procedural plant generator, which, in turn, is used to create a simple plant using only a few parameters. This can be useful when you need lots of plants in your scene but don't want them all to look the same.

In the next chapter, we'll be creating a procedural spider web using Geometry Nodes.

11
Creating a Procedural Spiderweb Generator

In the previous chapter, you've learned how to create a procedural plant using Geometry Nodes. In this chapter, we will take a step back from the complex subjects and focus on a simpler node tree. We will make a procedural spiderweb generator. This chapter will mainly focus on the logical-thinking part of your Geometry Nodes learning journey! You will learn about the calculation of a **Convex Hull** node and the deletion of geometry using the **Delete Geometry** node, and at the end of this chapter, we'll top this exercise off by adding group inputs to our project. This will all greatly improve your logical thinking, which is a crucial advanced skill to use with Geometry Nodes.

We will cover the following topics in the chapter:

- Creating a scene in our Viewport
- Creating our node tree
- Group inputs
- Organizing your node tree using Reroutes

Let's get right into the exercise.

Creating a scene in our Viewport

Let's start this chapter off by making a simple scene in our Viewport. We will do this in **Edit Mode** in the Viewport:

1. To do this, let's go to the **Layout** workspace and press *Tab* to enter **Edit Mode**. Alternatively, you can also choose to enter **Edit Mode** via the button shown in *Figure 11.1*.

Figure 11.1: Mode selection

2. For this exercise, we will take three **Suzanne** primitives and place them around our Blender Viewport. We went with the scene you can see in *Figure 11.2*.

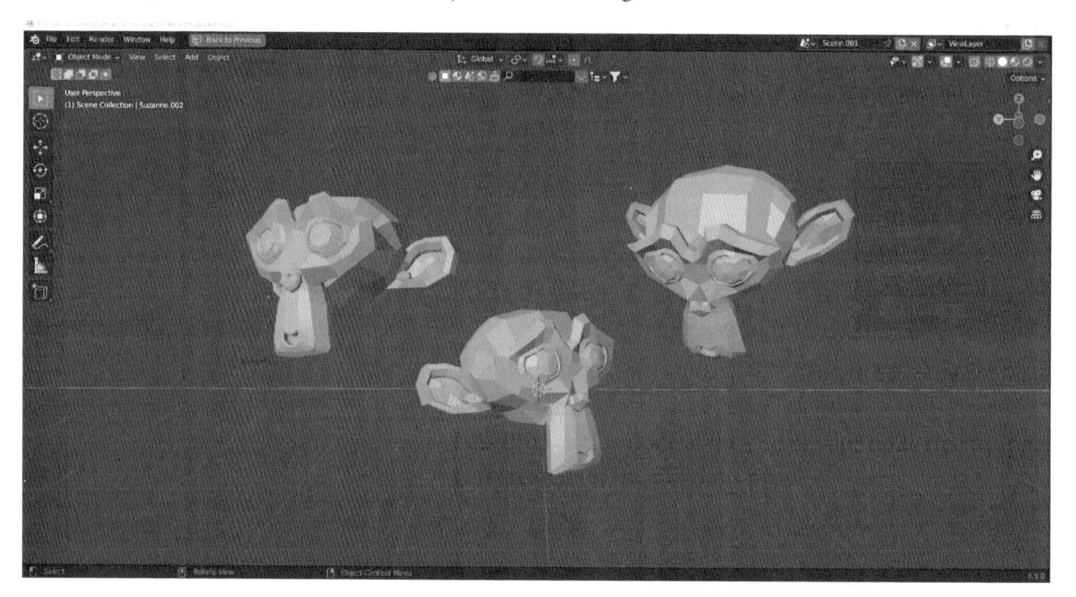

Figure 11.2: The Viewport

3. The next step is to join these models together by selecting all the models and clicking **Join** from the **Object Context** menu, as you can see in *Figure 11.3*.

   Alternatively, you can also use the *Ctrl + J* shortcut.

   Figure 11.3: Object Context Menu | Join

4. Now that we have completed our scene, we can head to the Geometry Nodes workspace to begin this exercise.

   Make a new node tree by pressing the **New** button, which you can see in *Figure 11.4*. Make sure you've selected the **Suzanne** object.

   Figure 11.4: Add a new node tree

   This button will add a new Geometry Nodes modifier to your **Suzanne** object along with a node tree.

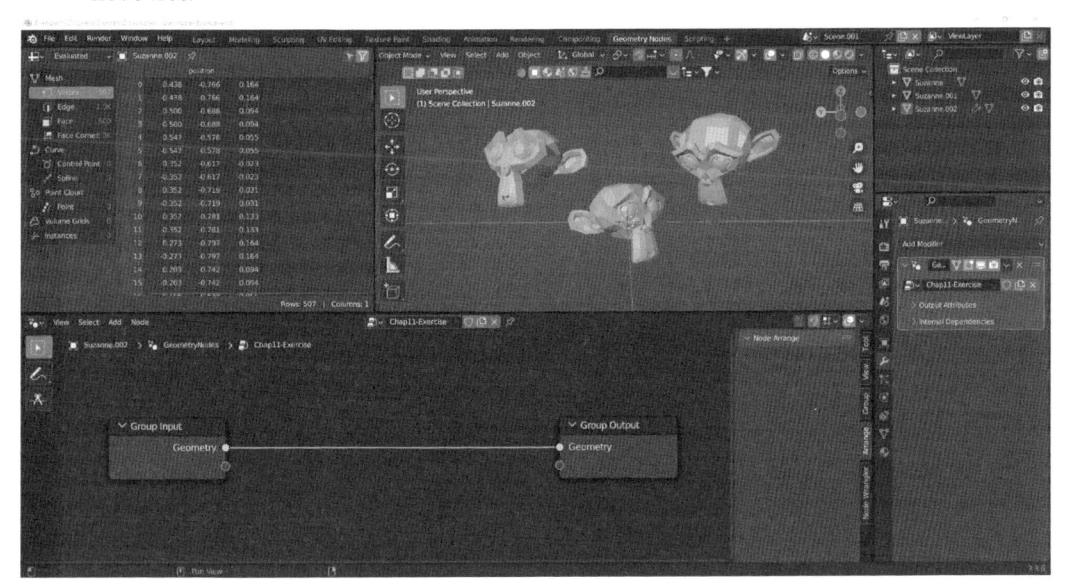

   Figure 11.5: The Geometry Node editor

With our Geometry Node editor ready to be used, we can move on to the next section, where we will be making the node tree for this procedural spiderweb generator.

Creating our node tree

To make a procedural spiderweb generator, we will begin our journey by making use of a convex hull shape; after that, we will convert this convex hull shape into a wireframe, and we will join the original mesh with this wireframe.

But first, let's learn a little about convex hulls.

What's a convex hull?

A convex hull is best explained as a version of a model that is cut from a block using only straight lines. This means that we won't have any crevices in the model. The following figure shows in simple terms what a convex hull means on a vertex level:

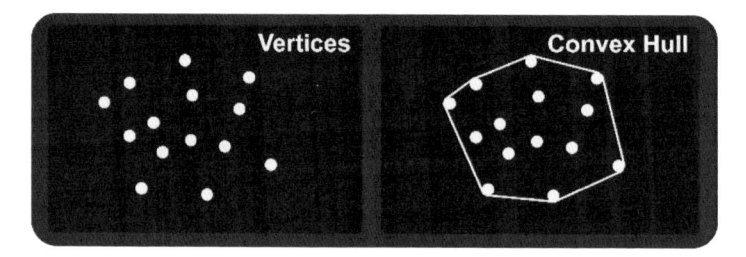

Figure 11.6: A convex hull calculation

In the following figure, you can see various examples of objects with convex hulls:

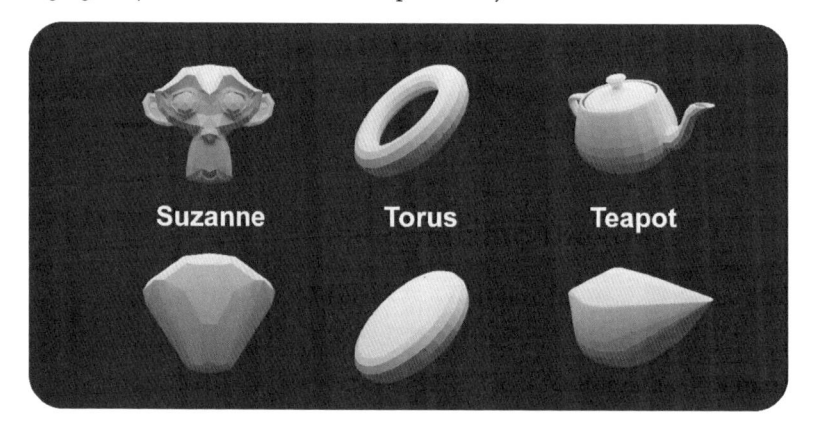

Figure 11.7: Convex hull examples

Creating a convex hull around our objects

Making a convex hull around our objects is very easy. There is a special node to do this in the Geometry Node editor, conveniently named the **Convex Hull** node.

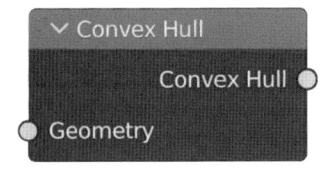

Figure 11.8: The Convex Hull node

This node will convert the inputted geometry into a Convex Hull, which is exactly what we need for this exercise.

Drop in the **Convex Hull** node between the **Group Input** node and the **Group Output** node.

We can see that we now have a convex hull in our scene.

Figure 11.9: The convex hull in our scene

Let's move on to the next step, where we will be converting this convex hull into a wireframe.

Making a wireframe from the convex hull

We will execute this idea by utilizing a **Mesh to Curve** node along with a **Curve to Mesh** node to create a wireframe effect. As mentioned in previous chapters, the **Mesh to Curve** node disregards any faces in its outputted mesh. This means that our convex hull will turn into a wireframe:

1. Let's start by dropping in a **Mesh to Curve** node after the **Convex Hull** node.
2. This is followed directly by a **Curve to Mesh** node to add thickness to the curves.
3. Drop this node in after the **Mesh to Curve** node. Don't forget to tick the **Fill Caps** option.

This is how the current node tree should look:

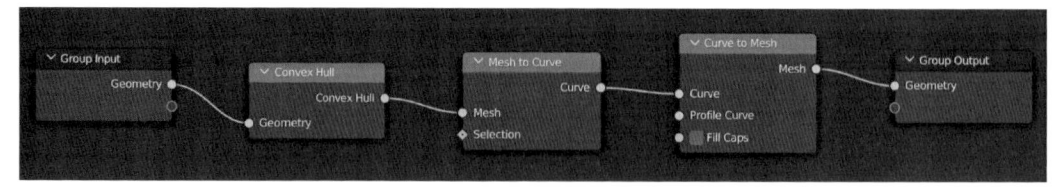

Figure 11.10: The current node tree

If we take a look at our Viewport, we can see that there is not any thickness yet. However, we can see a wireframe model of our convex hull.

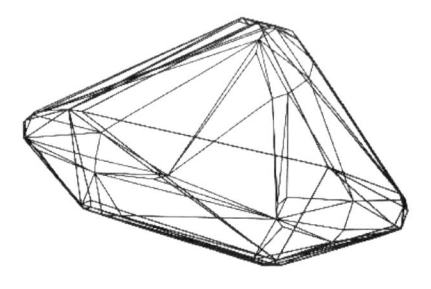

Figure 11.11: A wireframe model of our convex hull

4. The reason why we do not have any thickness is that we did not input a **Profile Curve** node yet. Let's choose a **Curve Circle** node as our **Profile Curve** input, but you can experiment with different curve primitives, as shown in *Figure 11.12*.

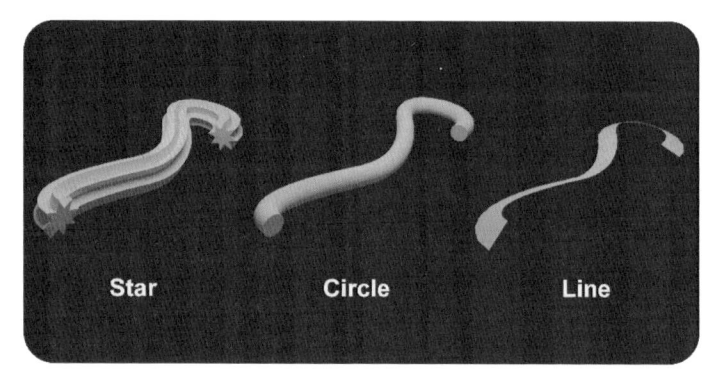

Figure 11.12: Curve profiles

Keep in mind that our spiderweb will have a minuscule thickness, which will not be very noticeable in the final render.

5. Once you've plugged the **Curve Circle** node into the **Profile Curve** input, set the **Radius** value of the **Curve Circle** node to `0.01`. This will define the thickness of your spiderweb strand.
6. To minimize the strain on your computer's CPU and RAM, let's also minimize the resolution of this **Curve Circle** node. By using a value of `5`, we reach a golden compromise between quality and performance.

Once you've executed these steps, you're ready to move on to the next step.

The next step is to combine the wireframe with the original mesh that we created in the *Creating a scene in our Viewport* section.

Let's use a **Join Geometry** node to combine these two meshes, as we did in previous chapters.

Drop in the **Join Geometry** node at the end of the node tree and connect the **Group Input** node's **Geometry** output to the **Join Geometry** node, along with the **Curve To Mesh** node.

If you've executed these steps correctly, you will now see your convex hull wireframe along with your original model.

As you can see in *Figure 11.13*, this is how your current model should look.

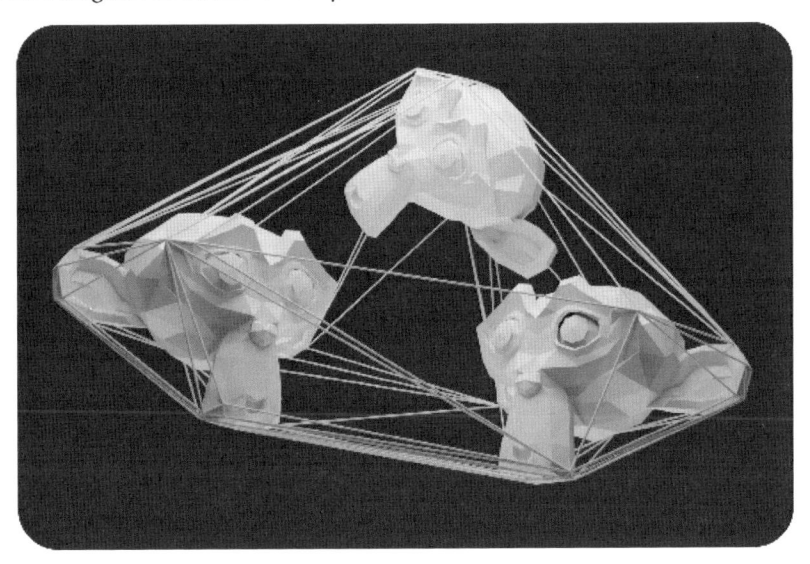

Figure 11.13: The current model

Let's also take a look at the node tree we have so far. You can see this in *Figure 11.14*.

Figure 11.14: The current node tree

Once the wireframe has been joined with the original model and you have a new model, it's time to add some detail and randomization.

Adding detail and randomization

Now, it's time to add some detail to your wireframe; we can do this by subdividing our convex hull before it's turned into a wireframe.

We can execute this using the **Subdivide Mesh** node. Let's drop this node between the **Convex Hull** node and the **Mesh to Curve** node.

Using the **Level** value on the **Subdivide Mesh** node, we can control the iterations of our spiderweb – in other words, how deep the middles are filled with topology.

In *Figure 11.15*, you can see what the various levels look like:

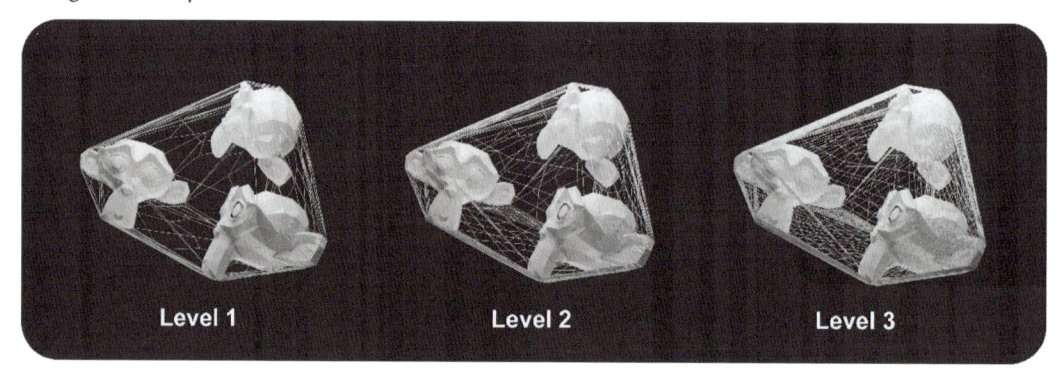

Figure 11.15: The levels

This is how the current node tree should look:

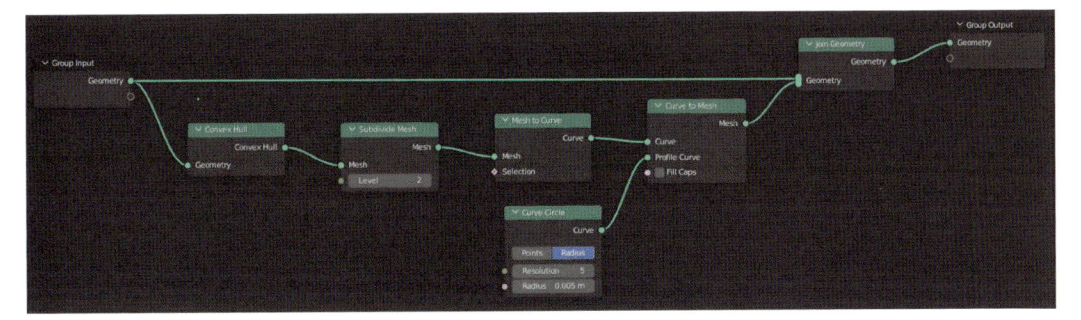

Figure 11.16: The current node tree

There's one problem in our model though – our spiderwebs look too consistent, and we need a way to randomize this. Luckily, we can use a **Random Value** node in this scenario too.

We can delete the geometry of our convex hull to add randomization. For this, we can use the **Delete Geometry** node.

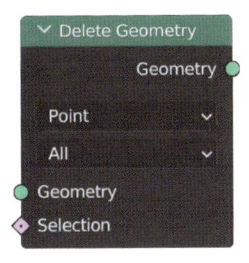

Figure 11.17: The Delete Geometry node

As the node title suggests, this node will delete points, edges, and faces using the **Geometry** input. The edited mesh will be outputted in the **Geometry** output.

Using the **Selection** Boolean input, we can define what parts of the mesh should be deleted. This is handy because we can use a **Random Value** node set to **Boolean** to control the probability of points that we will delete.

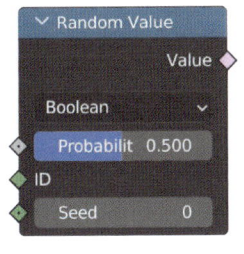

Figure 11.18: The Random Value node set to delete

Let's now start wiring these nodes into our node tree:

1. Firstly, start by dropping in the **Delete Geometry** node between the **Convex Hull** node and the **Subdivide Mesh** node. We want to drop **Delete Geometry** node there because we want to delete the geometry of the convex hull itself, not the geometry from the subdivided convex hull.
2. After that, let's connect the **Random Value** node that is set to **Boolean** to the **Selection** input of the **Delete Geometry** node.

   Once you've done that, your node tree should look like this:

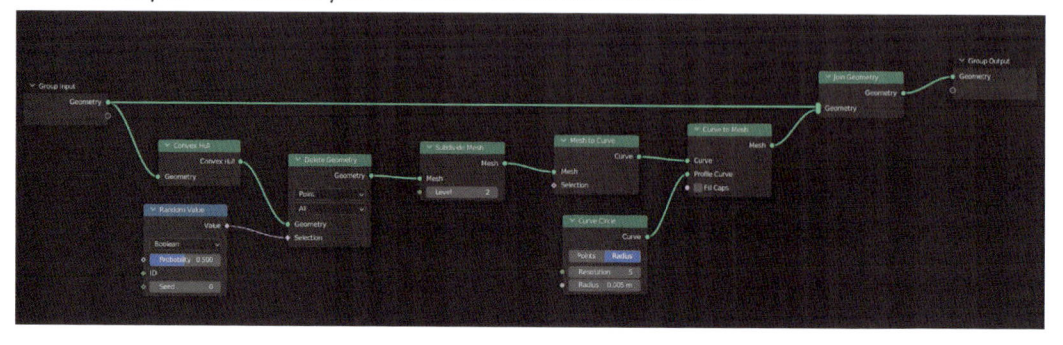

Figure 11.19: The current node tree

Using the probability slider, we can control how much of the geometry gets deleted. This can easily be turned into a Group Input slider for easy access, which we will cover in the next section.

Group inputs

Let's start adding group inputs to our node tree. This is an important step of the procedural workflow, allowing us to obtain an easy-to-modify procedural object with values accessible from the modifier stack.

There are four values that we want to include in our **Group Input** node:

- The **Probability** input of the **Random Value** node
- The **Seed** value of the **Random Value** node
- The **Level** input of the **Subdivide Mesh** node
- The **Radius** value of the **Curve Circle** node

As mentioned in previous chapters, we can add group inputs by sliding the gray node connection from the **Group Input** node to the inputs that we want to include.

Once you've added all these group inputs, it's time to rename them. Open the right-hand panel of the Geometry Node editor, head to the **Group** tab, and start renaming the entries to the following names:

- ``Randomization``
- ``Seed``
- ``Detail``
- ``Thickness``

This is how your modifier should look after making these changes:

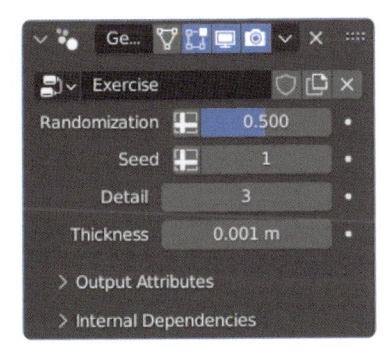

Figure 11.20: The Geometry Nodes modifier

As you can see in *Figure 11.20*, we now have easy access to the most important sliders and values in our Geometry Node editor. This is useful when you want to hand over your project to someone else. They do not need to understand your node tree to change the properties of the procedural model.

This is how the current node tree should look:

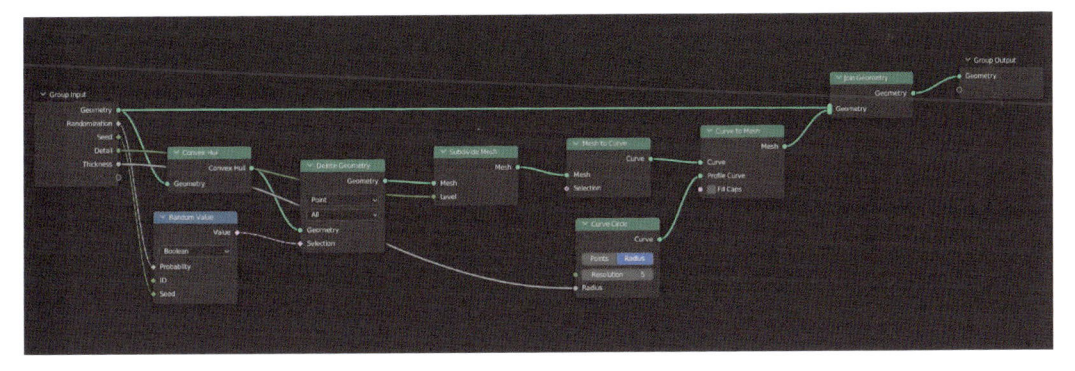

Figure 11.21: The current node tree

In the final section, we will look at how to utilize Reroutes to clean up a node tree.

Organizing your node tree using Reroutes

As mentioned in past chapters, a **Reroute** is basically a free-standing node connection that can be used to guide node cables to other directions, group multiple node connections, and so on. We can also utilize Reroutes to clean up our node tree.

Beware though – this can be a really tedious process that requires a lot of thinking.

We can add Reroutes by one of two methods – we can either add them via the **Add** menu, or we can add them by pressing / on our keyboard, although this requires the **Node Wrangler** add-on to execute.

We can add Reroutes to the corners of hard-to-see node cables to guide these node cables in another direction. We can also use Reroutes to make the curves of these node cables more natural.

> **Tips**
> You can move Reroutes by pressing *G*. You can also copy them with *Shift* + *D*.

Play around with these Reroutes until you get something that looks like the following result:

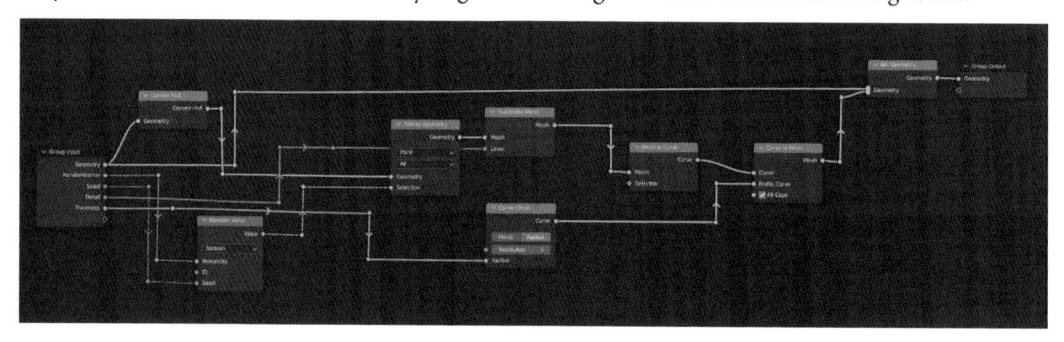

Figure 11.22: A tidy node tree using Reroutes

Using Reroutes to clean up your node tree is a crucial step in your workflow because it will help you greatly in finding bugs or parts in the node tree that you might want to append later.

And that's how you cable-manage your node tree by utilizing Reroutes!

Now, you can see the final render:

Figure 11.23: The final render

And that brings us to the end of this exercise! In this chapter, you've learned how to create a procedural spiderweb using Geometry Nodes by utilizing convex hull calculations.

Summary

In this chapter, you've learned how to create a procedural spiderweb generator using the Geometry Nodes feature in Blender. The process begins by creating a simple scene in the Viewport using several **Suzanne** primitives and joining them together. Then, a node tree is created by using the convex hull shape and converting it into a wireframe using the **Mesh to Curve** and **Curve to Mesh** nodes. The final step is joining the original mesh with the wireframe to create a realistic spiderweb effect. Throughout the process, we emphasize the importance of logical thinking and organization in creating the node tree by comparing mathematical examples to real-world phenomena, as we did with spiderwebs and convex hulls.

12
Constructing a Procedural LED Panel

In the previous chapter, you learned how to create a procedural spiderweb by making use of convex hulls.

In this chapter, you'll learn how to create a procedural LED panel by using **named attributes**. We will need these named attributes to save attributes inside of our Blender project so that we can link various Blender workspaces together.

We will start off this chapter by explaining what named attributes are.

But before that, these are the topics we will cover in this chapter:

- What are named attributes?
- How do LED panels work?
- Creating a node tree
- Adding group inputs to the node tree

What are named attributes?

Named attributes can be thought of as variables inside your Blender project.

Attributes can be used in many parts of Blender. For example, attributes are used in weight painting, the positions of points, and vertex groups. A lot of things are controlled using attributes – for example, the Geometry Node editor, the Material nodes editor, and some entries in the Physics simulator in Blender. In this exercise, we will be using them to link the Geometry Node editor and the Material Nodes editor.

The node that we'll be using to store these named attributes is called the **Store Named Attribute** node.

The **Store Named Attribute** node will store the result of a value on **Geometry** in an attribute name. On which geometry this information is stored is dependent on the **Geometry** input socket.

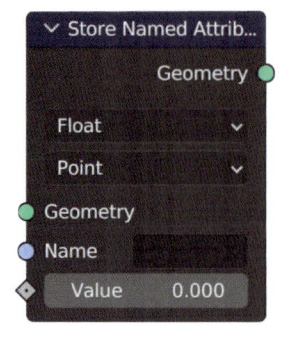

Figure 12.1: The Store Named Attribute node

The **Geometry** output of this node will just output the geometry with the named attribute saved.

Now that you know the techniques we'll use in this chapter, let's quickly go over the basics of how LED panels actually work in the real world. This will help you better understand what you're doing once we start building the node tree.

How do LED panels work?

LED panels come in a lot of shapes and forms; you have OLED, AMOLED, LCD, and a lot more variations of each of these. These panels work by using subpixels to mix colors together.

Subpixels are the underlying colors of your monitors, which are **red, green, and blue**, often shortened to **RGB**.

These RGB values can be combined into any color imaginable.

Figure 12.2: RGB mixing

Not all devices use RGB though; most printers use **Cyan, Magenta, Yellow, and Key** (**CMYK**) color mixing, since mixing light and mixing dyes work differently.

LED panels work by dimming and brightening each of these R, G, and B subpixels to create the desired color. In *Figure 12.3*, you can see how LCD pixels are arranged.

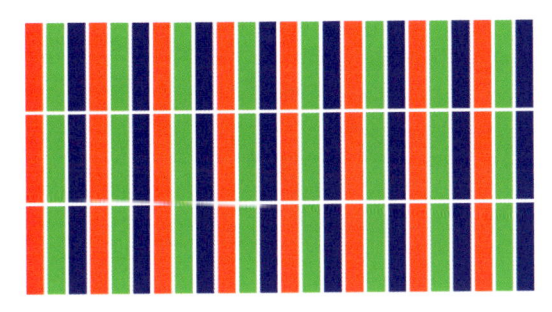

Figure 12.3: A subpixels array

Now that we know how an LED panel works, we can start making one in Blender using Geometry Nodes:

1. Let's start by opening a brand-new Blender project.
2. Head over to the Geometry Nodes workspace and add a new node tree to the default cube.
3. Let's delete the **Group Input** node, since we won't be needing it because we'll be working with node primitives instead.

Once we've done that, we can start creating the node tree.

Creating the node tree

We will create three subpixels that we will instance using a grid. After that, we will extract the R, G, and B channels from an image to send that information to the Material editor to edit the materials accordingly. Then, we will have a working LED panel.

Now that we know about the techniques that we're going to use, let's start by building the node tree we'll need for this exercise.

Creating a single subpixel

Let's start off this exercise by creating a single subpixel:

1. Start by adding a **Grid** node.
2. Since we want three pixels on the **X** axis, as shown in *Figure 12.3*, we will need to use a value of 0.333 (1 divided by 3). For our **Y** axis, we'll use a height of 1.

Make sure to only use 2 vertices on each axis. Since we'll be instancing this object a lot, we do not want to put too much strain on our computer.

This is how the node should look:

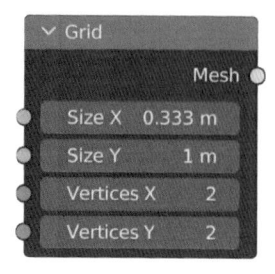

Figure 12.4: The Grid node for a subpixel

You can connect this **Grid** node to the **Group Output** node to visualize this subpixel.

In the next section, we'll see how we can instance this grid to the shape of an LED panel.

Creating an array of pixels

To execute this step, we'll need to use another **Grid** node. This time, we'll be adding a grid that contains 100 x 100 vertices. The size should be the same as the vertex count. Here's what that node looks like:

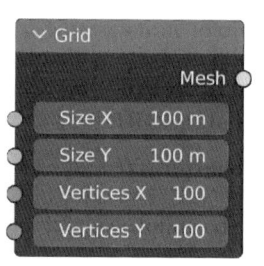

Figure 12.5: The Grid node for instancing

Now, we'll use this grid to instance pixels onto:

1. Let's connect this node to the **Group Output** node to visualize it.

   We can see that we now have a square. The only problem is that there are no subpixels visible yet.

2. To get this node to function as we want it to function, we will need to add an **Instance on Points** node after the **Grid** node (*Figure 12.5*). You will see that everything will disappear. This happens because we did not define an instance yet.

3. Then, drag the first **Grid** node (*Figure 12.4*) into the **Instance** input of the **Instance on Points** node.

This is how the current node tree should look if you've executed these steps successfully.

Figure 12.6: The current node tree

If you take a look at the viewport, you can see that we have rows of pixels.

Figure 12.7: Rows of pixels

This will be your red channel. In the next section, you'll be making the green and blue channels.

Creating an array for every subpixel

Let's now create a channel for every subpixel. We already have the red channel.

Creating the other ones is not as difficult as you might think. We only need to copy the **Instance on Points** node twice. Don't forget to connect the two **Grid** nodes to their respective inputs as we did for the red channel.

This is how that should look if you've executed the steps correctly:

Figure 12.8: The current node tree

We don't see anything happening yet; that's because the other **Instance on Points** nodes have not been outputted to the **Group Output** yet.

Let's fix that by adding a **Join Geometry** node to combine the three **Instance On Points** nodes, as shown in *Figure 12.9*.

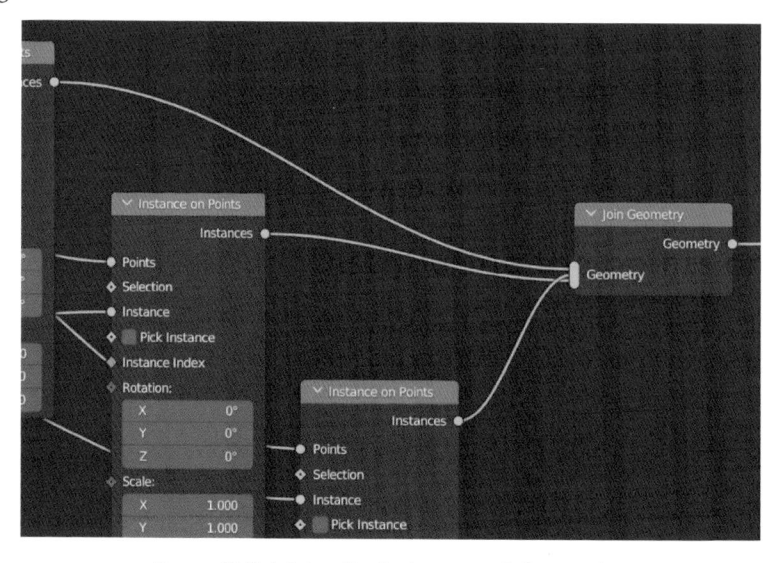

Figure 12.9: Joining the Instance on Points nodes

You will see that, still, nothing is happening.

This is because the three **Instance on Points** nodes are being intersected with each other. To solve that, we can execute both of these steps:

- Drop in a **Transform node** of 0.333 on the **X** axis after the second **Instance on Points** node
- Drop in a **Transform node** of 0.666 on the **X** axis after the third **Instance on Points** node

This will make the three channels move away from each other in the way that we want it. Since every subpixel is 0.333 on the **X** axis, moving them by 0.333 each time will put them side by side.

Figure 12.10 shows how the current node tree should look.

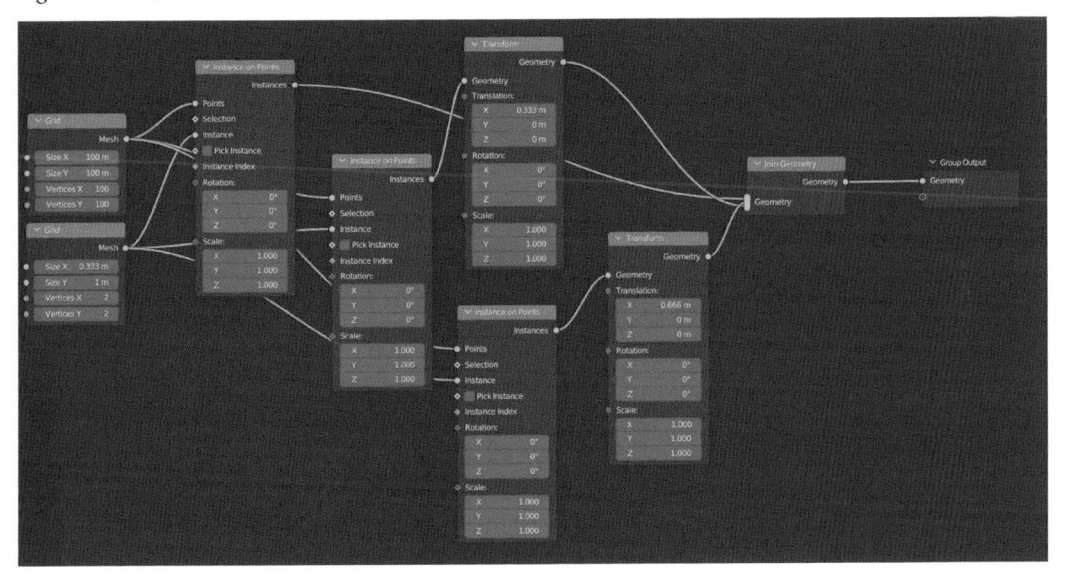

Figure 12.10: The current node tree

And now, we have the base mesh for the LED panel!

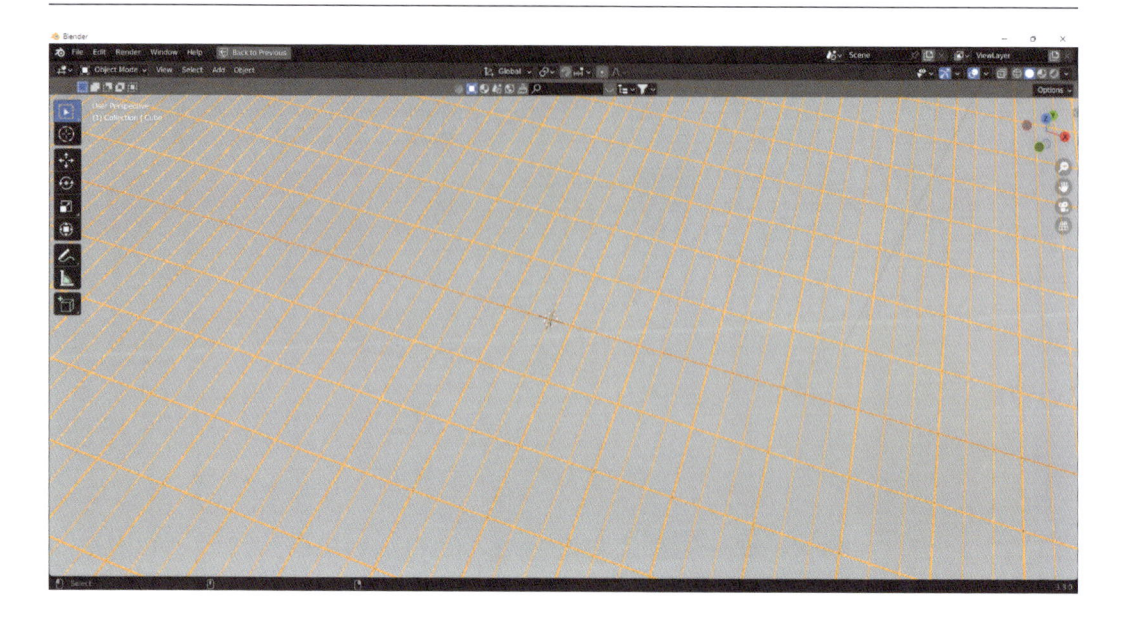

Figure 12.11: The base mesh for the LED panel

In the next section, we will be setting up the **Named Attributes** to transfer the color data of each R, G, and B channel to the Material editor.

Storing the RGB values in named attributes

So, let's begin the process of storing the RGB values:

1. To get started, we first want to use a **Realize Instances** node to convert the instances we've generated to a usable mesh. This is mainly done to avoid problems further on.
2. Drop in a **Realize Instances** node after every **Instance on Points** node.
3. Let's now add an **Image Texture** node. This will allow you to import images into your Geometry Node editor.

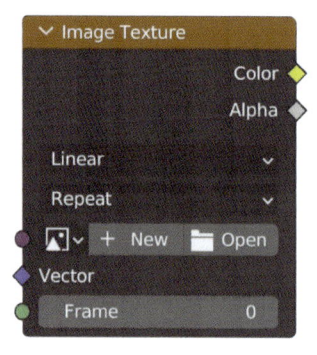

Figure 12.12: The Image Texture node

4. To open an image, you can press the **Open** button that can be found on the **Image Texture** node.

5. You have probably already noticed that this node has a **Color** output. This output consists of three sub-values: red, green, and blue.

   We can separate these values using a **Separate Color** node (also called **Separate RGB** in older versions of Blender).

   Let's connect the **Image Texture** node to the **Separate Color** node, as shown in *Figure 12.13*.

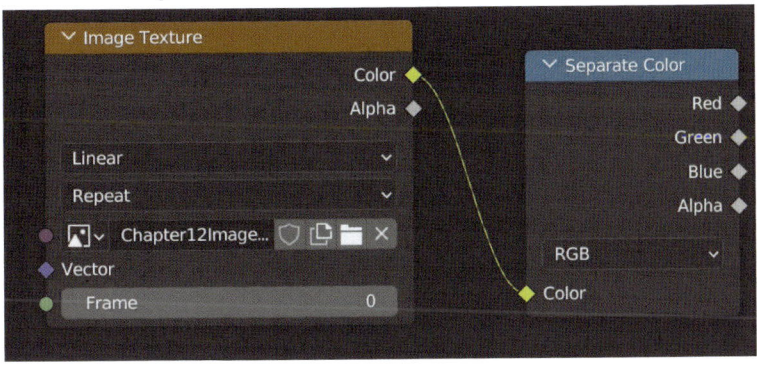

Figure 12.13: Image Texture to the RGB values

Now that we have each **Red**, **Green**, and **Blue** value as a separate output, we can put these in the correct named attribute to send this value to the Material editor:

1. Right after every **Realize Instances** node, let's add a **Store Named Attribute** node. This will allow us to store values.

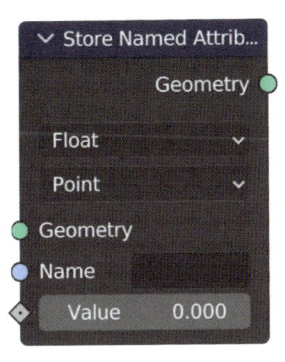

Figure 12.14: The Store Named Attribute node

2. You'll notice that the **Store Named Attribute** node has a **Name** socket. This is the name that we'll use to reference our value to the Material editor. You can think of it as adding an attribute name to your Blender project.

198   Constructing a Procedural LED Panel

Let's add the initials shown in *Figure 12.15* as the names for each of the **Store Named Attribute** nodes.

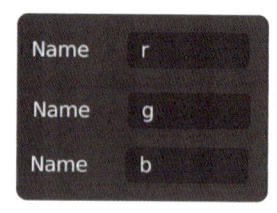

Figure 12.15: The Store Named Attribute names

3. Make sure that your **Store Named Attribute** node is set to **Face** and not **Points**. This will make sure it uses the **Face** as a guide for where to edit the materials. If you don't change it, the LED panel won't work.

4. When you type in the letters, you'll see a plus symbol appear. Make sure to press it; otherwise, it won't be saved as a named attribute.

Figure 12.16: The plus symbol

5. Lastly, we'll need to connect the **Red**, **Green**, and **Blue** outputs from the **Separate Color** node to the **Value** input of the respective **Store Named Attribute** nodes. Do this for each of the three channels.

If you have followed these steps correctly, this is how your current node tree should look:

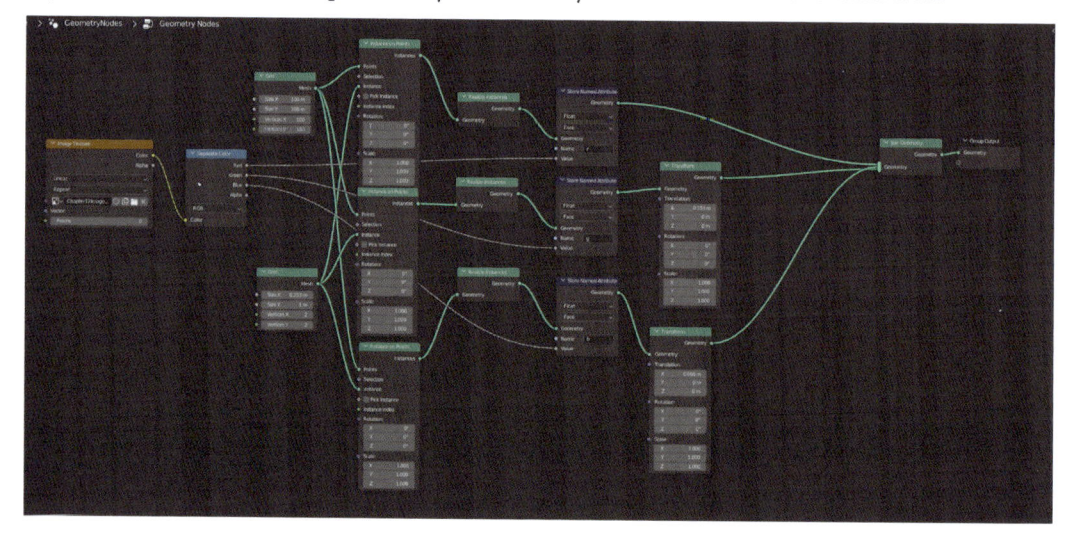

Figure 12.17: The current node tree

Now, we have everything set up to start work on the materials.

Creating materials

Now, it's time to create materials for our subpixels. To do this, let's head to the **Shading** tab. You might notice that there is a default material called **Material**. We will not be needing this, so you can remove it using the **X** button.

Figure 12.18: The default material

Let's also open the **Material Properties** panel, which can be found on the right of your screen.

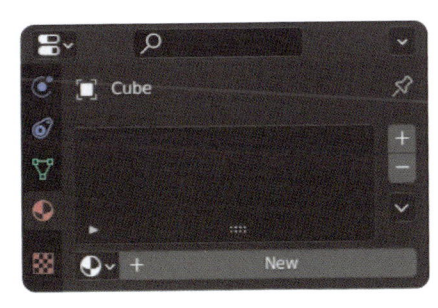

Figure 12.19: The Material Properties panel

Let's create three materials: `Red`, `Green`, and `Blue`. For each of the RGB materials, follow the following steps:

1. Delete the default **Principled BSDF** shader and change it with an **Emission** shader.
2. Connect this **Emission** shader node to the **Material Output** node.
3. Set the color of the **Emission** shader to the color of the correct subpixel color: **Red**, **Green**, or **Blue**.

This is how your **Material Properties** tab should look:

Figure 12.20: The Material Properties panel

Once you've executed these steps correctly, head back to the Geometry Nodes workspace to link these materials to the subpixels:

1. Drop in a **Set Material** node after every **Store Named Attribute** node. This will allow us to set the material of each subpixel separately.
2. Let's also select the corresponding material for each of these nodes: **Red**, **Green**, and **Blue**.

If you've followed all these steps correctly, this is how your node tree should look:

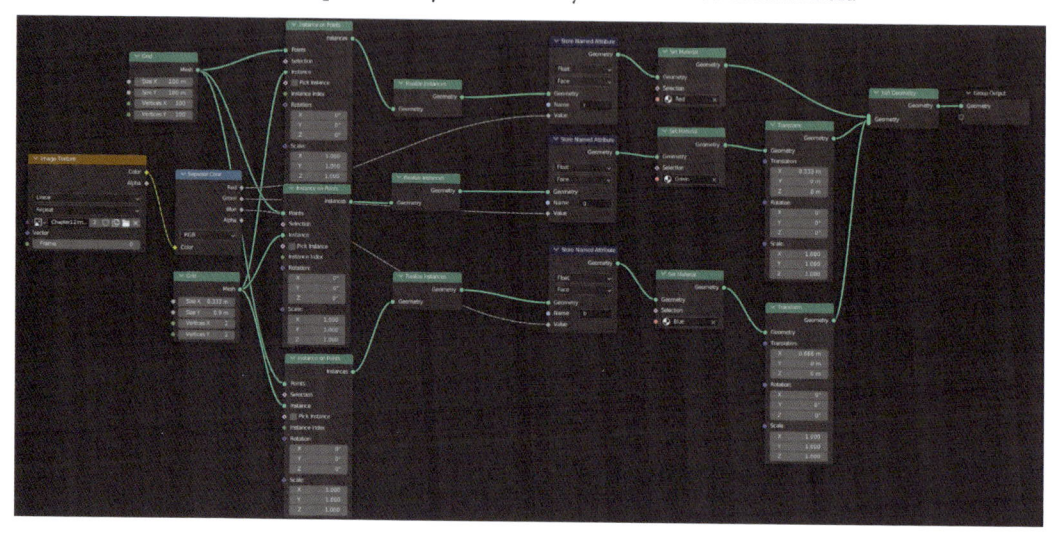

Figure 12.21: The final node tree

You might notice that nothing has happened yet. This is probably because you're still in the **Solid** view. To switch your renderer, press the button at the top of the screen, as shown in *Figure 12.22*. This will allow you to switch your view to the **Rendered** view.

Figure 12.22: Switch to the Rendered view (marked red)

We will now see the subpixels appear. The only problem is that we cannot see our image yet. This is because we still have to link the named attributes to our materials. We will do this in the next section.

Linking the named attributes to the materials

Let's now link the named attributes to the materials:

1. To do this, let's go back to the **Shading** workspace and add an **Attribute** node. This will allow us to read out an attribute.

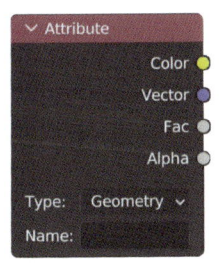

Figure 12.23: The Attribute node

2. In the **Name** socket, add the respective channel name; this will be either r, g, or b, depending on which of the materials you are editing.
3. After that, all you have to do is connect the **Fac** (factor) output of the **Attribute** node to the **Strength** input of the **Emission** node.

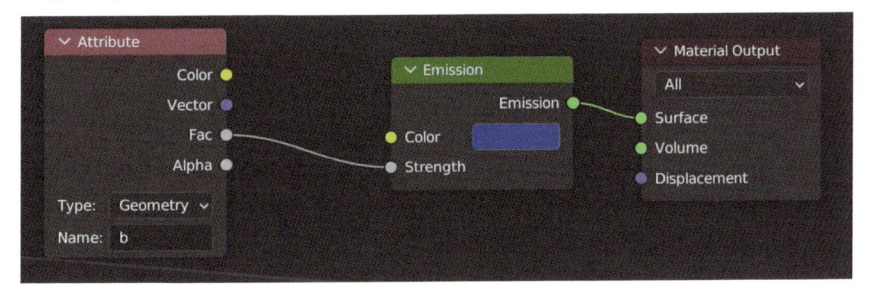

Figure 12.24: The Material node tree

Do this for every channel. Once you have done that, you can see that your LED panel works!

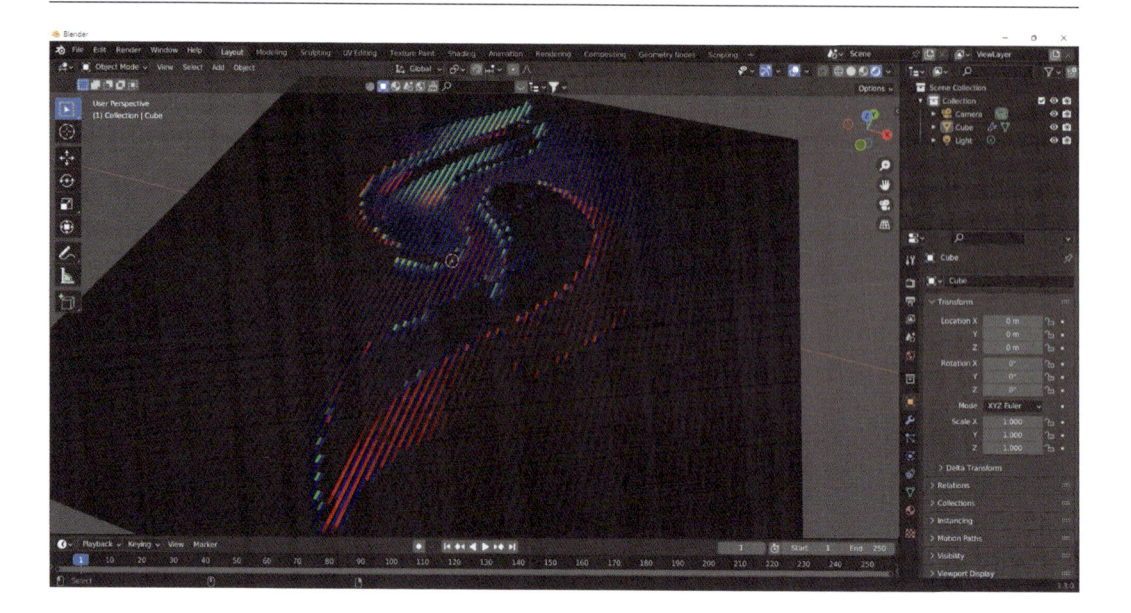

Figure 12.25: The final result

Our LED panel is now done. We are not totally finished with this exercise though; we can still add group inputs to make the node tree easier to use.

Adding group inputs to the node tree

Now that you've successfully made a LED panel, it's time to add group inputs to your LED panel. This will allow you and end users to easily change and adapt attributes in your Geometry Nodes project.

For this LED panel, we will create group inputs for the following attributes:

- **Size X**
- **Size Y**
- **Brightness**

Let's get right into adding these group inputs:

1. The first step in adding group inputs is, of course, adding the **Group Input** node. This will allow us to add easy access to the most used attributes right in the modifier stack.
2. To add the **Size X** attribute, we just have to take the gray node connection of the **Group Input** node and drag it to the **Size X** field of the **Grid** node (*Figure 12.26*).
3. You'll see that a new entry will be created on the **Group Input** node. Take the node connection of this new entry (**Size X**) and drag it to the **Vertices X** field as well.

We do this to ensure that **Size X** and **Vertices X** are the same value, which is very important in this project because, otherwise, we'll have overlapping pixels.

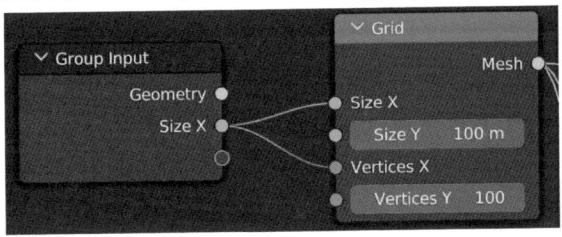

Figure 12.26: Size X in Group Input

4. Now, let's do the same but for **Size Y**. Drag the gray node connection of the **Group Input** node to the **Size Y** field of the **Grid** node. This will, once again, create a new entry in the **Group Input** node. Drag the node connection of this new entry to the **Vertices Y** field as well.

This is how that should look:

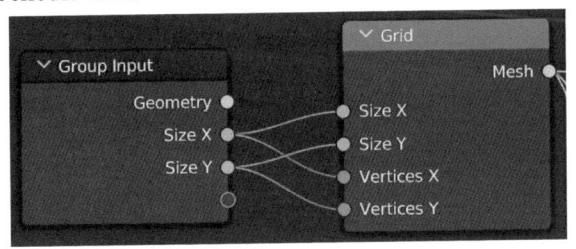

Figure 12.27: Group Input resolution

And that's how you add the option to change the resolution of your LED panel.

5. Now, let's add an option to change the brightness. We can use a **Vector Math** node, set to **Multiply**, between the **Image Texture** node and the **Separate Color** node.

6. In the top socket of the **Vector Math** node, we'll put the **Image Texture**'s **Color** output.

7. For the bottom socket, we'll drag the gray node connection from the **Group Input** node to the bottom socket.

If you've executed these steps correctly, this is how this part should look:

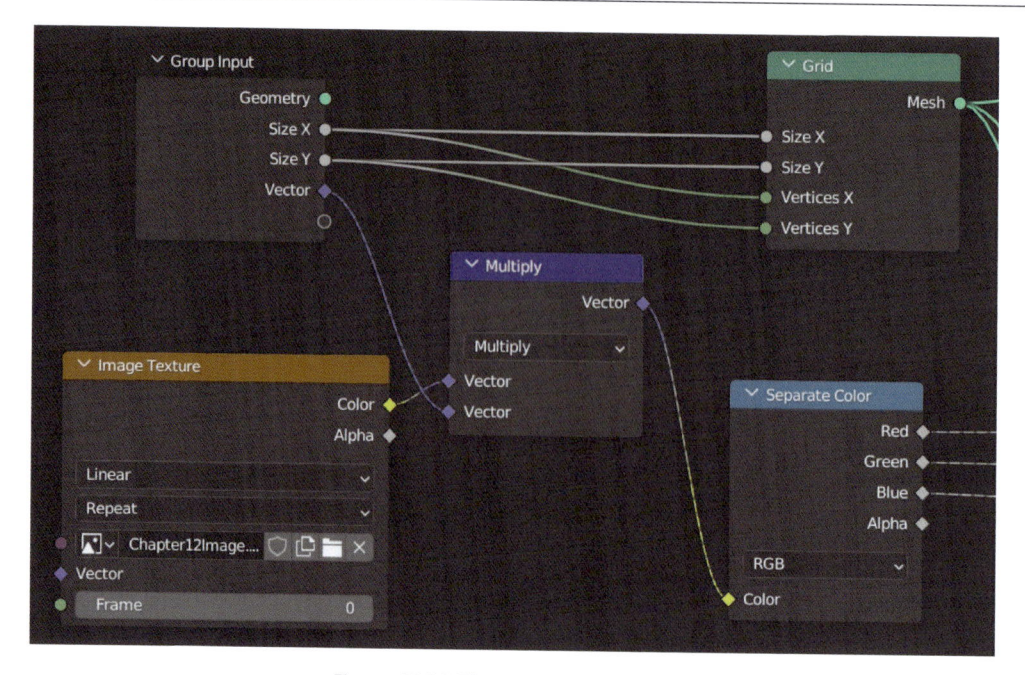

Figure 12.28: The group inputs setup

And that's how you add group inputs to the LED panel!

If you now take a look at your modifier stack, you'll see the values that you've defined appear.

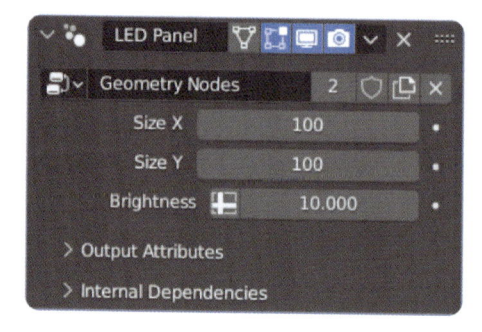

Figure 12.29: The Geometry Nodes modifier

There is still one more thing we need to do; we need to rename the **Vector** value `Brightness`. Along with that, we also want to convert it into a single-value field instead of a three-value field.

To do that, head to the **Group** options by opening the right-hand side of the Geometry Node editor (which can also be done by pressing *N*) and clicking on the **Group** tab.

Let's select the **Vector** entry and change its name to `Brightness`. Let's also change its datatype to **Float**.

And that's everything there is to it! That's how you create an LED panel in the Geometry Node editor!

Summary

In this chapter, we've learned how LED panels work and how to create them. We've also learned how to work with named attributes. In the next chapter, we'll take a look at some tips and tricks we can use in the Geometry Node editor. These tips and tricks will show you small operations you can do in the Geometry Node editor to advance and enhance your workflow.

Part 5 – Best Practices to Improve Your Workflow

As you reach the final stretch of this book, get ready to level up your skills with our last section. From tips and tricks to tackling the most common problems, this part will have you mastering Geometry Nodes in no time.

This section comprises the following chapters:

- *Chapter 13, Tips and Tricks for the Geometry Nodes Editor*
- *Chapter 14, Troubleshooting the Most Common Problems in Geometry Nodes*

13
Tips and Tricks for the Geometry Node Editor

Now that you have finished all the expert exercises, it's time to move on to the chapters you can use to improve and enhance your workflow. This is the first chapter that will help you with this.

In this chapter, we'll teach you how to perform various tasks in the Geometry Node editor, such as remeshing, using volumes, utilizing weight paint, and making use of geometry proximity. These intermediate topics will enhance your workflow by making use of these tips and tricks.

These are the topics that we will be covering in this chapter:

- Converting a mesh to a wireframe
- Remeshing in the Geometry Node editor
- Using volumes to model in the editor
- Aligning instanced objects along a normal
- Linking weight paint with **Geometry** Nodes
- Making use of geometry proximity
- Exercise – making two meshes merge together

All of the topics covered will help you get acquainted with some small details about the Geometry Node editor, one section at a time.

The first thing you'll be learning is how to convert a mesh to a wireframe using only **Geometry** Nodes.

Converting a mesh to a wireframe

First up is the method to convert a mesh to a wireframe, which we have already used in this book. For example, we used it when we wanted to make the tesseract cube in *Chapter 6, Working with the Spreadsheet*.

Let's repeat the basics one more time. The idea is that we want to take a mesh and disregard all the faces from it. This is the first step in making a wireframe effect.

Luckily, this can be done using the **Mesh to Curve** node, which disregards all the faces in its received input.

After that, we can use a **Curve to Mesh** node to convert these curves back to a mesh.

Don't forget to utilize the **Profile Curve** socket; otherwise, your node will not work as intended.

Usually, you'll use a **Curve Circle** node as your profile curve. It's best to use a low-resolution **Curve Circle** node, since the shape of it will be used in the wires of your wireframe mesh. It's also good to use a low radius so that your model does not intersect with its other edges.

Now that you've got a basic idea, let's now demonstrate this method:

1. To get started, let's add a **Suzanne (Monkey)** mesh to our Blender project.
2. After that, head to the Geometry Nodes workspace and add a new node tree to this object.
3. Now, add a **Mesh to Curve** node. Add this node between the **Group Input** and **Group Output** nodes.

   You'll see that your model has already turned into a wireframe.

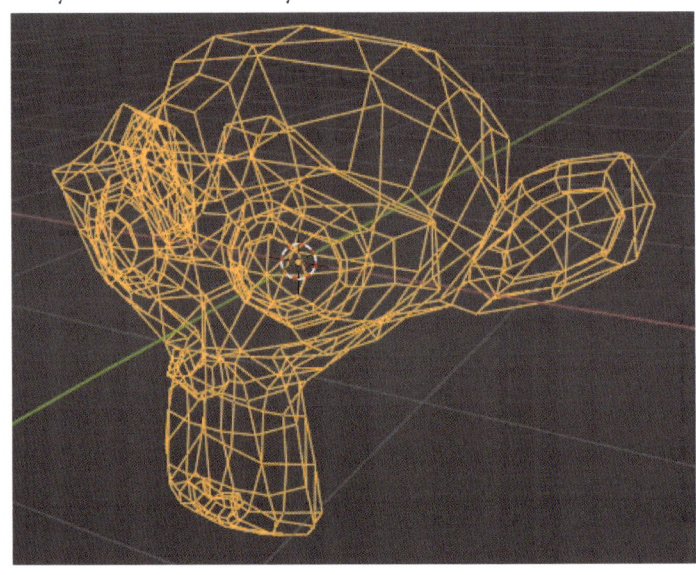

Figure 13.1: The Suzanne object wireframe

4. However, we're not finished yet; if you want to render this, you'll need faces to be present in your model. Right now, that is not the case. We can do this by adding a **Profile Curve** socket.

5. To give these curves a profile, let's use the **Curve to Mesh** node. Drop this node in between the **Mesh to Curve** node and the **Group Output** node, as shown here.

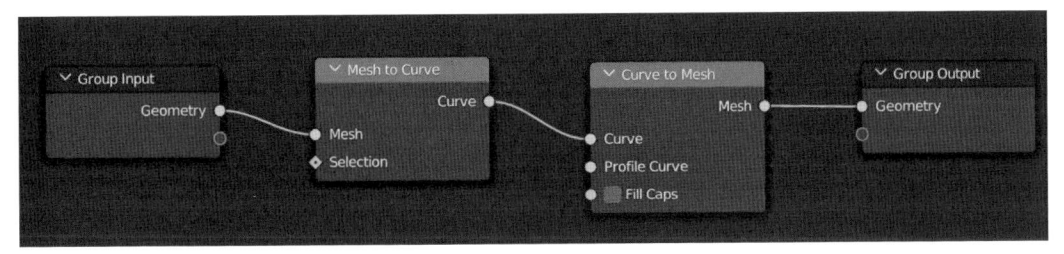

Figure 13.2: The current node tree

6. If you look at your viewport, you can see that nothing has happened, since we do not have a profile curve defined yet. Let's add in the **Curve Circle** node and plug it into the **Profile Curve** input of the **Curve to Mesh** node.

7. On the **Curve Circle** node, let's use a resolution of 4, since that will define the shape of a square. For the radius, let's go with a small amount, such as 0.01 meters. The lower this value is, the thinner your wireframe will be.

You'll now see that the wireframe has appeared. Now, there's only one thing left to solve.

8. If you take a close look at the model, you might notice that the shading behaves weirdly. This is because **Shade Smooth** is automatically applied when using the **Curve to Mesh** node.

To turn this off, we can make use of the **Set Shade Smooth** node, with the toggle named **Shade Smooth** turned off.

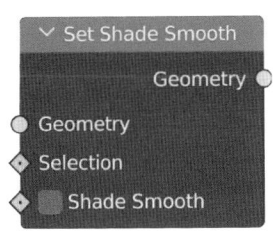

Figure 13.3: The Set Shade Smooth node

That's how you make a wireframe effect using only **Geometry** Nodes!

Remeshing in the Geometry Node editor

Let's now learn how to create a **Remesh** modifier in the Geometry Node editor. This might be easier than you first thought.

When we take our mesh – in this case, the same **Suzanne** mesh that we used in the previous demonstration – and convert it to a volume, we'll have a volume version of our mesh. This can be used to then convert back to a mesh. This will make Blender recalculate the faces to work like a Remesh modifier!

So, let us begin:

1. Once again, let's create a new Blender file, and let's add a **Suzanne (Monkey)** mesh.
2. Once you have done this, head over to the Geometry Node editor and add a new node tree to this object.
3. Now, let's drop in a **Mesh to Volume** node between **Group Input** and **Group Output**.

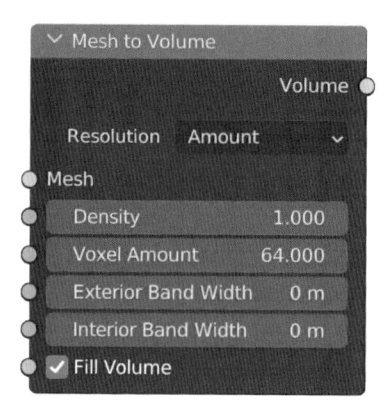

Figure 13.4: The Mesh to Volume node

This node will convert the input mesh into a usable volume.

By default, this node will use an **Exterior Band Width** value of 0.1. This is not what we want; we want an **Exterior Band Width** value of 0 meters, since we do not want any of our mesh to show outside of the model that we defined.

4. Once you've configured this node as you need it, it's time to add the **Volume to Mesh** node.

Remeshing in the Geometry Node editor   213

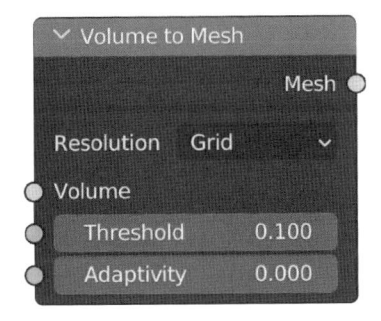

Figure 13.5: The Volume to Mesh node

This node will convert a volume back into a usable mesh. Drop this node in between the **Mesh to Volume** node and the **Group Output** node.

This is what your current node tree should look like:

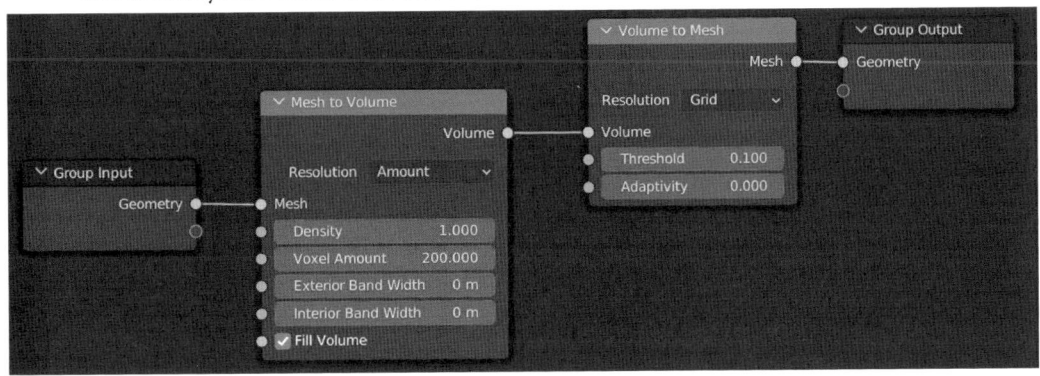

Figure 13.6: The current node tree

If we now look at our viewport, we can see that our **Suzanne** object has been remeshed.

5. There's one more thing we need to do, which is to give the **Mesh to Volume** node more detail/geometry to work with. We can do this by using the **Subdivision Surface** node.

   To make this node work as intended, let's drop it in between the **Group Input** and **Mesh to Volume** nodes.

   This node will basically smooth out your input mesh by adding more geometry.

Keep in mind that this algorithm for smoothing does not work on all models though.

Using volumes to model in the editor

Let's now take a look at a whole different part of the Geometry Nodes workflow, the **Volume Cube** node.

Figure 13.7: The Volume Cube node

This node allows us to custom-model objects in the Geometry Node editor, thanks to the squared node connection on the density value. We can define whether there should be geometry at every given point, thanks to this feature. At the end of this chapter, we will show you an excellent example of this node.

When we pair this with a **Volume to Mesh** node from the previous demonstration, we can create some very abstract art pieces.

In the following demonstration, we will apply a **Voronoi distance** pattern to the **Density** value of the **Volume Cube** node. This will create the effect of a block of cheese!

Now, let's create a new Blender project and add a **Geometry Nodes** node tree to the default cube.

We won't be needing the **Group Input** node, so you can go ahead and remove that:

1. The first node that we're going to drop in is the **Volume Cube** node, as shown in *Figure 13.7*. This node's name describes pretty well what this node does; it places in a cube that's made of a volume. This allows us to apply calculations to it, which can give some interesting results. First of all, plug the **Volume Cube** node into the **Group Output** node to visualize this node.

2. When you do this, you'll see that the volume is now visible. Although we do not need a volume as our final input, we need it to be a mesh. Let's add a **Volume to Mesh** node to fix that. Let's drop this node in between the **Volume Cube** node and the **Group Output** node.

3. Now that we have successfully set up this project, we can experiment with our Voronoi texture.

   Let's add in a Voronoi texture and plug the **Distance** value into the **Density** value of the **Volume Cube** node.

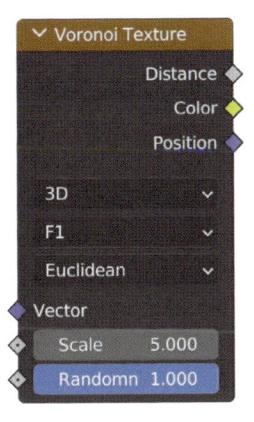

Figure 13.8: The Voronoi Texture node

Note that not a lot of things happen. This might be because you have to change the threshold value of the **Volume to Mesh** node to visualize any result. Along with that, you might want to change the **Scale** value of the **Voronoi Texture** node.

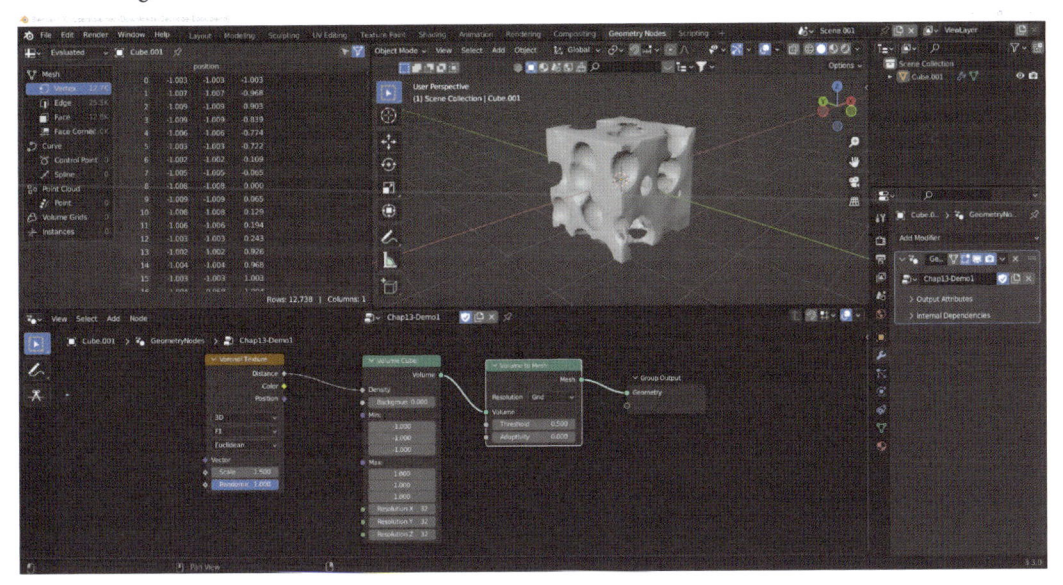

Figure 13.9: A Volume Cube demonstration

We can now see that we have a block of cheese in our Geometry Node editor!

Of course, we can do a lot of epic things with this method, so be sure to play around with this trick because, at the end of this chapter, we'll build on this method with an exercise.

Aligning instanced objects along a normal

You might have noticed that when you want to instance objects onto a curved surface – for example, a torus – the objects you instance will not curve along with the normal of the mesh.

To fix this, you'll need to make use of two nodes:

- The **Position** node: This node will just output the position in space as a squared node connection.
- The **Align Euler to Vector** node: This node will convert any input vector value to an aligned vector value. For this exercise, the input of this node is the **Position** node.

So, let's start this journey by creating a simple instancing example:

1. Open a new Blender project and add an Ico Sphere. Don't forget to add a **Geometry Nodes** node tree to this Ico Sphere as well. Once you've done that, you're ready to move on to making the node tree.

2. Let's start by dropping in an **Instance on Points** node between **Group Input** and **Group Output**.

   Once you do this, you'll see that your Ico Sphere disappears. That's because we do not have an instance object yet.

3. For our instance object, let's take a cube that's stretched on the **Z** axis, as you can see in *Figure 13.10*.

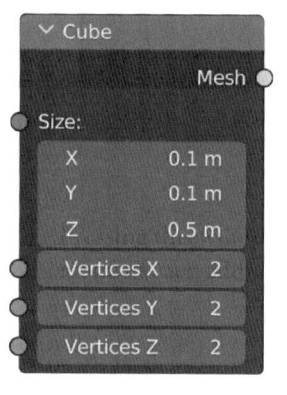

Figure 13.10: The Cube node

> **Important!**
> Don't forget to use a **Join Geometry** node at the end of your node tree to visualize your original mesh!

If you now take a look at your viewport, you'll get the following result:

Figure 13.11: The result

This is, of course, not what we want. We want the poles to be aligned with the normal of our Ico Sphere.

4. To do this, let's add a **Position** node and connect it to the **Rotation** input of the **Instance on Points** node.

5. The previous step did something, for sure, but it's not quite the result that we want. This is because now, we're just converting the position into a rotation. We need to somehow read out the normal to convert this value into a rotation.

This can be done using the **Align Euler to Vector** node.

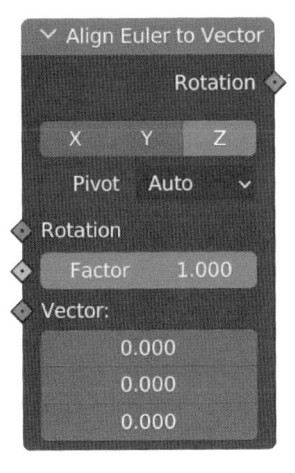

Figure 13.12: The Align Euler to Vector node

6. Let's drop the **Align Euler to Vector** node in between the **Position** node and the **Instance on Points** node. Make sure that the **Position** node is connected to the **Vector** input.
7. By default, this node will not always work. For this specific demonstration, we need to align our objects on the **Z** axis with an automatic pivot.

This is how the current node tree should look:

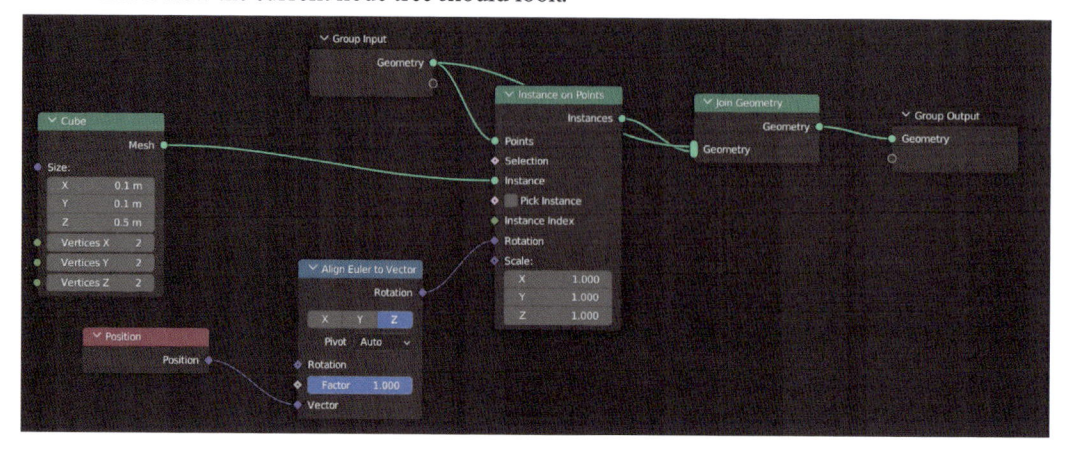

Figure 13.13: The current node tree

When we now look at our viewport, we can see that our long cubes have been correctly rotated along the normal of our Ico Sphere!

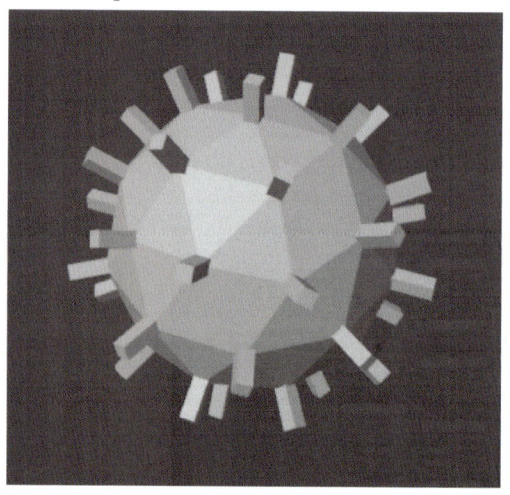

Figure 13.14: The finished result

That's how you align an instanced object along the normal of another object.

Linking weight paint with Geometry Nodes

One of the most important parts of the Blender workflow is making use of the **Weight Paint** feature in the viewport.

Figure 13.15: Weight Paint

This feature allows you to mark regions of vertices with a specific weight value. Normally, this **Weight Paint** feature is used to define where hair should be instanced, using hair particles. But let's say that we want to link these weight values in the Geometry Node editor? How do we do that?

Luckily, this is really easy to do.

You might remember the named attributes from the previous chapter. Luckily, **Weight Paint** is also saved as a named attribute in the Geometry Node editor and can simply be added by adding a **Named Attribute** node to your node tree.

Figure 13.16: The Named Attribute node

Now, we'll show a logical use case of using weight paint in a Geometry Nodes project.

In this demonstration, we'll be showing you how to utilize weight paint in a procedural terrain generator. This can be useful when you want to design a terrain and you need to define roads in it. Using weight paint, doing this is as easy as drawing a line.

Setting up your project

So, let's begin setting up our project:

1. Let's start by adding a 10-meter by 10-meter plane by pressing *Shift + A* in the viewport.
2. After that, subdivide this plane until you have enough resolution. The more resolution you add, the more detail you'll have in your terrain.

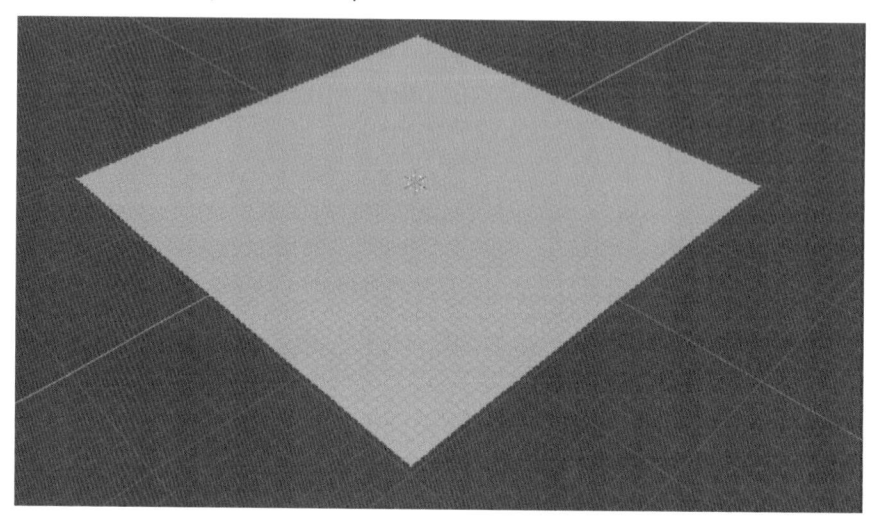

Figure 13.17: A subdivided plane

3. Next up, let's head over to the Geometry Nodes workspace and add a new node tree.

Let's get noding!

Building the node tree

Now, we can begin building our node tree:

1. Start by dropping in a **Set Position** node between **Group Input** and **Group Output**; this will determine the displacement of our terrain.
2. Of course, we do need to drive this **Set Position** node with an **Offset** value. For that, we'll use a **Combine XYZ** node, since we only want the displacement to happen on the **Z** axis. Plug this **Combine XYZ** node into the **Offset** input of the **Set Position** node.

3. Now, go ahead and build the set of nodes visible in *Figure 13.18*. These nodes are used to calculate the terrain generation and consist of a **Noise Texture** node that has been multiplied to give us a hill effect.

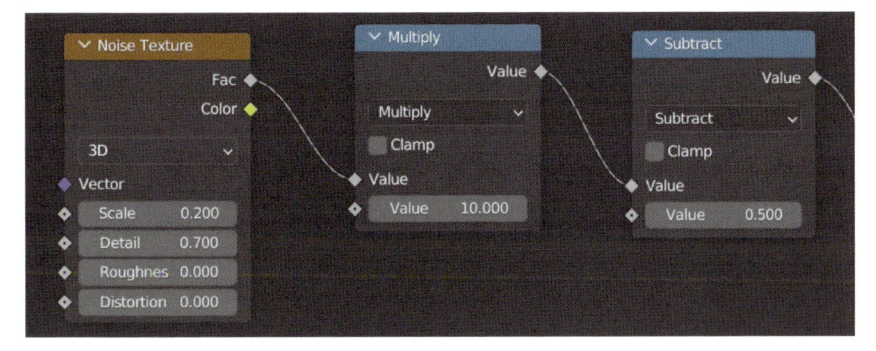

Figure 13.18: Terrain calculation

4. The output of the **Subtract** value will be plugged into the **Z** input of the **Combine XYZ** node. This will make the displacement only happen on the **Z** axis.

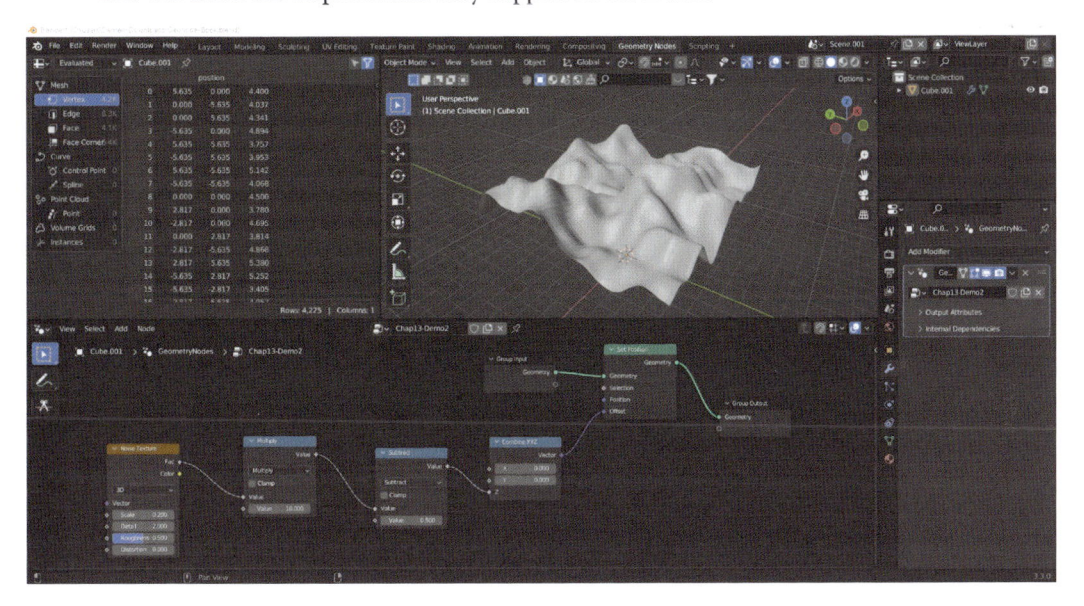

Figure 13.19: The current node tree

We'll now see that our terrain has started generating.

Let's now start on the fun part of this demonstration – deciding where the roads should generate:

1. Enter **Weight Paint** mode by changing **Object Mode** to **Weight Paint**.

Figure 13.20: The Weight Paint option

Once you see your mesh appear blue, you're ready to start drawing your roads!

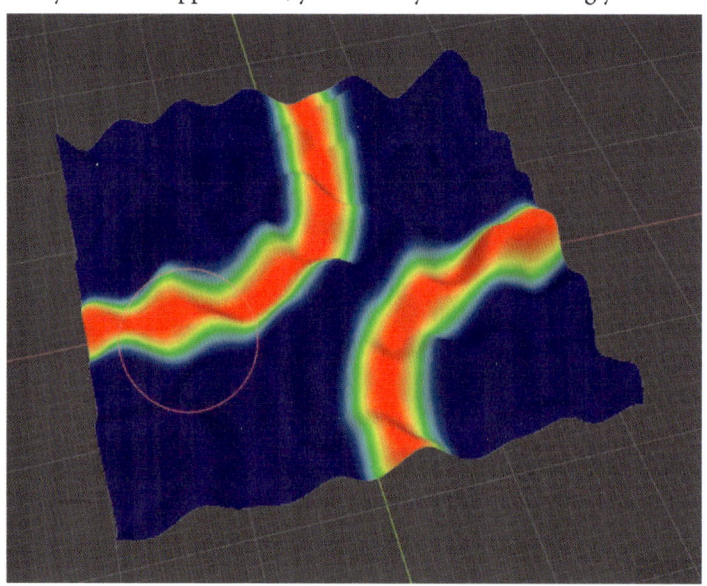

Figure 13.21: Drawing roads using Weight Paint

2. We can see that our painted area will become red, as you can see in *Figure 13.21*. Let's now modify our geometry script a little. We want to remove the terrain where the Weight Paint has been drawn. This will create a road.

   To do that, let's add in a **Math** node set to **Multiply** between the **Subtract** node and the **Combine XYZ** node.

3. Now, it's time to reference our **Weight Paint** to our Geometry Nodes project. To do that, we can utilize a **Named Attribute** node.

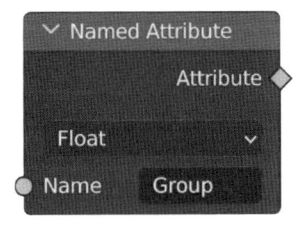

Figure 13.22: The Named Attribute node

Let's add the **Named Attribute** node and select **Point | Group** as our named attribute from the dropdown.

Figure 13.23: The named attribute selector

4. After you've done that, connect the **Attribute** output of the **Named Attribute** node to the second input of the **Multiply** node you've just added.
5. Once you've done this, you can see that the exact opposite of what we want happens; everywhere where there's weight paint, the terrain is visible. Fortunately, we can reverse these values using a **Map Range** node.

Drop in a **Map Range** node between the **Named Attribute** node and the **Multiply** node.

Let's use the following configuration for the **Map Range** node to get it to work as we want it to:

Figure 13.24: The Map Range node

Once you've done this, you'll see that our terrain generator works!

If you follow the preceding steps, even when you draw in **Weight Paint** mode on the mesh, the roads will appear accordingly. That's how you link **Weight Paint** with the Geometry Node editor!

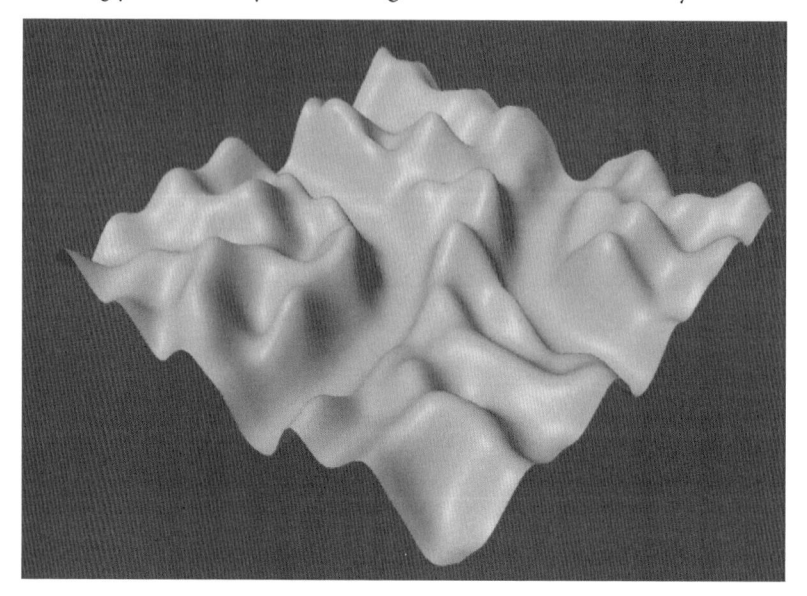

Figure 13.25: The finished demonstration

In the next section, you'll learn how to utilize geometry proximity in your projects.

Making use of geometry proximity

Geometry proximity is a function in the Geometry Nodes toolset that allows you to compute the distance of input geometry, such as vertices, edges, or faces.

There are two approaches to using geometry proximity:

- Manual calculation
- Using the **Geometry Proximity** node

You don't have to make use of the node though, which does not work for every use case, and sometimes, you'll have to calculate the geometry yourself.

You'll only really be needing the manual calculation when you are working with empties, since they do not contain any geometry. Any other use case will probably make use of the **Geometry Proximity** node.

Let's show you how to make use of each of these two methods.

Manual calculation

Let's first start by explaining how the manual calculation of geometry proximity works. You'll need this method mainly when working with non-geometry objects, such as cameras, empties, speakers, and other non-geometry objects.

This involves taking the original position and using vector math to calculate the distance to an empty.

This is how you can do it:

1. Let's start by creating a new Blender project. Then, head over to the Geometry Node editor to add a new node tree to the default cube.
2. We want to instance tons of cubes on a 5 x 5-meter grid. To do that, let's start by deleting the **Group Input** node and swapping it for a **Grid** node.

   We want this grid node to be 5 x 5 meters. Using this size, we'll need about 70 vertices on each side. In the following figure, you'll see what parameters we've used for this demonstration.

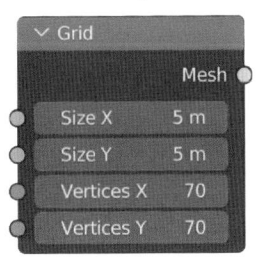

   Figure 13.26: The Grid node with parameters

3. Since we want to instance tons of little cubes on this grid, let's use an **Instance on Points** node to begin the instancing process. Drop in this node after the **Grid** node.
4. To get the instancing process to start, we'll need to define the instance object, which will be a **Cube** node.

   Add in a **Cube** node of 0.05 m on all axes, and plug the **Mesh** output into the **Instance** input of the **Instance on Points** node.

   This is how the current node tree should look:

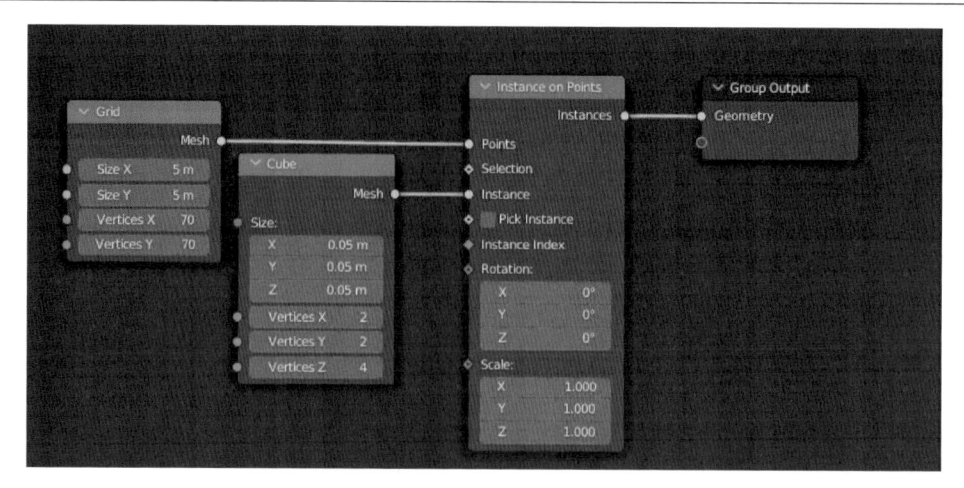

Figure 13.27: The current node tree

5. Now, it's time to get started on the fun part. We want the cubes to scale on the **X** axis when it's close to an empty, so you can go ahead and add an empty with the shape of your choice.

6. To configure this empty, we'll first have to set up a few things:

    I. Firstly, let's add in a **Combine XYZ** node and plug it into the **Scale** input to separate the **X**, **Y**, and **Z** values.

    II. Give the **X** and **Y** values a value of 1; otherwise, these will default to zero.

    III. To ensure our cube **Z** height will never hit zero, we'll need to add in a **Math** node set to **Add**, with a value of 1.

    Now, it's time to create the calculation for the proximity to the empty.

7. Let's add in two nodes, the **Position** node and the **Object Info** node. Make sure this **Object Info** node has been set to reference the empty. It's also important to use **Relative** positioning, since we want to acquire the position relative to the position of the grid.

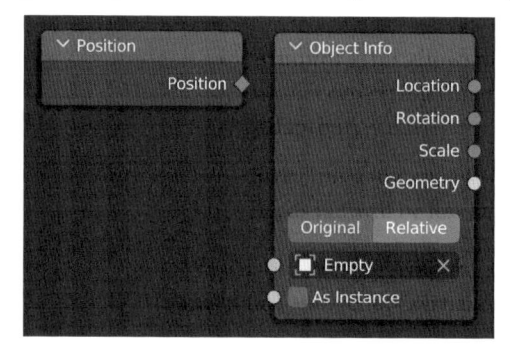

Figure 13.28: The nodes you'll need

8. On top of that, to process these two nodes, we'll also be needing a **Vector Math** node set to **Distance**.

    The **Distance** node will process these two **Position** outputs and calculate the distance from these two points, using some complicated math. More information about this formula can be found at the following link: https://en.wikipedia.org/wiki/Distance.

9. Plug the **Position** and **Object Info** nodes into the **Vector Math** node, as shown here:

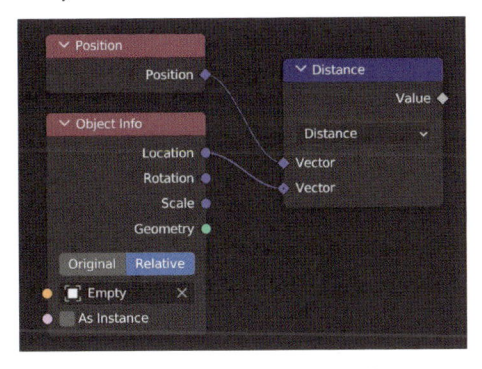

Figure 13.29: A manual calculation of proximity

10. Now, to make the whole calculation work, let's plug the **Value** output of the **Vector Math** node into the top **Value** input of the **Add (Math)** node.

11. We can see that barely anything happens when we do this. This is because the value that it produces isn't that big. To magnify this value, let's use another **Math** node, set to **Multiply**, and drop it between the **Distance** node and the **Add** node. Let's give it a value of 15.000.

    This is how the node tree should look:

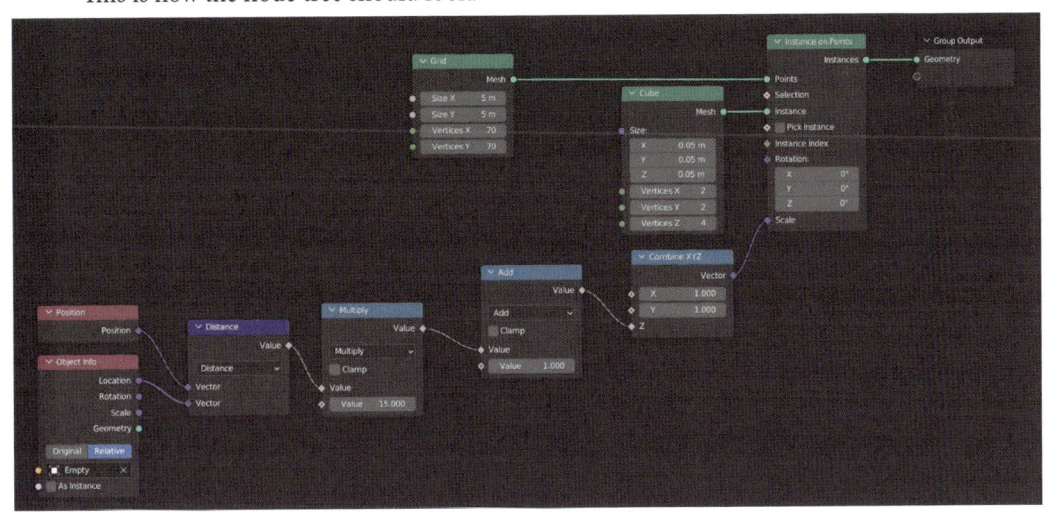

Figure 13.30: The final node tree

If you now take a look at your viewport, you'll see that the cubes are small wherever the empty is, since the distance value is the smallest there.

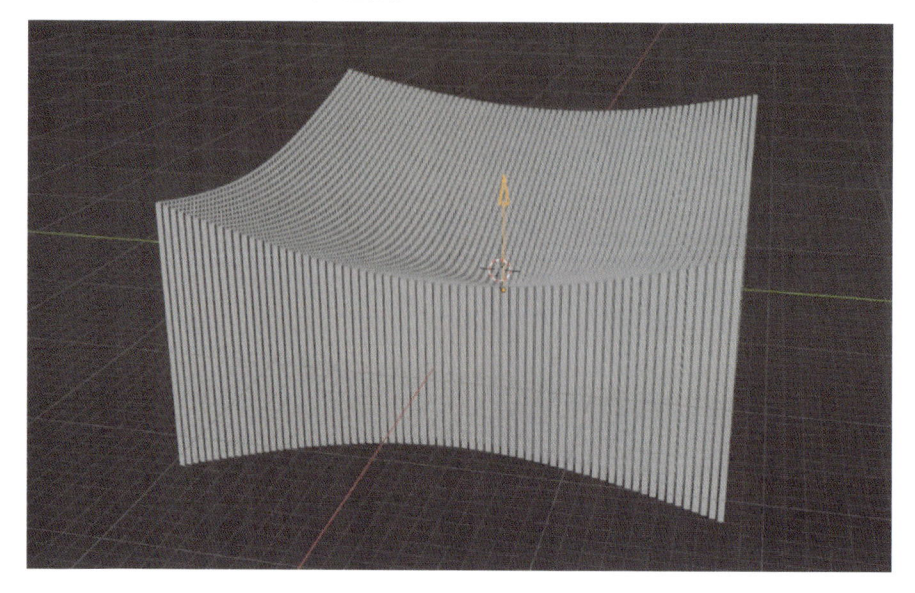

Figure 13.31: The final result

When we move the empty around, you'll see that the effects are immediately noticeable.

Using the Geometry Proximity node

Now, let's discuss how to use the **Geometry Proximity** node with an example.

To modify the original project, let's get rid of these nodes:

- The **Position** node
- The **Distance** (**Vector Math**) node

Let's also add a **Plane** using our viewport, and resize it so that it takes up half of the cubed area. This plane will be the object we'll use as our **Target** object. We can reference this plane by going back to our **Geometry** Nodes and selecting **Plane** in the **Object Info** node.

Now, let's learn how to use the **Geometry Proximity** node:

1. Add in a **Geometry Proximity** node and set the mode to **Points**. This will ensure that it will see every point of our plane as an object to calculate distance on.

2. Let's connect the **Geometry** output of the **Object Info** node to the **Target** input of the **Geometry Proximity** node, and then connect the **Distance** output of the **Geometry Proximity** node to the top value of the **Multiply** node.

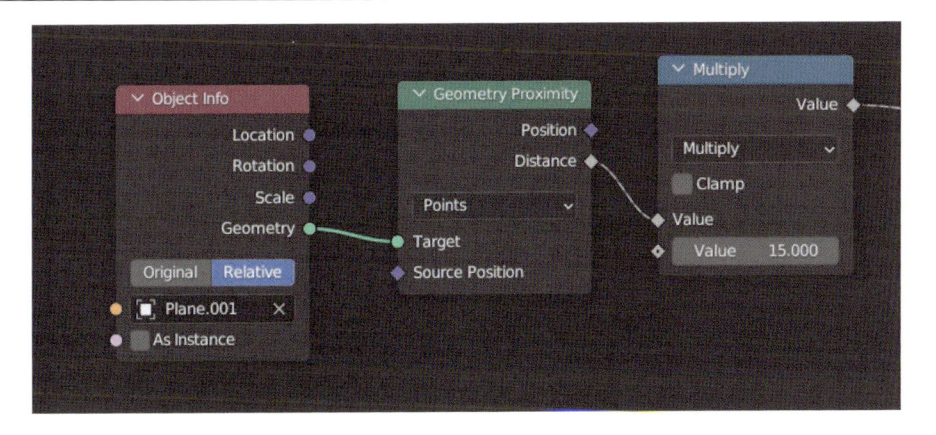

Figure 13.32: Using the Geometry Proximity node

You'll now see that it uses the plane to define the height of each instanced cube where, at each point, we see the cubes lower in height. This is the result we were expecting.

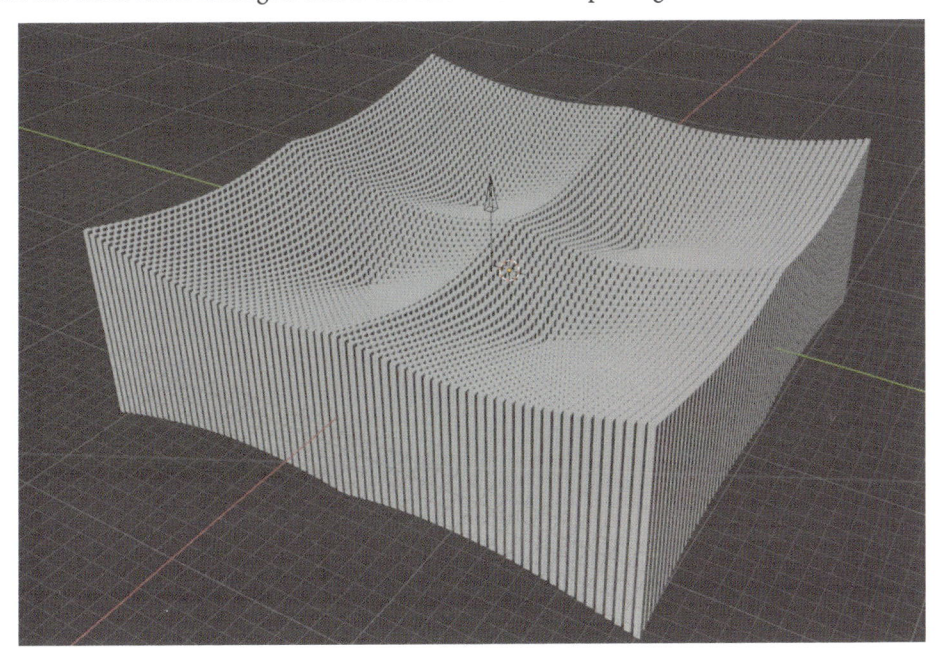

Figure 13.33: The final result

In the following exercise, we'll show you a really cool example of what you can do using **Geometry Proximity** nodes.

Exercise – making two meshes merge together

In this exercise, we'll take two cubes and merge them at places where they're the closest to each other. We will do this with the help of volume cubes, **Math** nodes, and **Geometry Proximity** nodes. Let's get right into it:

1. Let's start off by copying three cubes into our viewport.
2. After that, let's go to the Geometry Nodes workspace and add a new node tree to the second cube.
3. We won't be needing the **Group Input** node, since we'll be making use of a **Volume Cube** node instead, so delete this **Group Input** node and replace it with a **Volume Cube** node.
4. Now, it's time to reference our two other cubes in the Geometry Node editor. We can do that by dragging them from the outline into the editor.

    Alternatively, you can also perform this action manually by adding two **Object Info** nodes and linking the cubes respectively.

> **Note**
> Make sure the **Object Info** nodes are both set to **Relative** positioning.

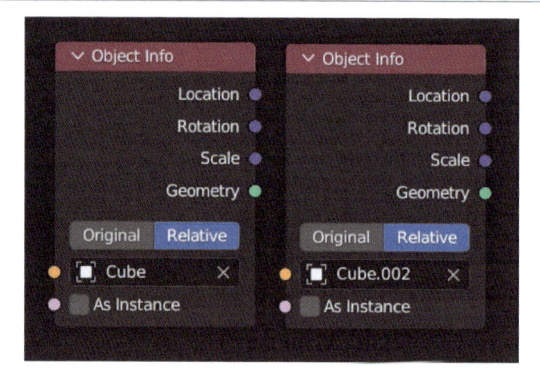

Figure 13.34: The Object Info nodes

5. After every one of these **Object Info** nodes, let's add a **Geometry Proximity** node. Make sure this node has been set to **Faces**.
6. The next step is to perform some calculations using a **Math** node. We'll need to make use of a **Smooth Minimum** formula.

    In simple terms, the **Smooth Minimum** function takes two input values and returns a value that is somewhere between the two input values, depending on how close they are to each other. This will create the merging effect that we're going for.

    If you want more information about this formula, check out the following link:

```
https://en.wikipedia.org/wiki/Smooth_maximum
```

Add in a **Math** node set to **Smooth Minimum** and connect both of the **Distance** values from the **Geometry Proximity** nodes to the **Value** inputs of the **Math** node.

The **Distance** value on the **Math** node will determine how much the cubes will merge together. Let's use a value of 5.

This is how the current node tree should look:

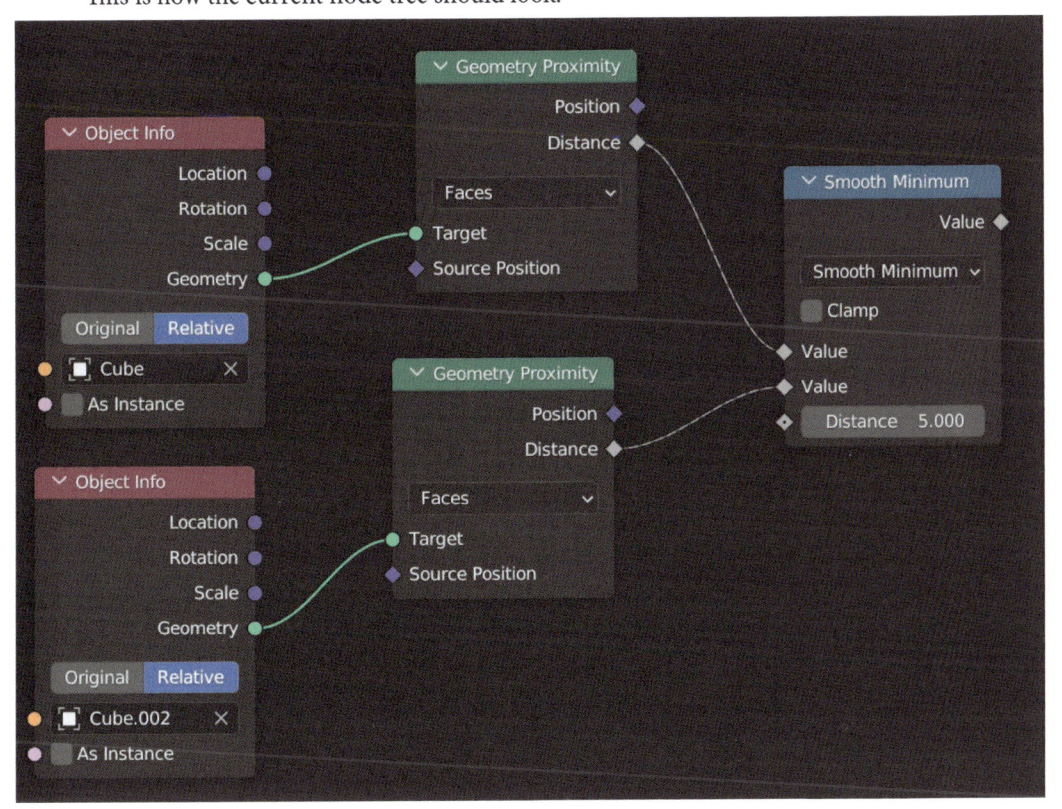

Figure 13.35: The current node tree

7. Finally, let's plug in the output value of the math node into the **Density** input of the **Volume Cube** node. This will make the math node determine the shape of this volume cube.

8. You'll see that nothing happens. This is because we have to modify the **Volume Cube** node a little:

    I. Firstly, the volume cube is way too small. It needs to cover both cubes. Let's give it a size of -5 on all minimum axis and 5 on all maximum axes. Let's also increase the resolution from 64 to 128 vertices on all axes.

    II. You'll now see that you have a big gray square. If this is the case, you're on the right track.

III. All you have to do now is add a **Volume to Mesh** node to convert the volume cube to a visible mesh. Let's use a **Threshold** value of `0.15`.

Now, if you move the cubes around, you'll see that they merge with each other!

> **Note**
>
> If the merging effect is not really visible, you might want to increase the **Distance** value on the **Math** node. This will increase the effect of the merging.

If you've followed these steps correctly, this should be your final node tree:

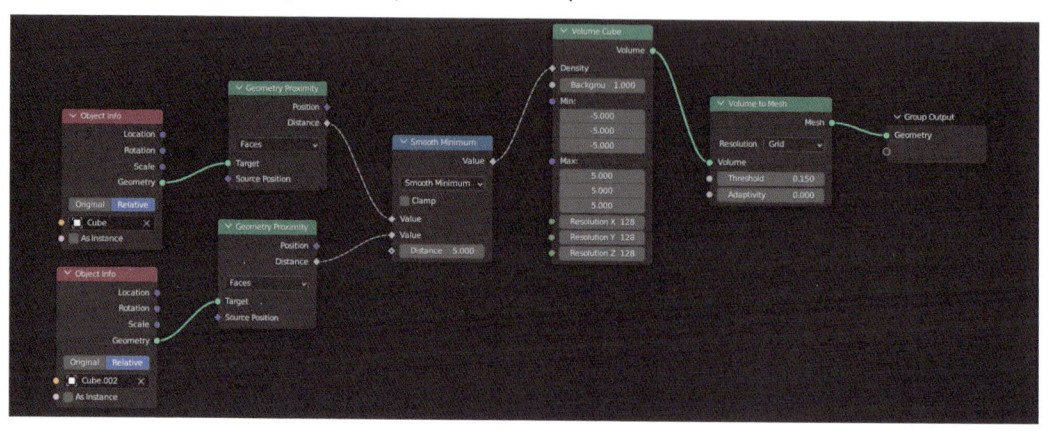

Figure 13.36: The final node tree

This is how the final result will look if you've followed the steps correctly:

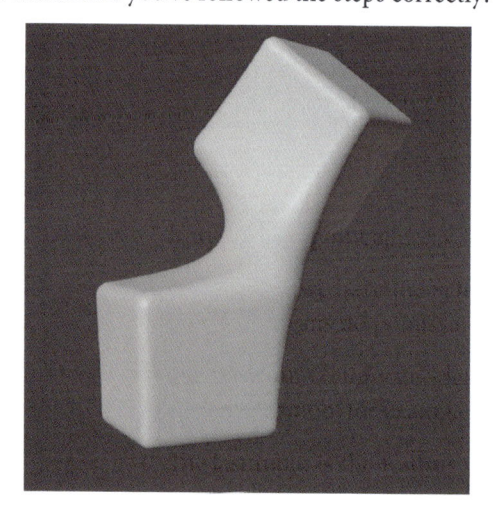

Figure 13.37: The final result

And that's how you merge cubes together using volume cubes, **Geometry Proximity** nodes, and **Math** nodes!

You can also replace the cubes with more complex objects. Remember that if you replace the object, you'll have to reselect it in the **Object Info** nodes.

If you want to add multiple objects to this calculation, you can add an extra **Smooth Minimum** math node after the first math node. You can repeat this step as many times as you want.

> **Note**
> If the effect suddenly stops at a border when moving the cubes, you can solve this by enlarging the area of the **Volume Cube** node.

And with this, we've come to the end of this chapter, where we learned how to utilize **Weight Paint**, **Geometry Proximity**, and more awesome tips and tricks with the Geometry Node editor.

Summary

In this chapter, you learned how to work with various aspects of the Geometry Node editor, such as volume cubes. Alongside that, you learned how to work with **Weight Paint** and **Geometry Proximity** calculations. To top this chapter off, you also learned how to merge objects together using the **Volume Cube** and **Geometry Proximity** nodes.

14
Troubleshooting the Most Common Problems in Geometry Nodes

We have covered a great deal about Geometry Nodes in this book, which hopefully has armed you with enough knowledge to handle most of the issues you might face while using Geometry Nodes. To tie everything up and ensure that your journey is even smoother, through this chapter, we will talk about some of the issues that you might still face while using Geometry Nodes. We will go over the most common problems you might face while working with Geometry Nodes, such as shading irregularities and a slow node tree. Then, we'll show you how to solve them. We will also talk about the common mistakes people make and how to avoid them. Let's get right into it!

Here are the topics we will be covering in this chapter:

- Exploring the most common problems in Geometry Nodes
- Common mistakes when working with Geometry Nodes

Exploring the most common problems in Geometry Nodes

The first problem we'll be troubleshooting is what you can do if your shading behaves weirdly.

My shading behaves weirdly

Shading issues are common in Blender, so it's important to address how to solve these. There are many possible causes of your mesh behaving weirdly. This can range from intersecting meshes and flipped normals to choosing the incorrect shading algorithm. Let's look at some probable causes for shading issues.

Intersecting meshes

The first cause of shading issues is that meshes are intersecting with each other. You can check this by carefully looking at each part of your **Geometry Nodes** tree. This can be the case when you are using a **Duplicate Elements** node, a **Join Geometry** node, or a **Mesh Boolean** node.

When there are intersecting meshes, you might notice a phenomenon called *Z fighting*. This is when you see a flickering mesh in your model.

Normally, this does not happen a lot in Geometry Nodes, but it is definitely possible. You can fix this by checking your Node tree for any nodes that might cause intersecting meshes, such as the nodes mentioned previously. Configuring the nodes so that the meshes don't intersect will solve this specific issue.

Figure 14.1: Z fighting

In *Figure 14.1*, you'll see an occurrence of *Z fighting*.

Flipped normals

Shading issues can also be caused by bad normals, also known as flipped normals.

A normal is used by Blender to see in what direction a particular piece of geometry is facing. In *Figure 14.2*, you can see how these normals look.

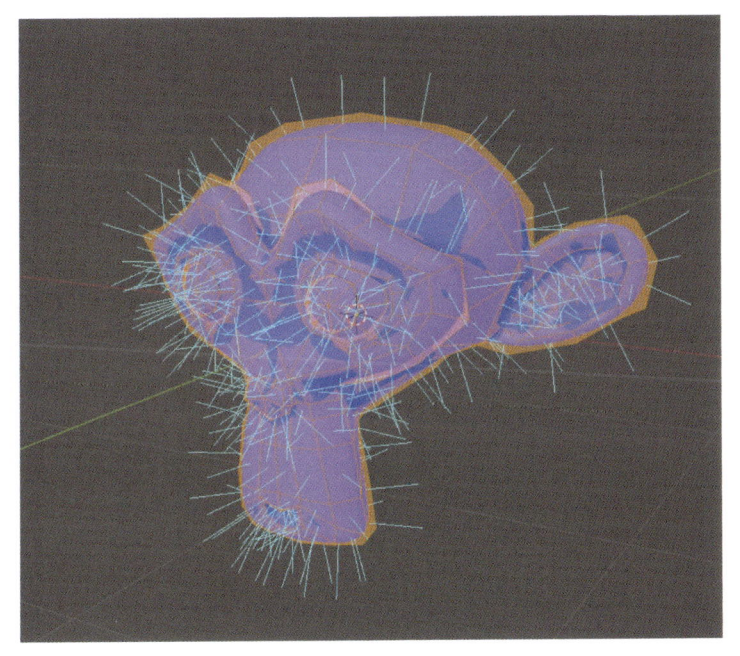

Figure 14.2: Normals

As we know, Blender can sometimes get this wrong and think that our normals are flipped inside out. Luckily, this is simple to troubleshoot and solve. There are two ways you could troubleshoot normals issues.

Using the Face Orientation view

This is the easiest way to determine whether something is wrong with your normals. It involves checking whether your mesh is inward or outward.

When looking at your viewport, you might have noticed the button shown in *Figure 14.3*.

Figure 14.3: Show overlays

Troubleshooting the Most Common Problems in Geometry Nodes

When you press the little drop-down arrow beside this button, you'll get a lot more options.

The only option we'll need to use from this menu for now is the **Face Orientation** one, which can be seen in *Figure 14.4*.

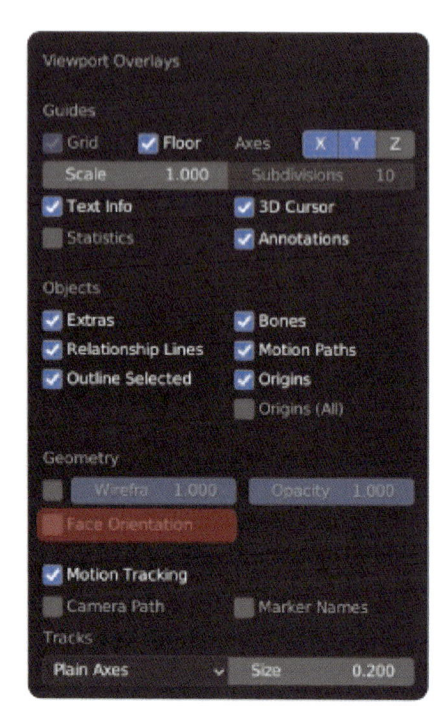

Figure 14.4: Face Orientation option

Clicking on this will color your viewport in red and blue.

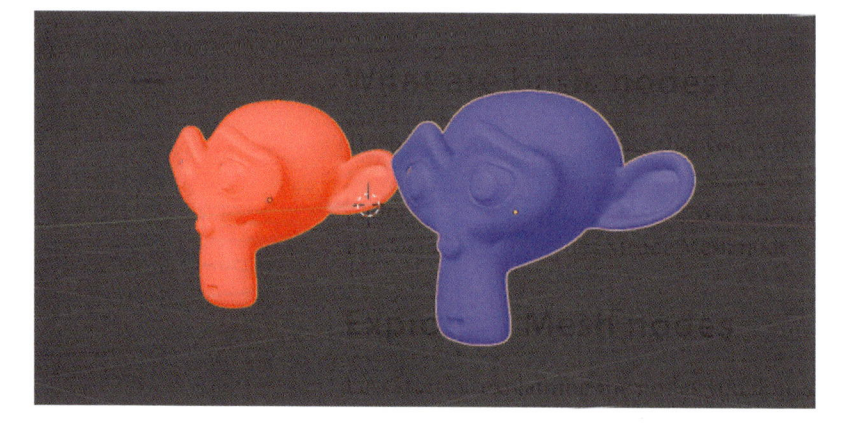

Figure 14.5: Face Orientation view

As you can see in *Figure 14.5*, we can easily differentiate between an object with the wrong normals and one with the correct normals.

A good rule of thumb is to say that everything that appears red to the camera is wrong.

We can fix this by flipping the red normals around, which of course can be done using a node in the Geometry Node editor.

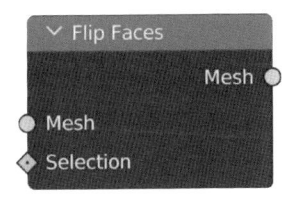

Figure 14.6: Flip Faces node

As you can see in *Figure 14.6*, the node we can use is the **Flip Faces** node, which is responsible for flipping the red normals to blue normals and vice versa. You can use this whenever your normals are inside out.

Displaying the normals

Let's say that the previous solution did not solve your normals problem; you can always take a closer look at your normals using the following procedure:

1. Start by pressing *Tab* to enter **Edit Mode**.
2. After that, you can go ahead and press the **Show Overlays** button, which can be seen in the following figure.

Figure 14.7: Show Overlays

3. Once you are in the **Overlays** menu, you'll see that new entries have appeared since we're in **Edit Mode** now.

4. We're particularly looking for the **Normals** entry in this menu. It is at the bottom of the menu.

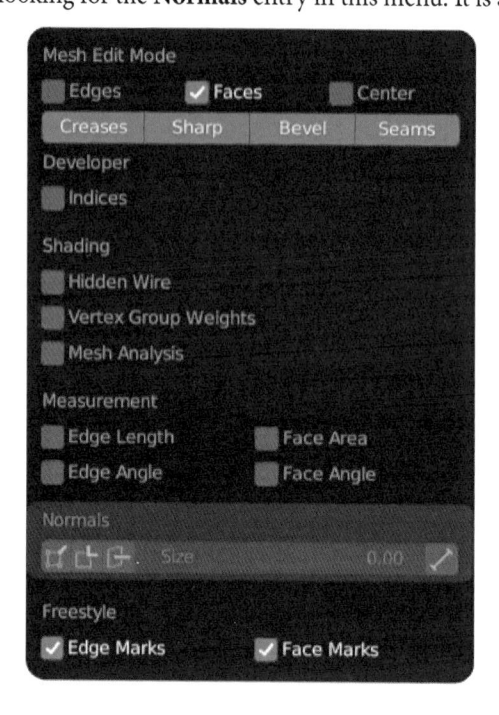

Figure 14.8: Normals entry

Below the **Normals** title, we see three buttons presented. These options will display either of the following normals:

- **Vertex** normals
- **Split** normals or **Edge** normals
- **Face** normals

The most common cause of shading issues is the Face normals. Clicking this option will add a line to every face indicating its normal.

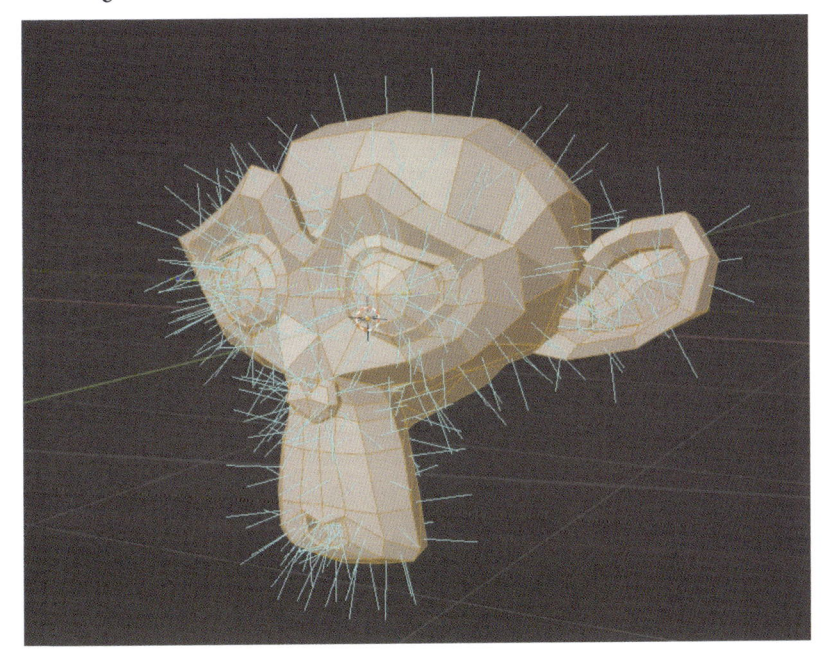

Figure 14.9: Face normals

That's how you view the normals of your models to troubleshoot normal issues. We can utilize the **Flip Faces** node to flip any normals that are facing the wrong direction. This node can be seen in *Figure 14.6*.

Set Shade Smooth

Another common shading issue is caused by shading algorithms. An example of this is the **Set Shade Smooth** node, which performs a complex algorithm to smooth out your mesh. Sometimes, these algorithms aren't suitable, for example, when there are hard cuts in your mesh that need to stay as hard cuts.

Luckily, there are some options to solve this.

The Auto Smooth option

In Blender, we have the option to let Blender calculate the angle of two faces and, by use of a threshold value, decide whether to shade smooth or shade flat.

This is really easy to apply. The first step in enabling this is adding a **Set Shade Smooth** node at the end of your node tree. Make sure that the **Shade Smooth** value is checked on the node.

In this quick demonstration, we'll use the node tree you see in *Figure 14.10*. As the input object, we'll use **Default Cube**, which we add to our project from the viewport.

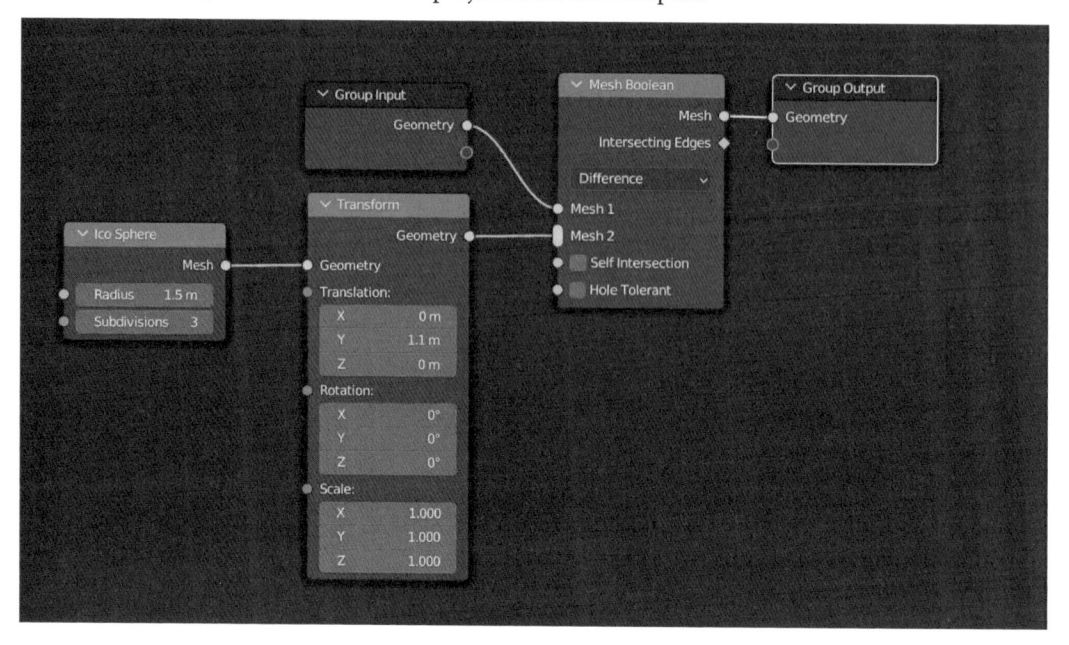

Figure 14.10: Demonstration node tree

The first step, as mentioned before, is to add a **Set Shade Smooth** node at the end of your node tree. Once you do this, you might notice that the shading has worsened.

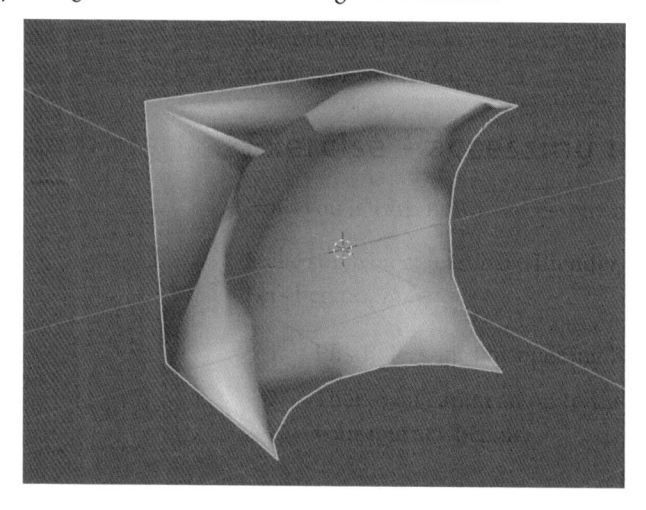

Figure 14.11: Set Shade Smooth

Exploring the most common problems in Geometry Nodes 243

This is because it is now shading everything smooth. We do not want that.

Instead, we want to let Blender decide what to unsmooth automatically. Let's show you exactly how to do that.

In the **Properties** panel, look for the green icon with the three dots, also known as the **Object Data Properties** panel. This can be seen in the following figure.

Figure 14.12: Object Data Properties panel

Once you've clicked on this menu, scroll down until you find the option called **Normals**.

Under this entry, you'll find the **Auto Smooth** checkbox. Once you tick this box, you'll see that the shading issues disappear.

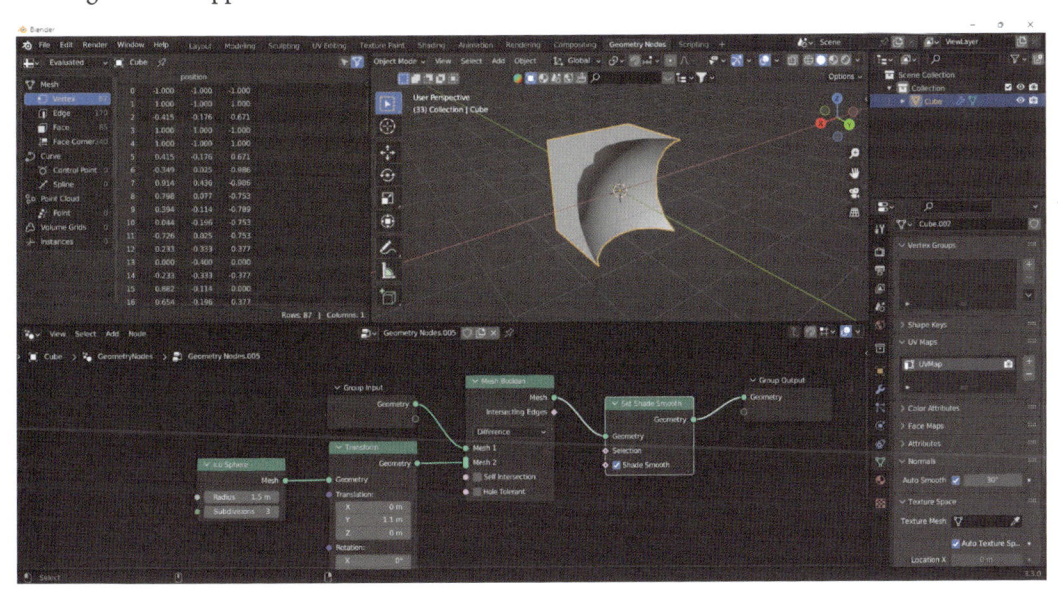

Figure 14.13: Shading issues are gone

Next, we'll look at manual calculation.

Manual calculation

Unfortunately, the previous option will not always work if you have complex node trees. Luckily, we can perform this calculation manually as well.

Let's uncheck the **Auto Smooth** checkbox and then go back to our node tree.

We will now create a part of the node tree where it manually calculates the angle of an edge and decides whether it's less than the given threshold.

We'll need two nodes to complete this calculation:

- The **Edge Angle** node

    This node will return the angle between any face as an **Angle** value.

- A **Math** node set to **Less Than**

    This math node will be used to see whether the angle is below our desired threshold. The output of this node is a Boolean, which we can put into the **Shade Smooth** input of our **Set Shade Smooth** node.

Let's start this demonstration:

1. We'll begin by putting both nodes in the Geometry Node editor, but don't connect them yet.
2. Once you've put them both in, let's connect the **Edge Angle** node to the **Value** input of the **Less Than Math** node.
3. For **Threshold**, we'll enter a value of 0.530. This equates to 30° in radians.
4. All that's left to do now is to connect the **Value** output of this **Math** node to the **Set Shade Smooth** input.

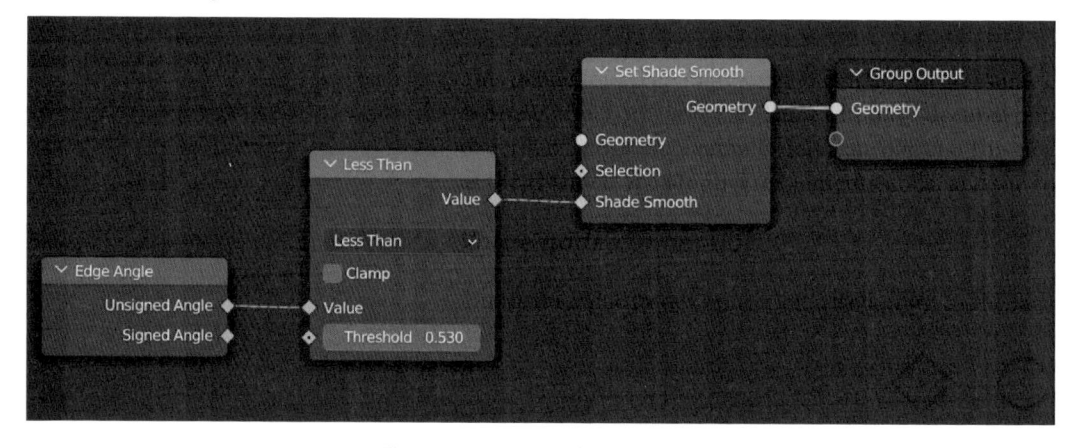

Figure 14.14: Manual calculation

That's all there is to it! That's how you solve most of your shading issues!

My node tree is very slow

Slow node trees can be the result of heavy operations, which can be difficult to troubleshoot. This can make your viewport experience very slow and unworkable. Sadly, this is a very common problem. Luckily, it's easy to diagnose and solve.

Let's now take a look at the possible causes of why your node tree can be slow.

Exploring the probable causes of a slow node tree

The speed of your node tree is dependent on a lot of values. These include the following:

- The number of subdivisions in your geometry
- The number of vertices, edges, and faces in your geometry
- The number of heavy calculations in your node tree

Here are some nodes that are quite performance-heavy for an average computer:

- **Instance on Points** node
- **Mesh Boolean** node
- **Subdivision Surface** node
- **Subdivide Mesh** node
- **Volume to Mesh** node

These nodes are especially dangerous because they are able to generate a huge amount of geometry with relatively low values. So, this can make your node tree really slow. Use these nodes with caution.

But if this is not the case, we can move on to the next step where we will perform some debugging using **Timing Overlay**.

Checking node tree speeds using Timing Overlay

In the following demonstration, we've done something that you should absolutely not do, which is adding an multiple **Subdivide Mesh** nodes. This node tree has been designed to show the effect of **Timing Overlay** easily.

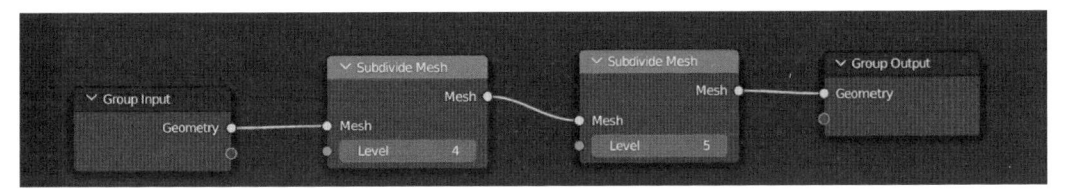

Figure 14.15: Subdivide Mesh load generator

But how do we now check the load of these nodes?

It's surprisingly easy to do. You might remember the **Show Overlays** button we used in a previous section; this button comes back in the Geometry Node editor. You can find it in the upper-right corner of the Geometry Node editor.

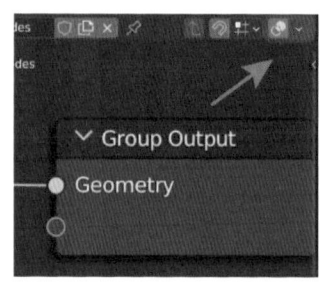

Figure 14.16: Show Overlays button

Go ahead and click on this button. You'll see that an extra menu with various options pops open.

Figure 14.17: Node Editor Overlays menu

We're looking for the entry called **Timings**, which will display the timings above each of the nodes, making it really easy to see where your node tree is being slowed down.

Once you enable this, you'll see these values appear on your node tree.

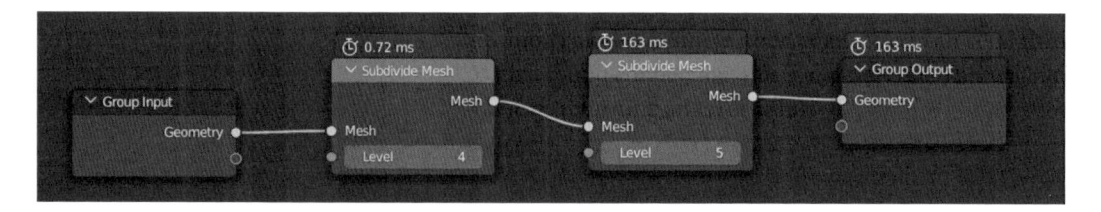

Figure 14.18: Timings overlay

We can see that primarily, the second **Subdivide Mesh** node slows down our node tree by 163 milliseconds.

At the end of our node tree, we see the **Group Output** node, which displays the total duration of our node tree.

In the next section, we'll take a look at the common mistakes when working in the Geometry Node editor, which are mistakes that everyone can make.

Common mistakes when working with Geometry Nodes

Everyone makes mistakes, so in this section, let's look at the mistakes that are the most common in the community.

When the chosen material doesn't appear on the model

This is a common mistake among beginners. Sometimes, when you're making use of node primitives, Blender will not put the material that you choose in the **Material Properties** menu on your model because Blender does not listen to the **Material Properties** menu when working with Geometry Nodes. Instead, you'll need to define your material in the Geometry Nodes node tree.

This can be done by adding a **Set Material** node in a **Geometry** line where you want the material to be changed, as demonstrated in *Figure 14.18*.

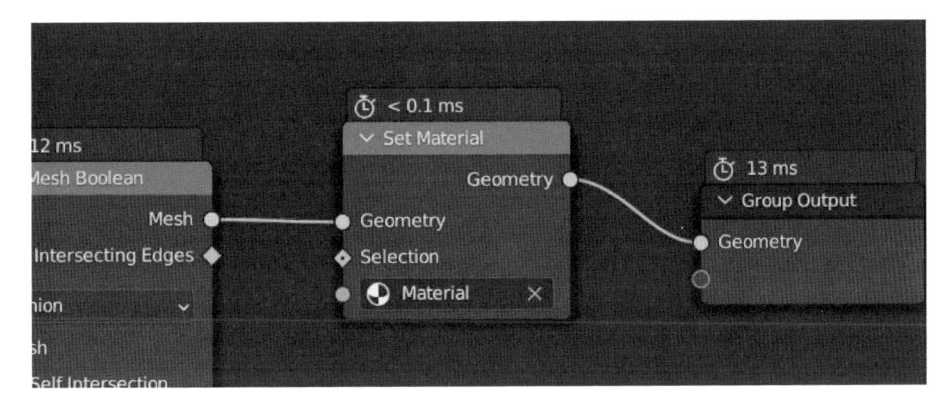

Figure 14.19: Set Material node

Onto the next mistake.

Applying a modifier makes parts of the mesh disappear

This problem is usually caused by instances. Instances will not be visible once you apply your Geometry Nodes modifier.

This can be fixed by dropping in a **Realize Instances** node at the end of your node tree, which will convert all instances to real geometry. This node can be seen in *Figure 14.20*.

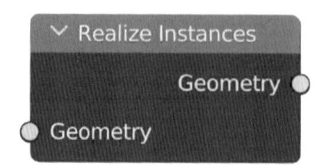

Figure 14.20: Realize Instances node

And that's how you can troubleshoot issues in parts of your workflow in the Geometry Node editor!

We've now come to the end of this chapter, where you learned about some things you can do to troubleshoot problems and avoid mistakes in the Geometry Node editor.

We've also come to the end of the book, which took you through Geometry Nodes in Blender.

Summary

In this chapter, you've learned how to deal with various cases of shading issues, along with the use of normals in Blender and how to utilize **Timing Overlay** in the Geometry Node editor. We also talked about how you can troubleshoot and solve some of the most common issues in the Geometry Node editor, such as shading issues and slow node trees.

We've now come to the end of this chapter.

Appendix
Important Shortcuts

You can always come back to this page to check out handy shortcuts if you've forgotten them. (Some shortcuts may be related to an add-on explained in *Chapter 3, Must-Have Add-Ons for Building Node Trees*.)

Shortcut	Goal
Shift + A	Bring up the **Add** menu
L	Select linked nodes
Shift + D	Duplicate selected node
Alt + 🖱	Auto-connect nodes
Shift + S	Switch node types
/	Add reroutes
O	Connect node to group output
Shift + W	Open Node Wrangler
Shift + Alt + L	Modify a node label
N	Bring up the right-hand menu
G	Move nodes

Index

A

add-ons
  accessing 37
  enabling 36, 37
  installing, in Blender 36
Align Euler to Vector node 216-218
Attribute node 201

B

Bezier Segment Node Primitive 51, 52
Blender
  add-ons, installing 36
Boolean input/output node connection 8
Booleans
  using, in mesh 141, 142

C

color input/output node connection 10
Combine XYZ node 118
Cone Node Primitive 47, 48
converter node 25
  Curve to Mesh node 25
  Mesh to Volume node 26, 27
  Volume to Mesh node 27
convex hull 178
  creating, around objects 179
  wireframe, creating from 179-182
Cube node 91
Cube Node Primitive 43, 44
Curve Circle node 210
curve nodes 48
  locating 48
Curve Primitives menu 49
  Bezier Segment Node Primitive 51, 52
  Curve Circle Node Primitive 50, 51
  Curve Line Node Primitive 49, 50
  Spiral Node Primitive 53, 54
  Star Node Primitive 52, 53
Curves
  noise, adding 117
  randomizing, with Random Value node 118-121
  thickness 124
Curve tab, Spreadsheet 83
  Control Point tab 83
  Spline tab 83
Curve to Mesh node 25, 125
  Fill Caps 25
  Profile Curve 25
  using 210

Cyan, Magenta, Yellow, and Key (CMYK) color mixing 191
Cylinder Node Primitive 47

D

datasets, Spreadsheet
  curve 83
  instances 83
  mesh 82
  point clouds 83
  volume grids 83
difference mode 142
  demonstrating 142, 144
Distribute Points on Faces node 20, 21
Duplicate Elements node 86, 91

E

Emission node 201
Extrude Mesh node 18, 19, 108-110
  demonstrating 138, 139
  random values, using with 140, 141

F

Face Orientation view
  used, for troubleshooting normals issue 237-239
Fill Curve node 106, 108, 110
flipped normals 237
Float Curve node 125

G

geometry input/output node connection 9
Geometry Node editor 4, 5, 99, 100
  input and output shapes 7
  multi-connection inputs 11
  node connection colors 8
  Remesh modifier, creating 212, 213
  standard Geometry Nodes blocks 6
  volumes, used for modeling 214-216
Geometry Nodes
  common mistakes, among beginners 247, 248
  shading issues 235
  slow node trees 245
  usage criteria 5
Geometry Nodes Modifier 4, 5
Geometry Nodes project
  creating 54-58
Geometry Node system 4
  accessing 11-13
geometry proximity 224
  Geometry Proximity node, using 228, 229
  manual calculation 225-228
  using 224
Geometry to Instance node 24, 85, 91
grassy field, creating
  blade of grass, modeling 71
  Geometry Node editor, setting up 72
  grass, removing 75, 76
  Group Inputs, for adding sliders to modifier 79, 80
  idea, sketching 70
  material, linking to mesh 76-78
  nodes 70
  node tree, cleaning up 78, 79
  points, distributing 72-75
  points, instancing 72-75
  terrain, modeling 71
  utilizing 70
Grid node 191
Grid Node Primitive 44

Index 253

Grid Primitive
  nodes, exploring 60
  node tree, building 60-62
  points, distributing 59
Group Input node 6, 202
Group Input 184, 185
  adding, to node tree 202-204
  experimenting with 68
  including 169
  Leaf Count, implementing 170
  Plant Height, implementing 169
  renaming 170-173
  utilizing 69, 70, 169
Group Output node 7

I

Ico Sphere Node Primitive 45, 46
Image Texture node 196, 197
input and output shapes, Geometry Node editor 7
  round input/output node 7
  squared input/output node connection 8
instanced objects
  aligning, along normal 216-218
instance node 23
  Geometry to Instance node 24
  Realize Instances node 24
  translating 23
Instance on Points node 22
instances
  randomizing 66-68
integer input/output node connection 9
intersect mode 141, 142

J

Join Geometry node 17, 216
Join Strings node 103

L

LED panels 190
  working 191

M

material input/output node connection 11
Material Properties panel 199, 200
Math nodes 110
mesh
  Booleans, using 141, 142
  converting, to wireframe 210, 211
  difference mode, demonstrating 142-144
  extruding 138
  noise, adding 144
Mesh Line Node Primitive 46, 47
mesh nodes 43
  exploring 15
  Extrude Mesh node 18, 19
  Join Geometry node 17
  locating 43
  Set Shade Smooth node 18
  Subdivision Surface node 16, 17
Mesh Primitives menu 43
  Cone Node Primitive 47, 48
  Cube Node Primitive 43, 44
  Cylinder Node Primitive 47, 48
  Grid Node Primitive 44
  Ico Sphere Node Primitive 45, 46
  Mesh Line Node Primitive 46, 47
  UV Sphere Node Primitive 44

Mesh tab, Spreadsheet 82
   Edge tab 83
   Face tab 83
   Vertex tab 83
Mesh to Curve node
   using 210
Mesh to Points node 21
Mesh to Volume node 26, 27, 212
multi-connection inputs 11
   geometry multi-connection input 11
   string multi-connection input 11
must-have add-ons
   exploring 29

N

named attributes 189, 190
Node Arrange add-on 34
   using 34, 35
node connection colors,
      Geometry Node editor
   Boolean input/output node 8
   color input/output node 10
   geometry input/output node 9
   integer input/output node 9
   material input/output node 10
   string input/output node 10
   value input/output node 10
   vector input/output node 8, 9
node primitives 41
   features 42
   locating 42
nodes 15
nodes, for converting strings into geometry
   Fill Curve node 106
   String to Curves node 105

nodes, for converting strings to usable mesh
   Extrude Mesh node 108, 109
   Fill Curve node 108
   String to Curves node 107
nodes, for creating strings
   String node 102
   Value to String node 102
nodes, for modifying strings
   Join Strings node 103
   Replace String node 104
   Slice String node 104
   String Length node 103
node tree
   array, creating for every subpixel 193-195
   array of pixels, creating 192, 193
   creating 146, 157, 191
   creating, for procedural spiderweb
      generator 178
   group inputs, adding 202-204
   group inputs, utilizing 169
   leaves, creating 162-166
   materials, creating 199, 200
   named attributes, linking to
      materials 201, 202
   organizing, with Reroutes 186, 187
   pot, creating 166-168
   RGB values, storing in named
      attributes 196-198
   single subpixel, creating 191
   stem, creating 158-161
Node Wrangler add-on 29
   quick access panel 32, 33
   shortcuts 33, 34
   using 30-32
noise
   adding, to Curves 117
   adding, to mesh 144-146
Noise Texture node 118

O

objects
    instancing, on points 63-66
    merging, Volume Cube and Geometry Proximity nodes used 230-233

Offset by Noise Textures 121-123

Offset by Random values
    Curves, randomizing 118-121

P

Point Cloud tab, Spreadsheet 83

Points nodes 19
    Distribute Points on Faces node 20, 21
    Instance on Points node 22
    Mesh to Points node 21

Position node 216

procedural spiderweb generator
    convex hulls 178
    convex hulls, creating around objects 179
    detail, adding to wireframe 182-184
    node tree, creating 178
    randomization, adding 182-184
    wireframe, creating from convex hull 179-182

procedural tree
    bushes of tree, creating 150, 151
    creating 146
    finalizing 152, 153
    node tree, creating 146
    tree trunk, creating 147-149
    tree trunk randomization 149, 150

Profile Curve socket 210

R

random values
    using, with Extrude Mesh node 140, 141

Realize Instances node 24, 196

Remesh modifier
    creating, in Geometry Node editor 212, 213

Replace String node 104

Reroutes 186
    used, for organizing node tree 186, 187

Resample Curve node 118

RGB mixing 191

RGB (red, green, and blue) 190

rotated tesseract cube
    creating 90
    material, adding 96, 97
    nodes, using 91
    node tree, building 91-96
    sketching 90

Rotate Instances node 91

round input/output node connection 7

S

Scale Instances node 91

scene
    creating, in viewport 176-178

Separate Color node 197

Set Curve Radius node 125

Set Position node 118

Set Shade Smooth node 18, 241

shading issues, Geometry Nodes 235
    flipped normals 237
    intersecting meshes 236

simple lightning bolt 135
    basic idea, sketching 129
    emissive material, adding 134, 135
    node tree 132

node tree, making 130, 131
thickness, adjusting 132, 133
Slice String node 104
slow node trees, Geometry Nodes 245
causes 245
Smooth Minimum formula 230
reference link 230
Spiral Node Primitive 53, 54
Spline Parameter node 125
Spreadsheet 81
datasets, exploring 82
items, filtering 84
nodes, using 85
node tree structure, building 86-89
usage 82
working 85
squared input/output node connection 8
Star Node Primitive 52, 53
Store Named Attribute node 190, 198
string input/output node connection 10
String Length node 103
String node connection 99, 100
String nodes 100-102
strings 99, 100
Strings system, used for making procedural countdown 109
basic idea, sketching 109
nodes, exploring 110
node tree, building 110-113
String to Curves node 105, 107, 110
Subdivision Surface node 16, 17
subpixels 190
Suzanne object wireframe 211

T

thickness, to Curves
advanced thickness control 127-129
basic thickness control 126, 127
controlling 124, 125
Translate Instances node 86
troubleshooting, normals issues
Face Orientation view, using 237-239
normals, displaying 239-241
troubleshooting, shading issue 241
Auto Smooth option 241, 243
manual calculation 244
troubleshooting, slow node trees issue
node tree speeds, checking with
Timing Overlay 245-247

U

union mode 142
UV Sphere Node Primitive 44, 45

V

value input/output node connection 9
Value to String node 102, 110
vector input/output node connection 8, 9
Vector Math node 118
viewport
scene, creating 176-178
Volume Cube node 214
demonstration 216
Volume Grids tab, Spreadsheet 83
volumes
used, for modeling in editor 214-216

Volume to Mesh node 27, 28, 212, 213
  amount 27
  grid 27
  size 27
Voronoi distance pattern 214
Voronoi Texture node 215

W

Weight Paint feature 219
  linking, with Geometry Node editor 219
Weight Paint, use case
  Geometry Nodes project, setting up 220
  node tree, adding to Geometry Nodes project 220-224
wireframe
  mesh, converting to 210, 211

Z

Z fighting 236

‹packt›

www.packtpub.com

Subscribe to our online digital library for full access to over 7,000 books and videos, as well as industry leading tools to help you plan your personal development and advance your career. For more information, please visit our website.

Why subscribe?

- Spend less time learning and more time coding with practical eBooks and Videos from over 4,000 industry professionals
- Improve your learning with Skill Plans built especially for you
- Get a free eBook or video every month
- Fully searchable for easy access to vital information
- Copy and paste, print, and bookmark content

Did you know that Packt offers eBook versions of every book published, with PDF and ePub files available? You can upgrade to the eBook version at packtpub.com and as a print book customer, you are entitled to a discount on the eBook copy. Get in touch with us at customercare@packtpub.com for more details.

At www.packtpub.com, you can also read a collection of free technical articles, sign up for a range of free newsletters, and receive exclusive discounts and offers on Packt books and eBooks.

Other Books You May Enjoy

If you enjoyed this book, you may be interested in these other books by Packt:

Blender 3D By Example - Second Edition

Oscar Baechler , Xury Greer

ISBN: 978-1-78961-256-1

- Explore core 3D modeling tools in Blender such as extrude, bevel, and loop cut
- Understand Blender's Outliner hierarchy, collections, and modifiers
- Find solutions to common problems in modeling 3D characters and designs
- Implement lighting and probes to liven up an architectural scene using EEVEE
- Produce a final rendered image complete with lighting and post-processing effects
- Learn character concept art workflows and how to use the basics of Grease Pencil
- Learn how to use Blender's built-in texture painting tools

Taking Blender to the Next Level

By Ruan Lotter

ISBN: 978-1-80323-356-7

- Use geometry nodes to quickly create complex 3D scenes and motion graphics renders
- Create realistic textures using physically based rendering materials
- 3D scan real-life objects using a normal camera and clean up the model using Blender
- Understand how to model, rig, and animate your own 3D characters
- Use rigid body simulations to create dynamic scenes
- Understand how to perform 3D tracking within Blender
- Become well-versed with compositing 3D renders into live-action footage

Packt is searching for authors like you

If you're interested in becoming an author for Packt, please visit `authors.packtpub.com` and apply today. We have worked with thousands of developers and tech professionals, just like you, to help them share their insight with the global tech community. You can make a general application, apply for a specific hot topic that we are recruiting an author for, or submit your own idea.

Hi!

I am Siemen Lens, the author of *Procedural 3D Modeling Using Geometry Nodes in Blender*. I really hope you enjoyed reading this book and found it useful for increasing your productivity and efficiency in using Geometry Nodes in Blender.

It would really help me (and other potential readers!) if you could leave a review on Amazon sharing your thoughts on this book.

Go to the link below or scan the QR code to leave your review:

`https://packt.link/r/1804612553`

Your review will help us to understand what's worked well in this book, and what could be improved upon for future editions, so it really is appreciated.

Best wishes,

Siemen Lens

Download a free PDF copy of this book

Thanks for purchasing this book!

Do you like to read on the go but are unable to carry your print books everywhere? Is your e-book purchase not compatible with the device of your choice?

Don't worry! With every Packt book, you now get a DRM-free PDF version of that book at no cost.

Read anywhere, any place, on any device. Search, copy, and paste code from your favorite technical books directly into your application.

The perks don't stop there; you can get exclusive access to discounts, newsletters, and great free content in your inbox daily.

Follow these simple steps to get the benefits:

1. Scan the QR code or visit the following link:

https://packt.link/free-ebook/9781804612552

2. Submit your proof of purchase.

That's it! We'll email your free PDF and other benefits to you directly.

Printed in Great Britain
by Amazon